TAKE A CHANCE ON ME

BETH MORAN

Boldwood

First published in Great Britain in 2021 by Boldwood Books Ltd.

This paperback edition first published in 2022.

1

Copyright © Beth Moran, 2021

Cover Design by Debbie Clement Design

Cover Photography: Shutterstock

Every effort has been made to obtain the necessary permissions with reference to copyright material, both illustrative and quoted. We apologise for any omissions in this respect and will be pleased to make the appropriate acknowledgements in any future edition.

A CIP catalogue record for this book is available from the British Library.

Paperback ISBN: 978-1-80415-271-3

Ebook ISBN: 978-1-83889-344-6

Kindle ISBN: 978-1-83889-343-9

Audio CD ISBN: 978-1-80048-846-5

Digital audio download ISBN: 978-1-80048-847-2

Large Print ISBN: 978-1-83889-342-2

Boldwood Books Ltd.

23 Bowerdean Street, London, SW6 3TN

www.boldwoodbooks.com

MIX
Paper from
responsible sources
FSC® C171272

For Matthew and Paul Robbins
The kind of brothers who meant that I never once wished for a
sister instead.

1

I've been on thirty-seven first dates in the past three years. Five made it to a second. Two of those to number three. One of them even became a nearly-relationship, managing to limp along for seven weeks.

I've met men who never bothered dragging their eyes up above my neckline, tried to 'loosen me up' with shots, came right out with it and asked if I was going to sleep with them before we'd finished our first drink. Men who talked about their exes the entire time. Or about themselves. Men who lied, men who pretended to have forgotten their wallet or, on one delightful occasion, took one look at me, turned around and walked straight back out of the pub.

I've spent evenings with men I found eye-wateringly boring. Wasted hours with some who were rude, patronising, creepy or, in one instance, later revealed himself to be horrifically racist. I lost a whole afternoon on a pleasure cruise with a man who wore a bala-clava to prevent non-existent government drones from getting a photo of his face. Two invaluable lessons learnt there: always ensure I have an escape route and never let my sister Orla set me up.

Around half my dates were fine. A good few were fun, interesting evenings, and I would have happily seen the guys again. But then he was busy, or I was busy, or he lived that little too far away or actually had just met someone else or was about to go travelling round the world for a year or...

So now, to this evening, and I was on what had turned out to be the Date of All Dates. Oh yes, this one topped them all. Not as in, 'So, kids, this was how your father and I met.' More like, 'I will be retelling this terrible date story for the rest of my life.'

The man in question? My reasonably attractive neighbour, Ralph Hutchens.

The reason I was still here, with a man who had arrived drunk, proceeded to get even drunker, undone every button on his shirt because 'it's hotter than a brothel in this craphole', asked the waitress for her phone number, then had the audacity to ask me why I was still single, at my age – 'You're what – forty?' (I'm thirty-three) – then proceeded to fall asleep, while crying, face-first into his pasta?

Reason one: it was the Saturday after Valentine's Day, and in my warped, semi-desperate mind even being out on a hideous date tonight somehow compensated for being at home alone every other night this week. Reason two: I wouldn't be home alone if I'd stayed in. My littlest sister, Bridget, was getting engaged at that very moment in the apartment we shared. Reason three: I was hungry, the food here was delicious, and the least Ralph could do was buy me dinner.

Dinner was one thing – I wasn't quite desperate enough to hang around for dessert. The instant he fell asleep I grabbed my coconut milk cheesecake, which the waitress had decanted into a takeaway box before I'd even told her I was leaving, handed her a decent tip and left Ralph Hutchens the bill.

I had, perhaps somewhat over-optimistically given my recent date track record, promised Bridget's boyfriend, Paolo, that I would be out until late that evening. Having spoken, in person, to my charming, funny and stone-cold sober neighbour on multiple occasions, I had stuck out the ninety-minute date for eighty-nine minutes longer than it deserved, but it was still only nine-fifteen when I arrived back at the Victorian house containing the two-bedroom apartment we called home.

Tiptoeing barefoot down the hallway, praying the music emanating from our open-plan kitchen-living space would drown out the creak of my bedroom door, I crept inside, unpopped the button on my jeans and crawled under the duvet. Realising that I had no cutlery to eat my dessert with, I improvised with a credit card, then opened my laptop to Netflix. An hour later, as I prepared to turn out the light and hopefully enter blissful oblivion, the messages started pinging through to our SisterApp WhatsApp group:

Orla, second eldest sister after me:

Hey, Emma, howd your V-day date go with sexy neighbour???

Sofia, sister number three:

Did you get home ok?

Annie, older than Bridget by a full twenty-two minutes, and therefore sister number four:

Kiss goodnight after walking you home? Or walking INTO your home??

And then a text message from my Italian mother, who had no idea I'd been on a date, but always seemed to know when I least needed some ex-fiancé gossip, written in her trademark, near-indecipherable style:

Today Pam queuing at pharmacy tells me Jake and Helen having
another baby. Pam say Helen is blooming again running marathons no
sickness. Can you believe it Jake married and baby 3 coming and you
still no man. Anyway, I gave them our love. See you Sunday, Mamma.

I sent a brief reply to my sisters, mainly to stop Sofia from
worrying – she was supposed to be keeping her stress levels down:

Home safe and sound. Chose not to kiss neighbour, who seemed a lot
less sexy after he had thrown up in plant pot. Will fill you in on Wednesday. You should all be too busy with your own men tonight to be
worrying about my lack thereof xxx

I deleted my mum's message. From my phone, at least. It wasn't
quite so easy to delete the pain jabbing between my ribs like a blunt
pickaxe. Although, a nice long cry while working my way through
half of my secret vegan chocolate stash helped. Okay, three-quarters
of my secret stash, but hey – as the eldest of five sisters, three of
whom were married before they turned twenty-five, and the fourth
of whom was currently getting engaged, I was feeling the old-spin-
ster-on-the-shelf pressure. That, with a big dollop of loneliness and
disappointment thrown in. I had really liked sober Ralph
Hutchens.

* * *

'Morning, Old One.' Bridget took one look at me, shuffling into the
kitchen in my threadbare hoodie and faded pyjama bottoms, and
jumped up to pour me a coffee, her dark bob swinging an inch
above her shoulders.

'Funny, that's what our delightful neighbour called me last
night.' I accepted the mug gratefully, and slumped onto a chair.

'I read the messages. Do I need to know details in case I cross paths with him in the foyer?' Bridget slid a croissant out of the oven and onto a plate. She knew there was no point offering me one – I hadn't eaten breakfast since Helen Richards called me The Emmapotamus in year seven.

'He was smashed off his face. Had been with his workmates at another pub somewhere, but it's hardly an excuse. I left as soon as he passed out. He probably won't even remember it.'

'That's gross.' Bridget's tiny nose wrinkled in disgust.

'It is. But this is your morning, if Paolo's repeated messages ordering me to stay away last night are anything to go by. Tell me everything!'

She grinned, holding out her hand to show me the ring, and I breathed a silent sigh of relief at how similar it was to the 'Dream Ring!!!!!!' she'd put on the SisterApp a few months before. Just in case it ever came in useful for us to know what kind of engagement ring she liked. Of course, we'd immediately forwarded it on to Paolo, with #takethehint.

'Wow, not a Haribo or a Hula Hoop! He must really mean it this time.' I held her hand in mine, nodding appreciatively. 'I hope he managed a better speech than the last time, too. What was it? "Please don't go to London, I want to marry you and have kids and stuff and if you go you might end up falling for some swanky southerner"?'

Bridget rolled her eyes, her grin downgrading to a quirky smile. '*This time*, he said I was the most amazing person he'd ever met, he'd known we were meant to be together since we were kids and he couldn't imagine not spending the rest of his life with me.'

'You don't sound massively thrilled to have been proposed to by the love of your life. Haven't you been waiting for this for, like, twenty years or something?'

'Well, yeah.' Bridget furrowed her brow. 'I think that's it. Getting engaged isn't some out-of-the-blue dream come true. I always knew we'd get married. I just, well, I suppose having had a couple of decades to plan it I thought he'd come up with something a bit more... memorable.'

'Right.'

Even though we Donovan sisters had a pact to never compare anything, whether it be dress size, bank accounts, or proposals, I could understand how she felt. Annie got the top of the Empire State Building, and Moses hijacked an outdoor cinema and played Sofia a film where he'd listed all the reasons he wanted to marry her. Orla and Sam were nineteen, dealing with a surprise pregnancy, and he still took the time to make her a treasure hunt.

Even my proposal had been more effort than a meal in the flat and some roses. Although a moonlit picnic didn't count for much when, three weeks before the wedding, I discovered Jake with his hand up my old school nemesis Helen Richards' shirt.

'Sorry. I sound like a spoilt bitch Bridezilla and it's only been one day.' She smeared an enormous blob of jam all over the remaining corner of her pastry.

'No, I get it. You don't want him to take it any more for granted, just because it's inevitable. You still wanted your moment.'

She shrugged. 'I guess it's about time I accepted that I've not chosen a romantic, grand-gesture type of man. But I love him to bits, and he loves me, and I can't wait to finally marry him. What does Mum always say? It's not the grand gestures that make a marriage, it's all the little ones in between.'

'Have you told her yet?'

'No. We thought we'd wait, get it all over with in one go at lunch.'

'Mum's radar'll spot your ring the second you step into church.'

Sunday mornings, the whole Donovan tribe went to the church that Sofia and her husband Moses ran in a deprived corner of

Nottingham. Well. Most of us did. My dad had come down with a horrible flu eighteen months ago, which then became post-viral fatigue, which then became something way more serious than that. As the weeks became months, instead of getting better, the chronic exhaustion and debilitating pain branched out into muscle tremors and agonising insomnia, and what was once lightning Irish wit became foggy and hard-going. After weeks of being told to wait it out and give it time, followed by months of tests and referrals and deeply offensive suggestions about wanting early retirement (to a man who arrived in England with nothing, and at the age of fifty-five owned a thriving hardware shop, which he loved only second to God, his wife and his girls), he finally got the answer we'd been dreading.

Dad had ME, otherwise known as Chronic Fatigue Syndrome.

Paolo took over running the shop, having worked there since he was fourteen.

Initially, Dad had made it clear that this was a temporary measure, repeating often to his regular clients, his family back in Ireland, the many, many friends he'd made since emigrating to Sherwood Forest, that it was only until he'd 'got back on his feet'.

Over the past few months, those comments had been made less often. When Dad had days he could barely get up on his literal feet, the life he'd given his all to build for himself, and more importantly for his family, began to fade into the past.

Still, nobody mentioned retirement. Or disabled. Or selling up.

What does a self-made man do, when suddenly everything he worked so hard to make is taken from him?

My father, like so many men his age, grieved in private. But we saw the stoop in his once-straight shoulders, and how we missed the twinkle in his Irish eyes.

My mother, of that same generation who would fuss for weeks about a speck on the carpet but, when it came down to it, revealed themselves to have a backbone of solid steel, knuckled down and, in addition to carrying on as the shop bookkeeper and administrator, learnt how to fill the car with petrol, work the hedge strimmer, replace a tile on their farmhouse roof and all the other things you never learnt to do when you had a handyman husband. She took for better for worse, in sickness and in health as a given, and never complained once about all this greedy, grasping illness had stolen from them. She did, on the other hand, complain often – in person and in writing – to the NHS, the welfare system, and our local MP. Last June, she also raised several hundred pounds for ME research by converting the barn behind the farmhouse into a pop-up tearoom for the day. Having nagged and cajoled most of the village to stop by for what turned out to be a huge success, this year she was planning to go even bigger and better.

As for the Donovan sisters, we dealt with this as we did with everything else: we talked it out, we hugged and cried and argued and eventually apologised or told each other to buck up, or to give ourselves a break. We cooked and ate and fell apart and picked ourselves back up again. We loved each other with the fierce Donovan love. We loved our mamma, Gabriella Donovan, even as she drove us crazy, and we loved our dad, Bear Donovan, even as his sad smile and shuffling walk broke our hearts. And we told them that, often. In words and cups of tea and phone calls and lifts to hospital and cakes and snarky, family jokes that no one else could get away with.

Our family was crushed, yes. But we were not beaten.

But there was a space on the end of the row every Sunday, and I didn't think we would ever get used to it. Or stop hoping that maybe next month, next year, Dad would take his place there again.

'I'm skiving this morning. We're having brunch with Paolo's parents, then we'll be over for lunch to break the news.' Bridget, who could never be accused of resembling a Bridgetopotamus even after eating breakfast, brunch and lunch, stuffed in a bite of a second croissant.

'I'd better go and sort myself out, then, try and look a little bit less like a washed-up old hag for the inevitable photos.' I dragged myself back up off the chair.

Bridget stopped me as I went past, wrapping both arms around my waist. 'I'm sorry that this means you'll be last,' she whispered into my shoulder. 'I hope it won't make it hard for you to be my matron of honour.'

'Oh, Bridget.' Was there anyone on this earth as sweet as my baby sister? I kissed the top of her head. 'It's not a race. I might never get married, and I'm fine with that. You'd better enjoy every second of this engagement, because I'll be there doing all the planning and the organising and the ticking-off-checklist parts that you hate. And who knows? I might have a gorgeous man to bring to your wedding as my plus-one. Or maybe I'll have fun flirting with the groomsmen.'

'You never know, you could end up married before me! We've still got to save a deposit for somewhere to live, let alone a wedding.'

I pulled away to look at her, smoothing back the stray lock of hair that always fell over her face, as I'd done a million times before. 'Maybe I will.'

That sister of mine always was the clever one.

2

'Where's Bridget?' Mum's Italian accent boomed at me from the end of one row of plastic chairs filling the community centre where the New Life Church, Nottingham met every Sunday morning and Tuesday night. 'She isn't going to miss lunch?'

Orla jerked her head round so fast her honey-blonde ponytail caught her husband, Sam, in the eye. Her raised eyebrows framed a curious smirk. Donovan Sunday lunches were mandatory, only to be missed on pain of death. Literally – when Orla was in hospital *in labour* with her first baby, Harry, who was now eleven, Mum took a gigantic spinach lasagne to the hospital waiting room in a cool-box, dragging us all along with her. She snuck loaded plates for Orla and Sam into the labour room, which Sam later reassured us he and the midwife very much enjoyed, Orla opting for gas and air instead.

Even Paolo had to leave an assistant in charge of Donovan's DIY, despite it being the busiest day of the week. And living in New York wasn't a good enough excuse, either. Annie video-called every Sunday, so Mum could show her that she'd made her favourite cannoli, as if this might prove so irresistible that Annie would hop on the next plane over. We'd given up trying to tell Mum that Annie didn't even like cannoli that much, it was her twin, Bridget's, favourite. Or would have been, had she not been served it every Sunday for fourteen years.

'No, Mamma,' I whispered back. 'She's busy this morning, but will be there for lunch.'

'Busy doing what?' Mum leant forwards, her gold and black striped 'church blouse' gaping to reveal far too much solid chest. 'She better not be doing more work for that snotty boss of hers. I'll be taking a visit to that university scientist department and reminding Mr Fancy Degree PhD Professor that there are laws about working on a Sunday.'

'Sofia's working today,' Orla pointed out. 'Those laws got over-turned decades ago.'

'Sofia never misses her family lunch!' Mum's eyes suddenly creased in sympathy. 'Oh, is it her diarrhoea again? I've told her that vegan diet is not natural. And she can still come for dinner, we've got two bathrooms.'

I didn't bother correcting her on any of those fronts, including that I was the vegan, not my sister.

'I said she'll be there. Shh, now! Sofia's trying to get started.'

Mum dutifully turned to smile at Sofia, who was standing on the small stage holding a microphone. Dressed in denim dunga-rees, her long chestnut hair tied in a messy bun held back with a red bandana, she smiled patiently as she waited to welcome the sixty or so people filling the hall.

'That's my daughter,' Mum whispered at full volume to the nearest rows, as if they didn't know already thanks to Mum making the same announcement every week. 'Always had the heart of an angel, right from a little girl. Working so hard to care for all the people in this church, she is married seven years and still not stopped to have her own family.'

'Mamma, *shut up*,' Orla hissed, to our mother's consternation. 'You're distracting everyone.'

We all stood as Moses began to lead the congregation in the first song.

Orla was the only one of us who would dare to speak to Mum like that, and only then because what she knew, and Mum didn't, and hopefully would never have to, was that Sofia and Moses had been trying to get pregnant for the past four years. The one round of IVF offered by the NHS had failed. Living on a pastor's wage, supplemented by Moses' occasional gigs as a wedding singer, going private was out of the question. Those of us who knew what they were struggling through could see the strain and the sorrow taking its toll on our beautiful sister and her husband. There had been many a SisterApp thread discussing the possibility of Moses going back to teaching music, Sofia finding something that paid enough to allow them to gradually save up. Any job that didn't end up with them feeding, clothing and in a thousand other ways taking care of half the people in their neighbourhood would help.

But it was their life, and, even if they could afford it, the IVF had been brutal. It was hard keeping a secret like this from our mother, but her idea of a secret didn't quite match most people's definition, so for the sake of Sofia's privacy we contained our mother as best we could.

* * *

Once the songs were finished and Sofia had given a talk, after Orla's three children had come racing out of their kids' group and I'd drunk a mug of tea while chatting with someone who kept calling me Brian while asking how my fish were getting on, we set off in the usual convoy out to Hatherstone, the village where we Donovan sisters had grown up. Riding in the back of Moses and Sofia's ancient Ford Escort, as the houses faded into the fields and forest of my childhood, I felt the pressures of grown-up city life fall away.

'I have another customer for you,' Moses said, turning off the main road onto the lane that led towards Hatherstone. Moses originally came from Jamaica, although he had numerous aunts, uncles and cousins living in the East Midlands, some of whom were actually related to him. Moses was the kind of man who created family wherever he went, and he also believed in supporting each other whenever the opportunity arose. A considerable chunk of my cake business had been built on Moses' family's celebrations, for which I thanked him with a triple-layer fudge gateau every birthday.

'Henry and Ruby have their diamond wedding anniversary coming up. Their great-granddaughter is going to call you.'

'Diamond?' Sofia whistled. 'What, that's like sixty years? I was impressed when we hit six.'

'Thanks, Moses,' I replied as we pulled up at my parents' rambling farmhouse. 'Tell her not to leave it too late. I've got a few weddings booked for March, and their ideas are ambitious to say the least. Nita's going to be in her element.'

Nita was my business partner at Emma's Cakery. I was the scientist, creating cake recipes that specialised in meeting various dietary requirements while also managing to bear the weight of Nita's handiwork – she was the artist, who transformed the tasty into visual triumphs.

'I thought you might bring a cake today,' Sofia said as we made our way across the broad gravel driveway to the wooden porch.

'Now, what possible reason would I have for bringing a cake?' I asked, eyes wide with innocence. Mum would never let me bring dessert, even though that meant I could make something vegan, so could actually enjoy eating it for once. She did, however, in the interests of supporting a family business, allow me to bring a cake on special occasions.

'I don't know, Emma, why don't we ask the lovebirds?' She grinned, waving at Bridget and Paolo, who had just pulled up in his van.

'Don't go ruining their big moment, darling,' Moses scolded gently.

'I'm only waiting to say hello,' Sofia replied, peering over at Bridget as if searching for a ring from twenty yards away.

'You can say hello inside,' Mum said, having flung the door open that second. 'Why are you all hovering on the doorstep like salesmen?'

She stood back to let us into the stone-flagged entrance hall. 'Moses, my second son.' She kissed him European style before letting him through. 'Singing beautifully this morning, as always. Emma. You look tired. Are you sure you're not anaemic? A good spoonful of beef stufato will put colour back in your cheeks.' She patted said cheeks as I walked past.

'Mum, these are what Irish cheeks look like. We didn't all inherit your Mediterranean complexion. And I'm tired because I've been working flat out all week.'

'Now, Bridget!' She had already moved on to the next sister. 'Paolo! Church was so quiet without you. I hope it wasn't your bowel problems again.'

'I told you it wasn't!' I called back from the doorway into the enormous kitchen. 'Oh, hi, Dad.'

'Emma.' My dad, who had been taking champagne flutes out of the dresser, put them down and came to give me a hug. 'How are ye now, my best girl?'

I leant into the warmth of his enormous chest, my head snuggling several inches below his beard. My father was not called 'Bear' for nothing. Breathing in the familiar scent of wool, woodsmoke and the faintest hint of turpentine, I blinked back the sudden prickle of tears. 'I'm fine.'

And I was – I was always fine, tucked inside his giant arms. 'You guessed, then?'

'Paolo came over last week to ask for my blessing. He might not do things fancy, that lad, but he does them right.'

'Does Mum know?'

'She's trying really hard to pretend she doesn't.'

'She could have picked a less embarrassing ruse than Bridget's dodgy stomach.'

'And since when did your mamma understand the meaning of embarrassment?'

We breathed together for a few moments, ignoring the chatter and laughter drifting in from the living room.

'Are you sure you're okay, now? It's been a grand arrangement, you girls sharing the flat together. I know you'll miss her something fierce. And, well, it's not expected, the eldest being last.'

'Sure, and, as Bridget said, it's hardly surprise news, is it? I'm thrilled for her.' I frowned against his bobbly old jumper. 'Possibly more thrilled than she is. Honestly, I'm fine. It's not like we have a limited allocation of family weddings per year, and she's taken mine.'

'All right, then. Let's not keep them waiting any longer.'

While I didn't have a Sam, or a Moses, or a Paolo, with Bear Donovan's rough hand in mine, I knew I would always be loved, utterly and unconditionally, and that was mighty fine indeed.

* * *

Due to patchy Internet connection, we made contact with Annie over dessert, the remains of dinner still sprawled across the oak dining table that Dad handcrafted after the twins had been born.

'Show me the ring!' she squealed through the laptop screen.

'Not from there, up close. Move the screen if you can't get any nearer.'

'Was there anybody who didn't know about this proposal?' Paolo grumbled behind his spoon of blackberry crumble.

'I think it's a twin thing,' I said.

'You've been a hanger-on to this family for twenty years,' Orla retorted, her four-year-old, Oscar, sitting on her knee while he scraped the remains of the custard jug into his bowl with rapt concentration. 'Don't pretend you didn't know what you were getting into, little brother.'

'Please don't call me that ever again.' Paolo grinned.

He ran a hand through his blond shock of hair and straightened his shirt before moving his chair closer to the screen. Even though Annie lived three thousand miles away, Paolo knew that for Bridget, having her twin's approval was everything.

'Where is he, then?' Annie's eyes darted across the screen, until she spotted Paolo waving.

'I like how your first priority was the ring,' he joked.

'My sister's stuck with both you and that ring for a long time. I already know what you look like.'

'Fair dos.'

'But seriously.' Annie pointed one long, manicured nail at him. 'While you may become Bridget's other half at some point in the near future, she's been my other half since we were twin blobs of gloop jostling for the juiciest section of womb wall.'

'A lovely analogy as always,' Bridget murmured.

'In short, you're marrying the joint top woman in the universe. Make her happy, treat her with the respect all women deserve, and you'd better love her nearly as much as I do.'

'Yes, ma'am.'

'Oh, and about bloomin' well time. It's weird me married and her not.'

'Antonia, did you see I made lemon cannoli? With pistachio sprinkles?' Mum moved us on to more important topics.

'Yes, Mamma. It looks lovely.'

'And where's Greg? We haven't seen him in so long I'm forgetting what his beautiful face looks like. Is he working? I keep telling you, he works too hard. You need to talk to him about this again, Antonia. I don't know what is going on these days, all these people working on a Sunday.'

'He's gone to the deli to pick us up some bagels, Mum. And you have no idea what hours he works, so please stop worrying about it.'

We might not have to worry about how hard Annie's husband worked – he was an accounts manager for an international advertising firm, of course he worked ridiculously long hours. But we sisters were starting to wonder about how rarely we saw him on Sundays, and how Annie's gushing reports on her loved-up wedded bliss were noticeably absent lately. At forty-four, Greg was nineteen years older than Annie. They had met on holiday in Rome, and, after a couple of short visits to meet his family and ours, she had gone to the US on a three-month spousal visa, marrying as required within the ninety days before flying back to England a week later for a lavish wedding reception. As used as we were to Annie's impulse decisions, we were also well used to them crashing down around her once the initial enthusiasm had worn off. We knew the pair wouldn't have married so fast if they'd not had to in order to live in the same country. We worried that, given a little more time and consideration, they wouldn't have married at all.

We liked Greg, and he had certainly seemed to love Annie. But a suit-wearing professional with a house in the suburbs who coached little league baseball was not who we'd envisaged her ending up with.

But we could hardly quiz her about it over roast potatoes and beef stew. I wondered if it would be too late to find out what was going on when she came home for Bridget's wedding.

* * *

Later that afternoon, Mum collapsed in an armchair to sleep off her efforts, while Paolo and Bridget played football with the kids in the garden. Leaving Orla and Sofia to clear up the remains of the mess, I went to take everybody's hot drink orders. Hearing Dad's voice coming from the study, I was about to open it when I caught Moses' deep reply.

'Thank you, Bear. But I won't take your money. Not even for this. If it is meant to be, God will make a way.'

'Maybe this is the way God is making?' I could hear the frustration in Dad's tone. There was a long silence. To my shame, I remained there, rooted on the spot, breath caught somewhere behind my pounding heart.

'I know that Sofia would do anything to have another chance, but, with respect, you didn't see what the last time cost her. Physically, and emotionally, I cannot put her through that again.'

'Don't you think you should make that decision together? She's a wise woman, she can figure out what's best. And if it gave you a child, wouldn't you both consider it worth it?'

'Of course.' Moses' voice broke on the words, and it tore at my chest to hear his pain. 'If I could do it for her, I would keep going as long as it took. If we could be certain... but the doctors have warned us, for her the chance is so slim. I couldn't take your money on a lost cause. And to hope again, only to have those hopes... to be told it was all for nothing... I can't risk putting her through that...'

Hearing Moses break down released my frozen limbs. I hurried back into the living room, where Sam was slumped across the sofa opposite Mum, head on his chest.

'Hey, Sam!' I spoke softly, not wanting to disturb Mum, but loud enough to jolt him awake.

'Oh! Emma. Was I asleep?'

'You must be getting old, needing a Sunday afternoon snooze. Welcome to your thirties.'

'Please don't tell Mamma, she'll not stop going on about how I'm working too hard.'

'Are you – working too hard? Or was it a late night last night?'

'It's never a late night with him, these days,' Orla said, walking in with two mugs of coffee. 'You should be out playing with your kids on a Sunday afternoon, not sat here snoring like a grandad.'

Sam sighed, sitting up straighter to accept a mug. 'I do get up with them at six every morning.'

'It's not a very sexy trait in a man, crashing out at nine-thirty on a Saturday night.'

'How do you know what time I went to bed? You were out with your new workmates until irresponsible o'clock.'

'Well, I might as well go out with them and be irresponsible as stay in with you like some boring elderly couple. We're thirty, Sam! Finally getting a bit of ourselves back now the kids are all at school. I've got the whole of my twenties to catch up on, and I want to make the most of it. I'd quite like a husband who wants to do it with me.'

Sam, who was the only person on this planet who knew exactly how to handle Orla, stuck his drink on the coffee table and yanked her down onto his lap, ignoring her squeals. 'You're the one who's acting like an old woman, nagging me all the time. Now stop moaning so I can drink my coffee and go and play with the wonderful children you gave me.'

'Come on, Cooper, you've faced worse.' Patrick Charles Cooper straightened his tie in the reflection of the entrance door, flicked the rain off his black mass of cropped curls and took a deep breath. It was true, he'd faced a lot worse. He just couldn't fathom why it would be helpful to remind himself of any of that at this moment.

'Are you going in or not?' an older man asked impatiently from behind, and Cooper turned to see a group of four or five people squashing under an enormous umbrella, their suits and evening dresses poking out from beneath raincoats.

'Uh, yes. Sorry.' He pulled open the heavy glass door, gesturing to the group to go ahead, before ducking in behind them. He gave his name to the member of staff, along with his sopping coat. Noting his position on the seating plan – good, right in the back corner with the other nonentities – he followed the crowd into the grand ballroom of the Nottingham Castle Hotel. Making his way past the banqueting tables, keeping his head down to avoid any of the IPD team, he reached the safety of the bar and tried to figure out for the hundredth time what he was doing here.

Ah yes, the lack of a job, that was a pretty good reason.

Having recently resigned from his research position at IPD, the top neuroscience research company in the UK, if not the whole of Europe, Cooper was currently well on his way to becoming broke, homeless and, more importantly, driven out of his mind with boredom. With no late-into-the-night working, impossible deadlines and the continual drive to justify his position at the company with the one thing that mattered – results – he had time to think about other things. And that was a dangerous and unpleasant road to head down. Cooper had worked very hard to make sure that he had no space left in his life for other things.

Now, they were laughing in his face when he woke up every morning, sneering at him from the other side of the sofa as he flicked mindlessly through the horror of daytime television, or scrolled through hours of drivel on the Internet.

Free time was Very Bad.

Bad enough that Cooper had swapped his faded joggers for a suit and prepared to endure the annual Henry Munch Conference Dinner, attended by some of the brightest and best in the world of neuroscience, psychology, behavioural sciences and other related fields, all hoping to scoop one of the awards given out on the night. While he wouldn't begrudge applauding most of the award recipients for a job well done, knowing that the ex-research partner who'd stolen his results had won one made his guts contract like a dying snake.

He forced his way through the meal, his rankings in the proceedings confirmed by the PhD students sitting to his left, and retired psychology lecturer on the other side. It became apparent by the end of the pumpkin soup that no one on the table could offer any potential job prospects. Unless the retired lecturer needed someone to cut her grass and fetch her prescription, that was. Which might end up being his best option. No, if Cooper wanted to leave here with some sort of a job lead, he was going to have to go looking for it.

So he did, weaving his way through the tables once the lemon tart had been served, not having to try too hard to avoid the IPD table, given that it was in the opposite corner to his own (in prime position, in other words). He paused to catch the eye of a few people he recognised, but most of them quickly turned away, or simply ignored him, not even bothering to pretend they'd not seen the disgraced golden boy.

Ouch. It had been a long time since Cooper had been shunned en masse. It felt as crap as when he'd been that kid with the stinky clothes and unwashed hair, lugging his school books in a worn carrier bag.

But then he saw her.

Cooper's battered and broken heart froze for a long moment before stuttering into life for the first time in four years.

He'd known she might be here – his rational brain thought it was more than likely; if anything it was a more compelling reason to come than needing a job.

And – *oh, Cooper, you are in trouble now* – she looked, if possible, even more breathtaking than the last time he'd seen her. To be fair, that day she'd been chasing his car down the street in a dressing gown and koala slippers. But, honestly, Bridget Donovan could wear his manky old school uniform and she'd still be the most beautiful woman he'd ever seen.

Her hair was shorter, a wavy, mahogany cut that didn't quite reach her shoulders, but her smile as she chatted to the other people at the table, the way her dark eyes glinted as she threw her hands about to emphasise a point, one of them still clutching a spoon – it was exactly the same.

He stood there, soaking her up, not even needing to approach, until a waiter carrying an oversized coffee urn politely asked him to move out of the way. At that point, as he shifted his gaze to avoid causing an accident, he felt her notice him.

This was confirmed by the sudden lack of oxygen in his vicinity. It was doubly confirmed when she stood up, waving the spoon even harder, and shouted, 'Cooper? COOPER! I can't believe it. This is amazing. Hang on, don't move, I'm coming over. Stay right there.'

As if he could have moved, even if he'd wanted to.

Tottering up to him, she grabbed his arm (yep, her touch still sent shivers of electricity careening through his nervous system) and dragged him through a pair of double doors into a corridor.

'Cooper! I can't believe it's really you, you're really here!' She poked him a few times in the chest, as if to double check, face beaming. Cooper swallowed painfully. It almost felt worth the whole past six weeks – giving up his job, his reputation, the six-figure salary – simply to make her smile like that, in this moment. Except, that would have been a meaningless gesture, as pretty much everything made Bridget smile.

He'd forgotten how perfect her teeth were.

'I mean, how? Why? Who are you here with?' She scanned around as if that would provide the answer.

Come on, Coop. Open your mouth and hopefully something sensible will come out.

Knowing that if he didn't say something soon, he might end up bending down and kissing her, he smiled back. 'Hello, Widget.'

Nice one, Cooper. Smooth...

If possible, her grin grew even wider. 'Hello.'

They stood there for a few more seconds. She wobbled on her heels. Bridget lived in Converse – she'd probably borrowed these spiky silver things from one of her sisters.

'So, in answer to my questions...?'

'Right! I'm looking for a job.'

Her forehead furrowed in sympathy. 'I heard you left IPD.'

'You heard I left or was pushed?' What was it about this woman that made Patrick Cooper tell her everything? Well, he'd started so he might as well finish...

'I wasn't pushed, I chose to resign. I was co-lead author on the whole Walberg study. The Cooper Walberg study, then. But Walberg's data stopped adding up. So I poked around a bit, and found out that a load more of IPD's studies were even worse. When I confronted them, it was either show my loyalty to the business, with a nice pay rise and a promotion in return. Or leave, with a destroyed reputation to cover their backs if I spoke up.'

'Wow. That's horrible.'

Cooper shrugged. 'Yeah. And now no one in neuroscience wants anything to do with me. I came here this evening hoping one or two far corners in academia might hate IPD enough to give me a chance, but, given that you and a retired lecturer are the only people to acknowledge me so far, I think it's been a waste of time.'

'Excuse me? A waste of time? The first time you've seen me, your once closest friend, in four years, and it's a *waste*?'

He wiped his mouth, trying to hide the sheepish grin. 'Not that bit, obviously.'

'And, more importantly, you were in Nottingham and you didn't get in touch? I can understand you not having time for your long-lost best friend when IPD are working you into the ground day and night, but given that you're now a man of leisure, in my home city, what possible reason do you have for not calling?' Even when she was telling him off, her cheeks dimpled with joy.

Because I'm in love with you, and seeing you with someone else kills me?

'Give me a break, I only arrived a couple of hours ago.'

'Hmph.'

'And I'm here now.'

Bridget pursed her lips, as if deciding whether or not to forgive him.

'Come on, Widget, you know I'm crap at all that stuff.'

'What, friendship?'

'Friendship, human interaction, basic communication, any kind of meaningful relationship...'

'Come on, then, let's get a drink and catch up on as much as we can before the awards start.' She linked her arm through his, and turned back towards the ballroom, but as she did someone stumbled out of the men's room.

'Ugh, quick, it's the professor.' Bridget started to pull him along, but it was too late.

'I know you,' the man called, as if that were a reasonable accusation. 'Stop!'

'Professor Cole.' Cooper stopped, turning with a sigh to address his old tutor.

'How do I know you?'

'Professor, this is Patrick Cooper,' Bridget started, the use of his first name making Cooper's innards shrivel.

'I know who *you* are! You're my assistant. Can you please assist me and this gentleman by running along and fetching two brandies? None of that cheap tosh. This fellow rings a bell and I want to know why.'

'I was your research student for two years, up until 2015,' Cooper said, preventing Bridget from 'running along' by squeezing her linked arm tightly against his body.

Suddenly the professor's face cleared, as far as possible when utterly intoxicated. 'Cooper! You turned down my postgrad post and sold your soul to IPD, leaving me Dr Donovan instead.'

'That's right.'

'Idiot.' The professor snorted.

'So it would seem.'

'Well, when you've come to your senses and realised that money is no substitute for greatness, give me a call. I can always make room for good talent. And I seem to remember you were outstanding. Dr Donovan, where are those drinks?'

'Professor, the awards are about to start – they're calling everyone to take their seats.' Bridget glanced anxiously at the busy bar.

'Well, bring them straight to the table, then.'

'Yes, Professor.'

'He's still an ardent feminist, I see,' Cooper muttered as he followed Bridget back into the ballroom. 'Don't bother getting him a drink – he's so off his head he won't notice.'

They paused inside the entrance as the nominations for the first award were called out to smattered applause. But Bridget wasn't listening; her eyes were shining again.

'Cooper.' She clutched his arm. 'He offered you a job! You have to call him, like first thing on Monday. Imagine it – the dream team back together. Cooper and Widget, uncovering the secrets of neuroscience one electromagnetic wave at a time.'

She peered into Cooper's face. It really wasn't helpful to have her standing so close to him. He could do a whole research study on how the proximity of Bridget Donovan could shut down a somatic nervous system.

'Why aren't you excited about this? This is the best possible solution. One, a job. Two, a job working in the same department as me!'

'And Professor Angus Cole.'

'Professor Cole loves you!' She'd lowered her voice to an impassioned whisper, to avoid disturbing the ongoing awards.

Cooper bent his head nearer to hers, only four inches below his six feet thanks to those ridiculous shoes. 'I don't particularly love him. Or the way he treats you. Why are you still working there?'

'Because he's the best in the Midlands, and, unlike you, I don't want to move away. My family are here, and that's worth putting up with an awful boss for.'

'And Paolo,' Cooper added, taking the tiniest of steps away, back into the cold and lonely void of not-near-Bridget.

'And Paolo.' Her shoulders squirmed a little. Paolo had always been a weird subject between them. After all, what boyfriend wouldn't be jealous of his girlfriend's straight, male best friend?

'Congratulations, by the way.' He nodded at her left hand.

'Thanks.'

'Only an engagement ring? I thought you'd be an old married couple by now.'

'Well, yeah. Dad's not been well, so Paolo's been busy taking care of the shop. And Annie got married last year. We didn't want to steal her thunder.'

'*Annie* got married!' He gaped. 'Now that would have been worth watching.'

'Well, if you'd stayed in touch, instead of disappearing into a lab never to be seen again, you'd have been invited to the wedding reception. It was every bit as fabulous as she is.'

'Never to be seen again? I'm here, aren't I?'

She beamed, clapping for the next prize-winner. 'Never to be lost again, I hope.'

Oh, Widget. I am so lost...

They watched the proceedings for a few minutes, Cooper simply soaking up the joy of being in Bridget's orbit.

'I'm really sorry to hear about your dad. It must be serious if he's stopped work—'

Then Cooper stopped, the other Donovans forgotten, as his subconscious tuned in to the winner of the next award. Every muscle in his torso went rigid, and there were a decent number of them these days, since he'd finally had time to start running again.

There was a thumping of feet and whoops from the IPD table, as Walberg pranced his way onto the stage to collect the award that should have been Cooper's, if anyone's, although if truth won the day, it would be nobody's at all.

'Ugh. I hate him. He looks like a sneaky weasel,' Bridget declared. 'You're better off without him and his fabricated research. Come and work for Prof Cole – he might be a boorish prig but he's an honest prig.'

'I think he's trying to get your attention.' Cooper pointed in the direction of the Nottingham University Neuroscience Department table, where the professor was beckoning Bridget over, making exaggerated drinking gestures.

'I'd better go and join him. He's convinced he's won the lifetime contribution award, and wants us all there to fake how delighted we are.'

She turned and grabbed Cooper's arm again. 'But don't go anywhere! At least, not until you've given me your number. Or, call me on mine – it's still the same. Find me on Instagram or something. DO NOT disappear again!'

Cooper smiled, hoping it hid the pang of longing in his chest. His terrible reputation might not have spread as far as New Zealand, or Siberia. He could find a job somewhere far enough away from Bridget Donovan so that he could manage to exist without her, couldn't he?

Bridget scurried to her seat, and the room fell silent as the host prepared to announce the winner of the award that every fledgling neuroscientist dreamed of receiving one day.

'And this year's Henry Munch Lifetime Achievement Award for an outstanding contribution to neuroscience and behavioural science goes to...'

Professor Angus Cole had downed his drink and already half risen to his feet by the time the name was announced.

'Professor Ernestine Lavinski!'

The room went wild.

While celebrity psychologist Ernestine Lavinski, better known as Prof Love, glided her way onto the stage, Professor Cole seemed frozen, backside hovering a foot above his chair, spine hunched as he gripped its arms.

Prof Love graciously accepted the gold trophy, holding it aloft as people cheered and whistled. Gesturing with a smile for the crowd to die down, she leant her willowy frame towards the microphone.

'Thank you so much. What an incredible surprise. I wasn't expecting this at all.'

'Why would you be? No one in their right mind would have expected you to win,' Professor Cole barked, causing a rumble of excited anticipation from the crowd. Nothing those neuroscientists loved more than a public spat between rival professors.

Ernestine blinked, her smile temporarily vanished before she spotted who had spoken, at which point her eyes took on a steely glint. 'As I was saying, thank you. Most of you know how much the noble study of psychology means to me.'

'Hah! Noble! Nothing but guesswork and common sense. Not fit to be classed as a science if you ask me.'

'Which no one did,' Ernestine pointed out. 'It has been a joy and an honour to devote my life to helping discover the secrets of how we think, and how our thoughts, alongside a myriad other factors, determine our behaviour; for example, why someone would indulge in gross rudeness, embarrassing themselves and a roomful of fellow professionals, when purely motivated by jealousy and an overwhelming feeling of inferiority.'

'INFERIORITY!' The professor pulled himself up to stand upright, tugging at his waistcoat as he smirked at the other tables, assuming they'd all agree with him. 'You haven't published a single piece of credible research in over a decade!'

'With all due respect, which in this case is virtually none, I have sold over three million books. How many people do you think read your latest paper on, what was it again? Oh, hang on a minute, nobody actually noticed or cared.'

Cooper could see Bridget frantically trying to persuade her boss to sit down. No one else moved or uttered so much as a delighted gasp, entranced by the impromptu after-dinner entertainment.

'How dare you insult this room of mostly credible scientists! Every single person here, most probably including you, knows that the only reason you won this award is the exact same reason three million gullible cretins bought your books!' He spat, both the words and some accompanying spittle. 'A charming smile, bewitching eyes and a media career as the notorious Professor Love! Lifetime contribution to televisual tripe, more like!'

'Oh, you're only bitter because I've made a highly successful career out of bringing people together, *contributing* to happiness, long-term loving partnerships and shedloads of fabulous sex! Three things your life has been sadly missing since I dumped you in 1986!'

Now, that *did* elicit a gasp from the entranced listeners. Somebody by the side of the stage tried to get the host's attention by making furious slashing motions across their neck. Cooper chuckled, admiring the host's impressive job of pretending to ignore them. This would send ticket sales for next year's event through the roof.

'Long-term partnerships!' Professor Cole tucked his thumbs into his waistcoat pocket, tipping his chin up slightly in classic lecture pose as he smirked, clearly about to launch his fatal blow. 'And how many of the so-called couples on that blind-date wedding show of yours have stayed together beyond the initial three months, Professor Lavinski? How much happiness, and let's go with short-term partnerships – let alone loving ones – or genuine acts of sexual intercourse did your outdated, pseudo-scientific, bunkum baloney of a supposedly infallible technique manage to produce?'

Professor Ernestine turned briskly back to the lectern, as if she had a hope in hell of returning to her acceptance speech.

'Anyone?' Professor Cole roared. 'Anyone care to make a guess? I believe it is precisely none!'

'I'm flattered you take so much interest in my career.'

Professor Cole was too busy chortling to respond.

'And I suppose, as a *proper* scientist, you could do better?' Prof Love was losing her cool, brandishing the award now as if considering whether she had the strength to hurl it far enough to hit her target.

The target raised his bushy eyebrows in gleeful surprise. 'Is that a challenge, Professor?'

Ernestine Lavinski narrowed her eyes, while the room held its breath. 'Yes.'

Bridget made another attempt to get the professor to sit down. She might as well have asked him to offer his congratulations to a well-deserving colleague.

'Match one couple, using your own method, give them a blind-date wedding, and if they're still successfully married by next year's dinner, I'll present you with this award myself.'

The room erupted into chatter, quickly shushing to await the response. Knowing that there was no way he could decline with his pride intact.

'And by what method will success be determined?'

Ernestine smiled, teeth glinting like a shark's. 'The renowned Lavinski evaluative tool for determining relationship health and satisfaction.'

Her rival let out a bark of laughter. 'Challenge accepted. Please proceed with your speech.'

* * *

Twenty minutes later, having manhandled her boss into the back of a taxi, Bridget found Cooper collecting his coat. 'Phone.' She waggled her fingers in the direction of his jacket pocket. 'Quick. Paolo's picking me up any second.'

Knowing it was a terrible idea, he handed over his phone. After all, what was a phone when he'd already handed her his heart?

'Usual passcode?' Not bothering to wait for an answer, she unlocked the phone, added in her number and then sent herself a message. 'Now get in touch, soon.'

Handing it back, she nudged him in the ribs with her elbow. 'Believe it or not, I've really missed you, Cooper.'

He ducked his head – a giveaway move for all the behavioural scientists milling around, but it was better than collapsing in a swoon into the cloakroom queue. Or wrapping his arms around her and kissing her. Especially seeing as Paolo had just stepped into the foyer. 'I sort of missed you, too.'

'Promise you'll message me!' She started to back away, hurrying towards Paolo once she'd spotted him waving, and almost instantly disappearing into the crowd of people by the door.

Cooper blinked at the polished floorboards for a few moments, giving his vision time to readjust to normal, non-Technicolor levels of beauty and brightness.

He shrugged into his coat, checked his pocket for the key to the Airbnb shack he was renting, and headed out into the rain, dragging the leftovers of his shredded heart behind him.

4

EMMA

Monday morning, I woke up to late February sunshine poking through the cracks in my bedroom blind. I'd painted the room a soft grey, with bright white trim on the Victorian coving and huge sash window. Most of the furniture I'd scavenged from my parents' farmhouse, using the space in Dad's old workshop to strip, sand and repaint the wardrobe and drawers in white, and my old book-case mustard yellow. With matching cushions, a pretty blind covered in tiny yellow and grey flowers, and a whole wall of photographs depicting my life from birth until Annie's wedding, my room was a perfect haven. On sunny days like this one, I could almost pretend it belonged to the quaint little cottage I hoped to buy one day. But if that dream was ever going to happen, I needed to stop daydreaming and get out of bed.

I downed a mug of coffee in between throwing on running gear, smoothing my dark blonde hair into a ponytail and sidestepping Bridget, slumped at the kitchen table prodding a bowl of porridge.

'See you later, Young One. Have a great day.'

'Mmph,' she replied, which after twenty-five years I knew translated as, 'Stop interacting with me, freak, no one should be this cheerful at 7 a.m.'

I set off on the four-mile run to the Cakery kitchen, located a short stroll from Wollaton Park. One of the advantages of having our premises in my business partner's converted outbuilding was that she always let me use her huge, guaranteed-to-be-hot-for-as-long-as-you-wanted-it, digital eco shower. Given that one of the disadvantages of owning a cake business was the constant need to consume sugar and fat in above-recommended levels, I ran to work most mornings, so the shower was pretty much essential.

Now dressed in my work uniform of black chef's trousers and matching jacket, I found Nita in the design room. As well as a design room, the building included a larger room for consultations and tasting sessions, with a counter where we also sold our off-the-shelf celebration cakes to walk-in customers. Behind that were the kitchen, store rooms and pantry. Thanks to a very generous loan from Nita's husband, the kitchen was state-of-the-art, exquisitely designed and perfectly equipped to create works of culinary art. Because I needed order, organisation and a clutter-free working environment, I chose to set up my office space in one corner of the kitchen. Because Nita, God bless her, needed spontaneity and inspiration in the form of mountains of scraps of material and vision boards, torn-out pages from magazines, dried flowers, branches and endless random oddments she'd found in car boot sales, she got the design room.

I didn't mind. The kitchen smelled like heaven, and two of the walls were full of giant windows overlooking her vast back garden. Without having bumped into Nita at a wedding fair three years ago, I'd still be whipping up cakes in the cramped confines of my apartment. I might have been unfortunate in my original, failed choice of life partner, but when it came to business partner, I couldn't have done any better.

'Morning.' I pushed the design-room door open with one elbow, carrying two mugs of tea, and sidestepped a pile of old apple crates, a stack of yellowed bridal magazines from the eighties and assorted baby shoes.

'Morning, boss.' Nita accepted the tea gratefully, glasses perched on the end of her delicate nose. Calling me boss was how Nita got away with leaving all the organisational and administrative side of the business to me. I plucked a stray purple feather out of her enormous black bun, and had a look at the sheet of paper she'd been sketching on.

'Baby shoes? Are these to go on top of a cake, or is the whole cake a big shoe?' If so, I'd have to think carefully which baking tin to use.

'No, we had an enquiry after you left on Saturday for a baby naming ceremony. They want to give everyone a cookie with the baby's name written on it. When I suggested a dummy shape she nearly had a fit. She is apparently "not that type of a mother".'

I winced in anticipation of hearing how Nita responded to that, but before I had a chance to ask, she rolled her eyes.

'Don't worry, I restrained myself. She's not the type of mother to force her child's delicate feet into shoes, either, but for some reason found that idea quaint rather than offensive. And we can get the name printed onto a ribbon lace, save writing it out a hundred times in icing. I wouldn't mind so much if she was called Ann or Mo. But Genevieve would give me repetitive strain injury. I'm going to try an old-style Silver Cross pram shape, too, but that would mean icing the names so it's a token gesture.'

'Well, they will look lovely.' I took a sip of tea. 'After the ten-thirty consultation, I'm heading to the wholesaler's. Is there anything else you need that's not on the board yet?'

'Could you get me some jar lids? As many shapes and sizes as they've got, please.'

'I won't ask.'

'Don't, it's just something I'm mulling over.'

'I've emailed you the preliminary info from the couple coming in this morning – Poppy and Mike. Please don't make any reference to poppies being part of the cake, she's expressly stated she doesn't want that. Or the lemon and poppy seed flavour. She said she's had enough poppy-themed everythings to consider officially changing her name.'

'Duly noted.'

'Oh, and did you remember I need to leave at four? Bridget wants me to look at a wedding venue with her, to dilute the Mamma factor.'

Nita, adding another few strokes to the sketch pad, frowned. 'About time, too. I thought she'd never get around to it.'

'She's been engaged less than two weeks.'

'And the rest. Hasn't she known this man for nearly her whole life? Why wait all this time if you've found the person you want to be with? I knew Vik for two months before we got married.'

'Two months?'

She shrugged, a smile playing at the edge of her mouth. 'When you know, you know. And when you aren't allowed to spend any time alone together before the wedding night, it adds a bit of incentive to get moving.'

'Was it an arranged marriage?' I sat down on the spare chair, nearly spilling my drink as I wobbled about on the pile of books that already occupied the seat. Nita and I had discussed many, many different types of wedding over the two and a half years we'd been working together. I'd seen the stunning photos of her own special day, but somehow we'd never talked about the details of how her marriage came about. I suppose that was one pitfall of this job – we focussed on the happy moments, rather than the hard work that comes before and after.

'No. It was an introduction, arranged by our families, but the choice was ours.'

I waited for her to go on, not sure which of the questions jostling to be asked were rude, or simply betrayed my own ignorance.

'We met three times before the wedding, each time the house crammed full of parents and grandparents, aunties, uncles and siblings. I was so shy I barely spoke a word.'

'He married you having barely spoken to you?'

'He tells people my pakoras won him over.' She smirked. 'But the truth is we fancied each other rotten. You can't arrange chemistry, but there it was.'

She let out a dreamy sigh. 'More importantly, he was kind. And we were both committed. Chemistry, kindness and commitment – good soil in which love can take root, and a family can grow.'

Nita handed me a tissue from the box on her desk to blot the tears welling up. I wanted to pretend they were all for Nita's benefit – we had celebrated her silver wedding anniversary not long after I met her, and Vik's face softened every time he looked at his wife, the hard-nosed businessman brimming with tenderness. But, honestly? Some of the ache behind my eyeballs was for me. I never expected to be thirty-three and still single. If things had worked out as expected, I'd be celebrating my own eight-year anniversary this year. I thought about Mum and Dad, my sisters and their husbands and husband-to-be, and I longed so deeply for the chemistry, kindness and commitment they had found that it stung.

I just wasn't sure how many more first dates I could put myself through before I found it, too.

* * *

Later that afternoon, I met Bridget and my mum at a boutique wedding venue a few miles outside the city.

'Emma!' Mum called across the car park, loud enough to set off dogs barking on a nearby farm. 'You look tired. Did you catch Sam's cold? Working too much compromises your immune system.'

I waited until I reached them before replying. 'Hi, Mamma, no, I'm fine. I took the whole weekend off, as you know since I spent yesterday with you. Hi, Bridge, how was uni today? Has Prof recovered from the weekend's revelry?'

Bridget shrugged her bag back up on her shoulder. Underneath her tan leather jacket she wore a vintage red and white polka-dot dress, with a matching scarf to hold her hair back. My skinny black trousers and grey jumper, which had earlier seemed stylish and sophisticated, now felt frumpy and stiff. Oh, well. Next to Mum's brightly patterned leggings and turquoise furry gilet, no one would notice.

'He has, unfortunately. What's even worse is that he remembers most of what happened. Including that insane blind-date wedding bet he made with Prof Love.'

I gasped. 'No – he isn't going to go through with it?'

'He has to – professional pride. And the worst thing of all is that—'

At that point, the events manager opened the main door. 'So, you must be the blushing brides? Congratulations!' she trilled, bouncing on her toes. 'You make a stunning couple!'

'Actually, we're sisters. I'm the maid of honour. Bridget is the bride.'

'Oh. Oh!' She ended up being the one blushing. 'I didn't mean to assume, it's just, well, isn't there a groom – or another bride – here?'

'He's working,' Mum boomed. 'No point taking time off to look at a venue when he'd happily marry Bridget in a pub car park. Leave it to the experts.'

'Oh, right. Well, we can offer you something considerably more attractive than a car park for the most special day of your life.' The woman started ushering us inside the ornate entrance hall.

'And Emma here is most definitely an expert,' Mum continued. 'She makes wedding cakes – perhaps you have heard of her?'

'Does she? How lovely. This way, please, ladies.'

'She has organised weddings for her three younger sisters. Plus, there was her own, of course. Although that one ended with a broken heart. Her childhood sweetheart ran off three weeks before the wedding with that Helen Richards – do you know her? Fuzzy red hair, like a squirrel, skinny arms and legs? No? Anyway, he was the love of her life and she has never brought another man home in eight whole years. And now, on top of this tragedy, her fourth and final baby sister is getting married. It is so hard for the eldest one to be the last one left. People can be so tactless, so who knows what the looks and the comments will be, everyone feeling sorry for poor Emma, all alone? Still, she can take care of me and her father in our old age, at least this is some consolation. Her father has ME. Perhaps you've heard of it? I sell raffle tickets to fund research, if you're interested. I have a whole book in my bag, here.'

To her credit, the woman's rictus smile never faltered. 'Anyway... this is the Forest Suite. You'll see we've set up a couple of table options for you. I'll wait in the office, give you ladies some time to have a good look around.'

'That's wonderful, thanks,' Bridget replied, before Mum could say anything else. 'Look, Mamma. What do you think of these chair covers?'

I loitered by the entrance while they strolled around the hall, admiring the moulded ceiling and the beautiful oak panelling. I knew that most of what my mum said was utter rubbish, and I had grown partially immune to her gross insensitivity over the past thirty-three years, as well as understanding that in some warped way it was simply her expressing her sorrow on my behalf. But, for some reason, I felt more bothered now than I had in a long time.

Not about Jake. I was glad to have escaped a mistake of a marriage. But maybe it was more that, as I had grown up as a Donovan daughter, my future had always been presented as including a husband and children at some point. Preferably, the earlier the better (although perhaps not quite as early as Orla managed it). Imagining a life without those things felt like boarding a spaceship to another planet. Although nothing in my immediate future had changed, I felt lost, and afraid, and at times verging on panicked about continuing on down this path of singleness indefinitely. I was not someone who enjoyed uncertainty or relished the unknown.

Why couldn't it have been Sofia or Annie who ended up the single one? I threw out as a muttered prayer. Even Bridget would have taken it on the chin and embraced the adventure.

'What do you think, Emma?' Bridget asked, coming over to link her arm in mine. 'Can you see the sisters doing it for themselves on this dance floor?'

'I think it's all lovely, but, more importantly, what do you think?'

Bridget scanned the room. 'Yeah, it's fine. Got everything we need. Enough space, some comfy chairs.'

'Fine?' I frowned. 'I'm not sure that's the reaction Mum was hoping for. It's a lot of money to spend on fine. If you're not that bothered, maybe we should go with Paolo's pub-car-park idea.'

She laughed. 'I'm pretty sure Paolo would rather be inside the pub.'

'Which pub?' Mum had come to join us. 'You want a reception in a pub, let's go and look at a pub. Why did you drag me all the way out here to this fancy place if you want a pub?'

'I seem to remember you were the one who made the appointment,' Bridget said teasingly. She was always so much more patient with Mum than I could ever be. 'But how about you give me and Paolo some time to chat about it, and when we've decided what we want, we'll let you know.'

'You cannot pick a date until you have a venue sorted, Bridget.' Mum shook her head, baffled. 'These places get booked up years in advance.'

We began walking back outside towards the car. I was sure usually the events manager would have been chasing after potential customers to try to close a deal, rather than pretending she hadn't noticed us leaving.

'Then we'll wait. Or we'll use the back barn at home. I've been waiting eighteen years, Mamma. A couple more won't hurt.'

Mum harrumphed as she slid into Bridget's passenger seat. 'I do not understand you, Bridget. This is supposed to be the most wonderful, exciting time and you're treating it like deciding what to have for lunch.'

'I've had a long day, Mamma. I'm very happy and excited to be getting married, I just want to do things my way, in my own time. Unlike Orla, Sofia and Annie, I've got no reason to rush. Stop panicking and enjoy it.'

5

COOPER

When Patrick Charles Cooper completed the personal statement section of his university application form, he was supposed to explain why he wanted to study a neuroscience degree. This presented something of a moral dilemma, given he had to tick a box and sign to confirm all the information was true and accurate. Being truthful in this instance would be the equivalent of writing, 'Please reject me, I've decided I'd rather forget my four A stars and keep working on a zero-hours contract at a filthy warehouse with men who scare the crap out of me, instead.' Because the truth was, he'd been fully intending to study economics until he went to the Nottingham University open day and ended up queuing for a panini behind the loveliest girl he'd ever seen. It might look even worse if he went on to say that he had trailed her, and another girl who was clearly her sister, all the way into a neuroscience taster lecture. Her sister sat scrolling through the Top Shop website on her phone (yes, he was sitting directly behind them), but the girl scribbled notes furiously throughout, and from what he could decipher over her shoulder they seemed to be directly related to what the mumbling lecturer at the front was saying. Cooper's life flipped one hundred and eighty degrees in one hour. If this girl – this *angel* – found neuroscience so fascinating, he wanted to know everything about it.

And being still mostly rational and sane, Cooper knew that his was not a rational or sane reason to abandon the career you'd been working towards for eight years. He didn't even know what neuroscience was. Neurones, whatever they were?

He also knew it came across as slightly sinister. No one wanted a fledgling stalker around campus. But for the record, he'd never done anything like this before. At twenty-two, Cooper had never had a serious girlfriend, never been in love – or, perhaps more relevantly, been infatuated or followed anyone anywhere. For a long time, he'd been too intent on survival, on hoping people might stop hating him rather than daring to hope anyone might actually like him. He'd done this by learning to slip through life for the most part undetected. Keeping his head down, working hard but not so hard he'd become a threat, keeping himself to himself through school, college and then four years of working low-paid, come-and-go jobs, before he'd summoned up the courage and paltry amount of savings to dare to consider applying to university.

And now this.

Since the open day, Cooper didn't know who he was any more. He didn't really do friends, beyond the occasional mate. He didn't do family, since the aunt who'd raised him after his mother died had dumped him and moved to New Zealand the moment he turned eighteen. He certainly didn't do romance. Romance was a luxury, for people who didn't spend all their time working and didn't spend every last penny on paying rent and bills. What was he supposed to do with a girlfriend? Cosy nights in at his dilapidated bedsit? Very sexy, flipping the sofa into a bed at the end of the evening. Eating Pot Noodle sharing his one fork. Pretending the place didn't stink of mould and stale food and what he was fairly sure was decomposing rat.

But now her.

And suddenly Cooper was hunting for clothes that looked halfway decent in charity shops. Paying to get his hair cut. Working another double shift at the warehouse to afford a decent backpack, even though he had no laptop to carry, and couldn't even splash out on a packed lunch to put in it. He was daydreaming – *dreaming!* – imagining conversations, introductions, first dates, speaking on the phone last thing at night. Heart stuttering whenever he thought of her, his breath catching in his chest, feeling a completely different sense of urgency from the background panic that had propelled him forwards for over a decade. When he closed his eyes at night, it was her long dark hair, her sparkling eyes, her joy and her *light* that he saw. When he woke up, it was with a smile, because now he had a reason to get out of bed, because she was out there somewhere, and every day took him closer to the day when he would find her again.

Was this what they meant by love at first sight? Or had he totally lost his mind?

Either way, Cooper was now enrolled at the University of Nottingham to study neuroscience. Whether the sunshine girl was there or not, merely being back in that lecture hall made him feel closer to her, and that made him happy. And after everything, Cooper wasn't walking away from the chance to feel a sliver of happiness.

It was two weeks before he saw her. Two weeks of wearing the same not-ex-kid-in-care clothes he'd carefully put together, of walking around the campus with a fixed 'I'm a nice, normal, friendly neuroscience student exactly like you!' expression on his face (it wasn't bad – he'd done a lot of practising). And then, just when he thought he was totally lost, she came right up and spoke to him.

'Hi!'

Cooper froze. His heart felt as though it had catapulted halfway up his windpipe. Her eyes were darker than he'd remembered. Nearly as dark as her hair, but with tiny rings of amber around the pupils. How could eyes be so captivating, say so much? Like, every thought in her head was exposed for anyone to see, and she didn't even care, because she had nothing to hide, no shame, no dirty secrets, no horrendous past. Nothing to prove.

'Hi!' he managed, in a sort of shouty croak.

'Are you doing neuroscience? Because I thought I recognised you from the open day, but the lectures are so full of people it's hard to spot everyone, and I keep ending up sat next to physiologists or biochems. I've got my first tutorial in three minutes and I'm totally lost.'

This could not be happening. The lonely, neglected boy still hiding inside Cooper keeled over in a dead faint. Girls like this did not talk to people like him. Not while smiling, anyway.

'Um, yeah. Is it with Professor Cole? The tutorial's in his office.'

'Yes! Oh, my goodness, that is so amazing. I'm so relieved. Can I walk with you?'

'Umm...' Cooper hiked his bag up higher on his shoulders, and checked his non-existent watch for no reason at all except that he was disintegrating inside and wasn't sure of the correct protocol for dealing with this.

Her eyes widened in horror. 'I mean, if you're, I don't know, busy having some alone time, or something, that's fine, I don't want to impose. I could always follow behind you at a distance.' She laughed, awkwardly. 'Okay, now I just sound like a crazy stalker. But that is totally what I'm going to do.'

'No! No, of course not, that's fine. It's just... I can't find it either.'

'Well, if we're going to end up in trouble for being late, might as well do it together, right? My dad always says that shite smells better when it's shared. And this way, I can push in front of you at the last second, so I'll not be the last to arrive. Oh, and I'm Bridget.'

'Cooper.'

'Cooper? Cool name! You must have interesting parents.'

'Yeah. It's a long story.'

Bridget smiled. 'Well, I'll look forward to hearing about it when we've got more than three minutes.'

When they arrived at their first tutorial with Professor Cole, twenty-three minutes late, both of them dishevelled and sweating, she had no need to push past because Cooper stood aside to allow her to go first. Of course, he found out soon enough that she was madly in love with her boyfriend, and was planning on getting married as soon as she graduated. That was fine. He never really expected to be loved by the sunshine girl. Simply spending a few days a week in her orbit was more than enough.

And now, seven years later, here he was standing outside the door to Professor Cole's office yet again.

* * *

Emma

With Monday night being my gym class, and Bridget spending Tuesday evening with Paolo, I didn't get the chance to ask her what the 'worst thing of all' that she was going to tell me about the professor's stupid bet was. However, this evening was Wednesday Wine at Sofia's, and there'd be plenty of time to find out.

Although the whole family got together every Sunday, so as sisters we saw each other often, the key phrase is 'whole family'. With Mum hovering about scavenging titbits for her to then carve into the concrete of our family history forevermore, plus offer up to everyone she met, we had learnt to add a certain level of spin to our conversations. Plus, we could hardly discuss husbands, potential future husbands, children, or the deepening heartbreak at the lack of children, on any sort of meaningful level given that the very people we would be discussing were milling around.

So, a few years ago Wednesday Wine was born. Wednesday lime and soda in Sofia's case. Around twice a month we convened to slob about in comfy clothes, eat copious amounts of snacks, laugh, cry, bicker and most of all to share whatever was uppermost in our heads and forefront in our hearts.

They were the highlight of my month.

How did people get through life intact without sisters, biological or otherwise?

Once drinks were poured and plates loaded up with nachos, we settled in to dissect the goings-on of the past couple of weeks.

'I'll go first,' Bridget said, cheeks pink with excitement beneath her Mediterranean complexion. I was relieved to see it. While I admired how Bridget's positive outlook enabled her to treat something as potentially challenging as organising a wedding as nothing to stress about, I was growing slightly irritated at her total lack of decision-making so far.

'Go for it,' Sofia agreed, cosied up next to her on the sofa. 'Oh, wait, is that Annie messaging, Orla?'

Orla looked up from her phone, slapping it face-down on the arm of her chair in a suspiciously hasty manner. 'Ur, no. Just someone from the gym.'

'Who from the gym?' I asked. Wednesday Wine had a strict 'emergency messages only' rule, with the exception of the weeks Annie was able to video call.

'A work friend. It's not a big deal. I do have friends, who sometimes message me, and they didn't know I'm on lockdown for the next two hours.'

'And what is the name of this friend?' Sofia asked. Come on, we were sisters. We could sniff out a story from the merest glint in each other's eye.

Orla shifted on her seat, attempting to take a nonchalant sip of Sauvignon Blanc, which only made us more interested. 'Jim.'

'Jim from the gym?' I asked.

'Do you call him Gymmy Jim?' Bridget added.

'A bloke from work is messaging on your day off?' Sofia asked, throwing Bridget and me a hard stare.

'A *friend* from work is following up on a previous conversation we had. He's one of the trainers, and I asked him a question about using the weights. Stop making it into a thing – I'm allowed male friends.'

'Of course, you're allowed male friends! Which is why we're all wondering why you're acting so guilty. What's really going on?' Sofia asked.

Orla gripped her wine glass, face flushing. 'What's really going on is that I finally have a life that doesn't revolve around my kids. I have a job now, and workmates, I'm getting my body back, and I'm loving it. For the first time since I was a teenager I'm starting to love me. None of you know what it's like to spend eleven years being nothing but a boring, knackered, frumpy mum when all my mates are off to uni and having amazing careers and going on mini-breaks and out drinking every weekend. So back off, it's just a message from a friend at work.'

'Okay. We get it. As long as he knows that's all it is,' Sofia said.

Orla rolled her eyes. 'Yeah, because a trainer at the gym who's got a body like Jason Momoa would consider being more than friends with someone like me.'

'What, someone strong and fearless and funny and wise, and

amazingly generous and loving?' Bridget asked. Orla might act tough, but she loved her three kids with a tenderness that she'd inherited from Dad, and they could never doubt for one second how fiercely devoted she was to them. We also knew that, secretly, she loved us that way too.

She snorted out a few drops of wine. 'I don't think that's quite how he sees me, Young One. But don't worry, even if he did it's cool. I'm not going to do anything stupid.'

Tolerably reassured for now, we allowed her to change the subject by calling Annie. I don't think I was the only sister, however, to notice her checking her phone several more times as the evening went on.

Initial hellos with Annie over with, she got straight to business. 'So, twin of mine, what's the wedding news? I need a date already, but I'm presuming the lack of info on SisterApp means you've not got one sorted yet.'

'Not yet. Now Hatherstone Hall is open for weddings, we're thinking we should have a look there. It'll be easier for Dad being so close, and we know Ginger organises great parties.'

'Okay, well, get a move on and let me know. I want to know every detail. In fact, video chat me when you look round. And you need to start looking for a dress – don't you dare choose any old thing without showing it to me first!'

'She could wear your old dress?' Sofia joked. While Bridget and Annie weren't identical, they were pretty close, both having inherited more than their share of the Italian genes, leaving Orla and me with the pale Irish skin and blue eyes. Sofia, as diplomatic as ever, had ended up somewhere in the middle. With chestnut hair and hazel eyes, there might have been questions asked if it weren't for her Donovan nose and wide, Barone mouth.

'It would save some money...' Bridget mused, pretending to

consider it. 'But might freak Greg out a bit. Is he there? Shall I ask him? We've not chatted in ages.'

'That's because when you're meeting to guzzle booze and eat cake in your pyjamas it's three o'clock here. He's at work, keeping me in the manner to which I've become accustomed. Speaking of which, I've a client arriving in a few minutes. Is that it for note-worthy news, or anything else I need to know about?'

'Nothing that can't wait until you've got more time,' Sofia said. Orla gave her hand a squeeze. No news was always heart-rending news as far as Sofia and Moses were concerned.

We said goodbye, topped up our drinks and settled into the more mundane business of the evening. To my relief, Sofia told us about the offer of a loan from Dad. I had been stressing out about whether to say anything, not wanting to interfere, but I had hated keeping such a potentially significant secret from her.

'What are you going to do?' Orla asked, face pinched. The biggest cost of doing IVF was not the money.

'I don't know.' She shook her head. 'Moses says he doesn't want to. But I'm sure that's for my sake. Plus, he'd feel terrible taking Dad's money, of course. But I know how much he wants a baby. There must be a part of him that wants to take the chance. If I was being totally unselfish, I think I'd persuade him, because it's what he really wants.'

'But it's not what you want?' I asked.

'I want it so much my body physically aches every minute of every day. But I don't think I'm strong enough to dare to hope again, only to be disappointed. And I'm so tired, of the longing and the emptiness and the questions. This thing which hasn't happened has taken up so much of our lives the past four years. I don't know how much more I can keep giving, only to have it sucked down another black hole. It's stupid, that I want it too much to dare to try. I've never let fear stop me from doing anything. But I know what this will cost me.' She stopped, grabbed a tissue from the box on the table and wiped the tears pouring down her face, and then passed the box round so we could all do the same.

'And then, when I carry out another baby blessing, or help out at the toddler group. When I sit with Oscar on my knee, and he snuggles in for a story, I wonder how on earth I could even consider *not* trying again. Other people try three, four, even more times until they get their baby. Why would I give up after only once?'

'Well,' Bridget sobbed, 'you know whatever you decide to do, we are with you 100 per cent.'

'You have to talk about all this with Moses,' I added. 'You're both so emotionally involved it's impossible to know completely what the other one's thinking.'

'Whatever you decide, you'll only get through it together if you're honest with each other,' Orla said, ignoring another message lighting up her phone screen.

'I know. And I will be. Thanks for listening, sisters.' She opened her arms, and we all crowded in for a hug.

'Now, can I tell you what I'll be doing for the next three months?' Bridget asked, once we'd done loving Sofia and were ready for a lighter topic of conversation.

'Planning a wedding?' Orla smirked.

'Yes!' Bridget smirked back. 'But not just my own wedding!'

'Eh? Whose, then?'

'I don't know!'

'Ugh. This isn't that bet the prof made?' I asked, aghast. 'He's not palmed it off on you?'

'He most certainly has. He's made this terrible compatibility questionnaire, of five supposedly not random but I reckon completely random questions to go along with an even randomer DNA test to supposedly match a perfect couple. I have to use it to find potential candidates willing to marry someone who they won't get to meet until the wedding. All so that he can win the Henry Munch award at next year's dinner.'

'What?' Sofia asked. 'What are you talking about?'

Bridget explained. It took a while as Sofia had never heard of the *Blind Date Wedding* television programme, or Prof Love, being far too busy transforming her community to watch reality TV shows. But as she did, a weird thought started to creep into my head and promptly popped out of my mouth before I'd had a chance to stop it.

'I don't think it's such a terrible idea. In principle.'

'What? Marrying a complete stranger?' Orla scoffed.

'Well, look what happened when I tried to marry the person I'd loved since I was eighteen? That hardly turned out well.'

'Maybe not for you!' Sofia replied.

'I was talking to Nita this week about her marriage. She'd met her husband three times before their wedding. She said it was chemistry, kindness and commitment that made it work, and from those things, love grew. I don't know, I guess I began thinking about how I'd made such a rubbish choice of partner myself. I've been on so many awful dates in the past few years. Maybe someone else, someone with a bit of a clearer view, could make a better job of finding me a good match.'

Bridget looked at me, unusually serious. 'I am not setting you up with a husband via Prof's ridiculous test.'

'Please don't! I don't want you to. I'm just saying, maybe it isn't such a terrible idea. In principle.'

'Does that mean I can set you up with some blind dates again?' Orla asked.

'No!' we shouted back at her. 'Your dates are hideous.'

'Anyway,' Bridget sighed, 'if you can think of anyone who might like to apply, anyone who's not a total loser, and would at least make a halfway decent husband or wife so I'm not left feeling guilty for the rest of my life, please let me know.'

'There's probably loads of people at church looking for a decent partner,' Orla said, eyebrows raised at Sofia in question.

'I'm not going to advise any of the congregation in my care to marry a stranger.' She laughed. 'Sorry, Bridget, but it doesn't seem like an ethical thing for a church minister to do.'

'I know. I don't think it's an ethical thing for me to do, either. But I like my job and I want to keep it.' She shrugged. 'Who knows? Maybe I'll be flooded with applications. You can pray for me at least.'

'I always do. But now I'll be praying for that poor couple, as well. May God protect them from making the worst mistake of their lives!'

At that point, we heard the front door open and a moment later Moses came into the living room. A teenage boy carrying a rucksack hovered in the doorway.

'Eli!' Sofia stood up, her face creased with concern. 'Let's get you into the kitchen and find something to eat.'

Moses shook his head. 'It's fine, darling. I can sort it. I just wanted to let you know Eli will be staying with us for a few days.'

'Does his dad know?'

Moses nodded, his face grim. 'Yes.'

'Okay. The spare bed is made up.' Sofia stepped forwards to give Eli a side-hug, speaking softly. 'You're welcome here for as long as you need, you know that, right?'

'Yes, Pastor.'

'If you're living under my roof, you need to stick to the rules, Eli. And the first rule is that you call me Sofia. Got it?'

The boy nodded, sheepishly, before allowing Moses to herd him into the kitchen. Sofia yanked Moses back again briefly. 'When are you going to start giving me some warning before you do these things?' she hissed.

'Babe, I had no choice, you should have been there,' he whispered back.

'No. I shouldn't. I had the day off.' Sofia folded her arms. 'You know I don't mind Eli being here if he needs a place to stay, but you have to start discussing these things with me first!'

'But if I know you won't mind, why do I need to discuss it?'

Sofia shook her head in frustration. 'Just go and get him something to eat.'

Knowing better than to ask for details, Orla, Bridget and I quickly finished our drinks and left our amazing sister and her husband, so bereft by their childlessness, to take on the role of surrogate parents yet again.

After a laughable excuse for an interview, Cooper had been offered the job he'd turned down four years ago. Only this time, because Professor Cole had driven away yet another lab technician, leaving a fully funded research project half finished, he'd been offered a significantly higher salary, and his own office, on the basis that he completed the work.

It was a third of what he'd been earning a few months ago, where he'd had his own lab to go along with the office. Even so, he could think of only one rational reason not to take it.

And this reason was exactly the same reason he knew he'd end up taking it.

Professor Cole wanted Bridget to have a co-worker overseeing this crazy marriage project, to provide a 'steadier male influence'. And as long as he was prepared to spend a day a week making sure Bridget didn't get carried away on a wave of girlish romance, plus pull something out of the bag with the abandoned research, he could do what he liked the rest of the time. If the rest of the time consisted of running a project to blow the Walberg study out of the window, he wouldn't be getting any complaints from his new boss.

He snuck onto Bridget's Instagram account, looking for friends from uni who might still live in Nottingham, and found Ben Baxter. He'd shared a house with Ben, Bridget and a couple of other girls in their third year. Ben had bordered on being a genuine friend. He was a decent enough bloke, but viciously cynical about long-term relationships thanks to his parents acquiring numerous marriages between them, so was unlikely to be living with a partner.

Cooper messaged asking if he wanted to meet for a beer.

Four days later, after a curt phone call from the prof strongly suggesting that if he didn't get back to him with an answer by the end of the day, the offer would be revoked, Cooper met Ben for lunch in Annie's Burger Shack, a favourite hangout back in their student days.

'So, where've you been, man? I don't think we've seen you since graduation.'

Cooper shrugged, pretending to be absorbed in the menu, despite knowing he'd order a Sloppy Joe as always. 'I've been locked away in a lab in Cardiff doing brain experiments, remember?'

'Right.' Ben nodded, as if suddenly remembering. 'And they don't have trains in Cardiff. Or the Internet.'

'So, what, you've stayed in touch with everyone?'

Ben grinned. 'No. But I've done better than you. Did you even know Bridget finally got engaged?'

He watched Cooper carefully over the top of his beer glass. Cooper had never outright told Ben, or anyone, how he felt about Bridget. But Ben had eyes, and a brain, so it had probably taken him a matter of days to figure it out.

'Yeah. I saw her, a couple of weeks ago at an awards dinner.'

'Nice. Was her delightful boss there?'

'He was.' Cooper put down the menu as the waitress approached. 'Which is sort of why I'm here.'

They gave their orders before resuming the conversation.

Ben pretended to be shocked. 'So you didn't ask to meet up because you missed me?'

'Of course, I missed you. Who wouldn't miss that face? But I also need a new job. And Prof Cole has offered me one.'

'What, the big-money sell-out didn't pay off? How does Bridget feel about that?'

Cooper took a swig of beer. 'It paid very nicely for four years, until it didn't. And why would Bridget care?'

'Well, after turning down the job so you could have it...' Ben raised his eyebrows.

'What?' Cooper's breath froze in his chest. 'She didn't do that. Bridget would never have considered leaving Nottingham.'

'Man, you didn't know?' Ben sat back, his face creased with guilt, and Cooper knew him well enough to recognise it as genuine. 'I thought she told you everything.'

'Why would she turn down a job at IPD and stay working for Cole? You know how he treated her.'

Ben put his drink down, his face serious. 'Because she knew you needed it more than her. The confidence boost as much as the career. I mean, no offence, man, but you were kind of... lost back then.'

Cooper's face felt numb when he tried to speak. 'I can't believe she turned down an opportunity like that for me.'

If he'd known he'd never have taken it. Which was, of course, why she never told him.

'You were her best friend, Cooper. Considering how far she went out of her way for people she didn't even like, it's not that surprising. Remember that time she invited Evil Stephanie to move in with us, and we had to stage an intervention to throw her out again?'

They moved on to more stories from the past, but the whole time Cooper's mind was whirring, processing what Ben had told him. As much as he could convince himself that Bridget would have always ended up staying to be near her family and Paolo, if that was true, then why hadn't she told him she'd been offered the job? He'd known she'd applied, but she'd made out it was for the experience, and because she was under pressure from her careers advisor, with no expectations of it resulting in anything.

Crap.

He should have known. There was no way he'd have been a better candidate than Bridget Donovan.

Eventually, when their meal had been reduced to a few chips and a smear of relish, Ben brought them back onto topic.

'Are you taking the job?'

'I think so.'

Cooper tried to look up, seem casual, stuff down the old feelings of being a nobody, with nothing, having to rely on pity and handouts. 'But I need somewhere to stay. I don't suppose you know anyone looking for a housemate?' He winced. 'One who won't be too bothered about a deposit or first month's rent in advance.'

'Sure.' Ben nodded, cramming in his last few chips. 'You can stay with me.'

'Seriously?' I mean, he'd been hoping, but not expecting...

'Yeah, why not? To be honest, there's not as much money in the low-budget documentary industry as I originally thought. Too many people deciding to film their own depressing stories about how everything's gone to hell, to save them paying me to do it. I've even turned to the dark side.'

'What? You're filming weddings?' Now, that did make Cooper laugh, remembering the bitter contempt with which Ben had viewed anyone lowering themselves to wedding photography.

'Yeah, well. Once I realised I can get two grand on top of a free holiday to go and film destination weddings, I decided to reassess my standards.' Ben downed the last of his beer. 'Four hundred pounds a month, and we split the bills. No leaving your crap everywhere.'

'Saturday all right to move in?'

'Deal.'

* * *

The following Monday, Cooper walked into the lab where he had done the bulk of his third-year research project. It was as if nothing had changed: the ceiling tile next to the fume hood was still falling down, and the pile of random boxes towered in one corner. Apart from a couple of new machines and some different equipment, the main difference was that the old lab assistant, Pat, who used to keep everything running smoothly, had been replaced by an Asian guy who looked about fifteen. With four years at IPD behind him, Cooper viewed what had once seemed so exciting and cutting edge as in reality quite tired and outdated – a lot more probably should have changed, and he hoped that he could help rectify that soon. But, if he was honest, all of that was a side issue. Bridget's dad used to say that bad workmates turned a dream job into a nightmare, and the right ones could make a terrible job worth getting up for in the morning. He knew that Bear Donovan would agree there couldn't be a better person to waste a year on a pointless, idiotic project with than his youngest daughter.

Bridget looked up from the papers she was squinting at, sitting on her favourite lab stool by the window, and broke into a smile that cracked his heart right open.

'What are you doing here?' She plopped off the stool and came to give him a quick hug.

'I can't believe you're still wearing that old lab coat.' They'd spent an afternoon using Sharpies to customise their white coats with cartoons of animals conducting scientific experiments.

Standing in the lab with her again, it was as if he'd finally come home.

'What, you mean at IPD they made you wear a boring plain one? I bet they didn't even let you wear the antler goggles, did they?'

He laughed. 'I'd forgotten about those. They were such a health and safety hazard. But, more importantly, please tell me you aren't refusing to use the office?'

Most of the twenty or so postgrads and postdocs used a communal office, where each of them had a desk and some storage space.

She shrugged, glancing back at the workbench beneath the window. 'I like working here. Why would I want a crowded office with no natural light or clean air?'

'Space? No students spilling acid on your stuff? A place to hide from Cole or take a mid-experiment snooze?'

'Please! As if the prof ever deigns to enter the lowly lab.' She put her hands on her hips. 'But what are you doing here? And if it's not for a job interview then I don't want to hear it.'

'I'd better not say, then.'

Her face fell. Noticing him watching her, she quickly forced a smile. 'Well, it's lovely to see you anyway. Do you have time to stay for a coffee?'

'Yes.'

'Great. Let's go to the café downstairs. They've started doing a yoghurty muffin thing that is so good it's worth facing the med-student crush.'

'Or, we could go into my office? I've got a proper coffee machine in there. And doughnuts.'

Bridget pointed at him, eyes narrowed. 'Is your office inside the Nottingham University Medical School Neuroscience Department?'

He couldn't help grinning. 'It is.'

'In the old cleaning cupboard that overlooks the morgue

entrance, which we always said only the no-hope losers would accept as their office?'

'The very same.'

'I am so happy that you ended up a loser and I need at least two doughnuts to celebrate the dream team being back together.'

'Ah, Cooper. I thought that was you. Is Dr Donovan bringing you up to date?' Professor Cole had appeared out of nowhere.

'We were actually about to have a meeting to discuss the project.'

'Make sure she provides you with a detailed plan. I want to know you're happy with the timescales. We need a wedding by t equals eight weeks.' He disappeared as quickly as he'd appeared.

Cooper did some quick calculations as they headed into the cupboard office. 'That's the May bank holiday.'

Bridget plonked herself in the creaky, clapped-out spinny chair that the lab assistant had pinched from Behavioural Sciences. 'Yep.'

She tried to spin around but the chair merely let out a loud screech and jammed stuck after moving a couple of inches. 'I tried to explain the inconvenient timing but he wasn't interested.'

'Good job he's handed things over to the new senior research assistant, then, isn't it?'

Bridget clutched her heart with both hands beneath her lab coat. 'I cannot tell you how relieved I am to no longer be dealing with this by myself. This is one of the best days of my whole life.'

Cooper turned his back and started fiddling with the coffee machine. He knew that wasn't true – Bridget had one of those lives and one of those personalities that found great days all over the place. But for him, sitting in his new office that managed to be stuffy and freezing cold both at the same time, sipping coffee and listening to Bridget explain her work on the compatibility project so far, her cheek stuffed with custard doughnut; knowing that this was where he was going to be for the foreseeable future – well, it definitely made his top three.

* * *

Everyone else on the course thought they were mad, but Cooper and Bridget knew that the only way to end up on the same final-year research project was to both apply to the one that no other student would want to go near. Any other professor or doctor, and it was too likely that they would end up on separate projects. So that was how, despite Professor Cole being a boorish, sexist, highly annoying grouch, Cooper and Bridget ended up spending several hours each week carrying out research under the vigilant supervision of Professor Cole's research technician, Justin.

A couple of months into the course, Cooper arrived late at the lab to find Bridget nowhere to be seen. Justin, lost in a journal, simply shrugged when he asked him about it. A few minutes later he found her, crouched on the floor in the back of the cleaning cupboard, head buried in her arms.

'Hey, Widget,' he whispered, moving a mop bucket out of the way so he could sit alongside her. 'What's happened?'

She lifted a tear-streaked face, so stricken with sadness in the shadows that Cooper's own eyes welled up. 'I had a one-to-one tutorial with Cole,' she sobbed.

'And it didn't go well?'

'He said my project was unviable. I've messed up the planning and I'm clearly incapable of executing the required standard. That some people are fine at parroting other people's theories in an exam, but when it comes to actual research in a real lab then that requires being able to think for yourself. He told me to switch to psychology.'

'Ouch.' Cooper reached out and gave her hand a squeeze. There was nothing wrong with psychology, unless you were Professor Angus Cole, who considered it to be a course designed to allow dimwits and women to get a degree. Neuroscientists performed science, psychologists merely thought about it.

'I told him it was too late, if I switched I'd have to resit this year, and probably second year, too, and he said well that was up to me but either way he wanted me out of his lab so why not make at least one intelligent decision since starting university and face up to my own limitations,' Bridget said all in one watery breath.

'What?' Even by Prof's standards, that was cruel. And untrue.

'Don't worry, he's sure I can find a nice little job to suit me with a psychology diploma. Oh, and me responding by crying is further proof that I'm not cut out for a career in the discipline of neuroscience.'

'He's an arse.' Cooper had to let go of her hand to avoid crushing it. His fists were itching to go and wipe that smug smirk off Cole's face.

'I love neuroscience, Cooper, it's all I ever wanted to do.' She broke down into a wave of fresh tears. 'I don't want a psychology diploma. I want to study actual brain tissue but how can I when he's thrown me out of the department?'

Cooper shifted position so he could wrap Bridget up in his arms. Pressing her gently against his chest, he stroked her hair, wiping her tears with the cuff of his jumper. 'You know he can't do that. You're top of the year.'

'Not in epigenetics.' She sniffed.

'Well, I couldn't let you be first in everything, could I?' He leant back to look at her face, gently wiping another stream of tears with his thumbs. What kind of monster could make someone as sweet as her cry, and then be so callous about it? 'You need to talk to the head of Life Sciences, Professor Johnston. He knows what Cole is like. He probably says this to every female student who ends up in his lab. I wouldn't be surprised if it's some sort of test to see if you had the determination to challenge him.'

'What if he's right, though? What if I'm not cut out for it? What if I need to make an intelligent decision and face up to my own limits?'

'He's not right. You know he's not right.'

'But that doesn't matter, does it? Because I've been thrown out either way, and even if Prof Johnston made him take me back, he's going to fail my project.'

Cooper handed Bridget a tissue from a box on a shelf behind him, tucking her hair back behind her ear. 'It'll be okay. We'll figure something out. I promise. If the worst comes to the worst, you can share my project, and we both know mine is awesome.'

'That's true.' She managed a watery smile. 'Thanks, Cooper. I don't know what I'd do without you.'

She looked up at him through her thick eyelashes.

And then it happened.

Crouched in the grimy shadows, surrounded by bottles of bleach and cobwebs, Bridget looked into Cooper's eyes and finally, after two and a half years, one month and nine days, he couldn't hold it in any more. He ignored the voice in the back of his head yelling at him to stop, that this would ruin everything, that, even if she did feel it too, it was never okay to kiss someone in a committed relationship. He flicked that voice a mental two fingers, and he leant forwards to do what he'd wished and prayed for ever since she'd bounced into his life and changed it forever.

For the tiniest moment, she gently pressed her lips back against his, into the kiss, and her body swayed towards him, so subtly he wouldn't have noticed if he'd not been so acutely aware of exactly where she was.

At the precise second that the door burst open to reveal Justin, silhouetted against the bright lights of the corridor behind him,

Bridget sprang away. When Cooper replayed that moment a million times in his head later on, he wanted to convince himself that she'd pulled away because the door opened. That microsecond made all the difference. But he knew he was kidding himself. The way her eyes widened in shock and horror, and how she scrabbled to her feet, pushing past him without waiting to see if he followed her, refusing to stop even when he chased her down the stairwell. The fact that she didn't answer his texts, and made an impromptu visit home for the weekend, pretending it was because of what Professor Cole had said, not what happened afterwards.

Add to that the awkward few weeks until Cooper got himself a sort-of-girlfriend, to show her that it was a stupid moment in a cleaning cupboard, caused by high emotion and the stress of final year. All the evidence made it perfectly clear to the second-best neuroscience student in the year that the only scientific conclusion was that Bridget Donovan had not wanted to kiss him, was not secretly in love with him instead of Paolo, and that he was a total idiot who had to get away from her as soon as possible in order to preserve his own sanity as well as his dignity.

So, yeah, four years later he was trying not to think about what happened the last time he was in this cupboard every time he sat at his desk.

The last weekend in March, I persuaded Bridget to go wedding-dress shopping. She readily agreed, on the basis that Mum was visiting her cousins in London for the weekend. The future bride and groom were still dithering about a date, and I hoped that, by engaging Bridget in one of the more fun parts of wedding planning, I might help kick-start her into sorting some of the rest.

Not that it mattered to me when they got married – I loved living with my sister, and dreaded the hassle of finding either a new flatmate or a cheaper flat. But not knowing when that needed to happen was stressing me out almost as much as it was annoying Mum.

We headed into Nottingham town centre and hurried through the drizzle to a boutique bridal shop on the fringes of Hockley.

'I can't believe it was only last year that we were here with Annie,' Bridget said, pushing open the heavy door to dash inside.

'You must have taken a sneaky peak at dresses for yourself. I did and I don't even have a boyfriend.'

'All I could focus on then was getting my PhD handed in. Can you remember? I was trying so hard to pretend Annie's inconsiderate timing wasn't completely stressing me out.'

'Well, it all worked out fine in the end, Dr Donovan.'

We started browsing through the dresses on the rails, and shortly afterwards the shop manager came over.

'Now, I've put my foot in it by asking this before, but you two look familiar. I never forget a bridal party. No! Don't tell me! Let me see...' She circled us like a lioness sussing out a weak spot to pounce on. 'Neither of you were the bride... both bridesmaids? No, I said don't tell me! Dark hair, I'm thinking... Italian... and one of you blonde and pale... But the same strong nose, full mouth... Oh, yes! You're that family of sisters. With the mother. And this'll be, what...? *Don't tell me!* There was the maternity empire line, buttoned sheath, and diamanté princess. So, this is the fourth of you to get married! You've both been bridesmaids three times before. So, whose turn is it next...? SHHH! I haven't said you can tell me yet! I'd say... you. The eldest sister finally gets to be the bride!'

She pointed one finger at me, triumphantly. 'Wait here for two minutes. I'll bring out some styles you'll love while Phoebe pours the bubbles. PHOEBE?'

And before either of us could protest, she'd disappeared into the back of the shop.

'Remind us why we always come here, again?' I muttered, yanking out a random dress and thrusting it at my sister. 'Here, this style will suit you.'

Bridget ignored the dress, and its formidable price-tag, wantonly squashing the flounces and frills between us as she reached over to put an arm around my shoulders, leaning her head against mine. 'We don't have to do this. It was your idea.'

I shook her off with a flap of my hands. 'I want to do this! I'm very excited to be wedding-dress shopping with my baby sister. I don't understand why being the oldest means for some reason I should have got married first, and the fact that I haven't means I must be upset about it. I'm not!'

The clearly off-her-rocker shop manager hurried back in, holding an ivory dress covered in tiny lace that looked devastatingly close to the dress that I'd tried on, cried in, ordered, paid for, had altered and then dumped at a charity shop still in its plastic wrapping eight years ago. She skidded to a halt in her black brogues, gaping at me, then glancing at the dress and back to me again. 'Now I remember!'

'That's why we come here,' Bridget mused. 'You've gotta hand it to her, she's freakishly good at finding the right dress.'

'Lace off-the-shoulder sheath, one of our most popular 2011 styles. But now I'm thinking second marriage, maybe we want to go calf-length chiffon? Something more mature?'

'It's *my* wedding!' Bridget snapped in reply.

The manager flinched. 'But you don't even seem stressed! At least, you didn't when you came in. Are you sure?'

'Yes, I'm sure!' Bridget waved her engagement ring furiously. 'So, either put that boring dress back and find something to better suit a woman prone to the odd snackccident, or we'll find a bridal shop where we don't have to play a game of guess-who before we can even start browsing.'

'Right.' The shop assistant didn't seem fazed. She was probably well used to overwrought customers, after all. 'PHOEBE! Hurry up with that bubbly, and please add a complimentary Danish to the tray! I've a challenge on my hands with this one!'

Ninety minutes later, after Bridget had ploughed her way through twelve dresses, two pecan plaits and a fair amount of bubbles for eleven thirty on a Saturday morning, we were done. When Bridget tried on the tenth dress, we knew, although she tried a couple more just to be sure. Of course, I cried. Bridget looked like a fairy tale, and at the same time absolutely her. Even she had to admit the ball-gown dress embroidered with hundreds of tiny multicoloured flowers looked stunning.

'It's perfect.' I sniffed.

'It is,' the shop assistant agreed gravely. 'When do you need to pick it up?'

'Um...' Bridget stopped twirling and caught my eye in the mirror's reflection.

'We can have this one ready for you in six weeks, including the minor alterations. Although I strongly recommend a final fitting in advance of the big day.'

'Can I let you know?'

'We still need to confirm the venue availability,' I interjected. 'But it will be some time in the next few months. Probably June-ish time.'

'Will it?' Bridget saw the look of suspicion on the manager's face and took a deep breath before answering her own question. 'It will. June. Ish.'

'Oh, look.' I grinned at her while typing away on my phone. 'Ginger's confirmed that Hatherstone Hall is open and available from the fifteenth June. Shall I confirm that date?'

Bridget furrowed her brow. 'The pop-up tea shop is the fifteenth.'

'The twenty-second, then?'

'No, that's too close to the pop-up. It'll be far too much.'

'It'll be fine – we can manage them both given this much notice.'

Bridget put her hand on my arm, to stop me typing. 'But Dad can't.'

Would it stop one day, the reminder slugging into my guts like a slow-moving sledgehammer, stirring up anger and sadness at how my dad was only allowed snatches of normal life, constantly weighing up every activity against how it would impact him for the rest of the week?

I hated it. I hated what his life had become.

I made a note in my phone right then to start planning my cakes for the pop-up. Maybe I'd branch out, add in some dainty sandwiches and mini quiches. Stick it all on a tiered cake-stand. People would pay stupid money for an afternoon tea.

'Let's do the week after. The twenty-ninth.' Bridget gave my hand a squeeze of solidarity. 'If he only pops along to the pop-up, which is the whole point, he should be okay to make the wedding a couple of weeks later.'

I nodded. He was as likely to be okay for that date as he was any other. We'd learnt the hard way that this battle could not be fought via mental or physical effort, as if he could somehow will himself to be well enough. If anything, the ultimate strength was in having the courage and the confidence to admit the need to stay home and rest despite all hopes and expectations to the contrary.

But another glance at Bridget in her dress was enough to stop me wallowing and shake me into action. If I wasn't mistaken, my sister had finally committed to a wedding date!

'I'll just confirm with Ginger... Send a quick message to Mum... SisterApp... oh, and Paolo... There, done! We have a date and a dress!'

I gave myself an internal high five, ignoring the slightly dazed look on my sister's face as we helped her out of the dress and sorted the deposit.

'Oh, come on, isn't that why you asked me to be your chief bridesmaid, because I'm an organisational maestro?'

Bridget squinted at me as we hurried back through the rain towards her car. 'I asked you because, not only do I love you because you're my sister and so I have to, I actually really, really like you as a friend, and I wanted you to be involved. Involved, not taking over. Plus, if I'd asked Orla she'd only have ended up falling out with Mum and Sofia would arrange a bring-and-share lunch in the back of the church. Which was fine for her, but Paolo's family would go mad without a catered reception.'

'But it was also because my planning skills are legendary. And actually you want me to take all the hassle away so you and Paolo can simply say yes or no to my carefully presented choices, then rock up all stress-free and enjoy it.'

'If that will make you feel better, then yes, that's also why.'

'Right. We'd better get back so I can put a timetable together. Oh, and, Young One?' We reached the car, and I paused with one hand on the passenger door. 'This is your wedding. It's going to be amazing, I promise. And at the end of it you'll be married to Paolo!'

Bridget beamed back at me, jiggling up and down on her heels. 'I know. I can't wait!'

I think that was the first time my baby sister ever lied to me.

* * *

Cooper

It was definitely getting easier. It *was* getting easier, walking into the lab every morning and seeing her hunched over her workstation, or frowning at a machine printout. Face scrunched in concentration as she titrated a precise number of drops of solution into a row of test tubes.

Some days, he even managed to stroll past the lab door, coffee in hand, and resist glancing to see if she was there.

So, he was getting used to it. That feeling of awareness that constantly hovered behind his shoulder when he knew she was just at the end of the corridor. How one ear couldn't help listening out for the squeak of her trainers, and how he subconsciously braced himself for the squeak to stop outside his cupboard-office.

This morning, he'd lasted until midday before the magnetic

pull of Bridget sucked him out of his office and into her lab. He found her slumped at her desk, head in her hands. No lab coat, instead a pair of raggedy boyfriend jeans and a rainbow-striped jumper.

'Working on the side project today, then?' He walked up, nudging her shoulder so she'd look up and see the offered travel mug.

'Unfortunately, yes.' She hauled herself upright, accepting a grateful mouthful of coffee with eyes closed in relief. Cooper reached out and unpeeled a clump of hair stuck to the side of her cheek, tucking it behind her ear.

'I've tried everything.' She began ticking the list off on her fingers. 'Facebook, Twitter, Instagram, all those social medias that people old enough to get married haven't heard of yet, the uni newsletter, notice boards. That horrendous radio interview. I even put an ad in the *Nottingham Post*.'

'And no one's replied?'

She shook her head. 'If only. Then at least we could shut the whole thing down and I could go back to the actual neuroscience I'm paid to be researching.'

She waved at a pile of forms on her desk. 'What the genius Professor Cole failed to consider is that relatively normal humans might apply to go on a TV show and have a blind-date wedding, because an army of production people and a team of experts, including a famous and very charming professor, seemingly legitimise it. They also happen to get a free wedding reception, an amazing honeymoon and a swanky flat to live in for three months. But when it comes to marrying a stranger to help an egomaniac win a drunken bet, with zero budget, even less credibility and absolutely no chance of being invited onto breakfast TV afterwards, the pool of hopeful applicants looks more like a swamp.'

Cooper pulled up a lab stool. 'Let's have a look.'

Bridget handed him the top form. Typed across the top of the page in bright green font were the words, 'GREETINGS EARTHLINGS!'

He stood up, glancing at his watch. 'On second thoughts, I think we'd better relocate this meeting to the Tav.'

Bridget's eyes lit up.

Cooper grabbed his jacket and rucksack, a discreet glance reassuring him that his expanding heart wasn't glowing through his shirt.

Bridget was his oldest friend, and he was happy they'd reconnected, of course he felt good about it. It was only natural for his bloodstream to buzz at the prospect of working with a colleague he respected and trusted again. He was revisiting one of his favourite haunts from the best days of his life, so he was bound to have a spring in his step.

All perfectly natural responses from a neuroscientific point of view.

So. Yeah. He was doing better, relearning how to be friends – and colleagues – with Dr Bridget Donovan. And he was sure (almost sure) that soon enough his heart would get on board with the programme.

* * *

Two hours later, while he was finishing off the remains of the Tav's legendary mac 'n' cheese, Cooper's phone buzzed:

Compatibility project update 2.30

'Great.' He showed Bridget the message. She immediately checked her phone.

'Well, sometimes it pays to be discriminated against. You can enjoy updating the good professor while I check in on how my cells are doing.'

'I don't think so. This is your baby, you're coming with me.'

Bridget grimaced 'Ugh! If this is my baby, that makes Cole the father!'

Cooper raised his eyebrows in alarm. 'Foster baby! You had nothing to do with its conception. I witnessed the hideous event in all its glory, remember?'

An older couple at the next table gaped, not even pretending not to listen.

That caused her to smile, which was of course, as always, the goal.

'How could I forget?' She leant towards the couple and lowered her voice conspiratorially. 'Him and a couple of hundred other people, laughing and heckling. Taking photographs! Shouting suggestions!' She shook her head in mock disgust as Cooper grabbed the folder of applications from the table and bundled her out of the pub.

* * *

They weren't laughing when, twenty minutes later, they sat, backs rigid, facing Cole across his enormous desk.

'You've had seven applications? In three weeks?' He swivelled his beady gaze from Cooper to Bridget and back again. Cooper could sense Bridget trying to force her breathing to remain steady. The red flush that always appeared when she felt upset had begun creeping up her neck.

'To be honest, Professor, I'm surprised we've received that many. This is an extreme piece of research,' Cooper replied, working hard to keep his tone professional.

'And yet Lavinski managed to get tens of thousands, even

knowing the whole spectacle would be broadcast on national television.'

'I think that's *why* she got so many,' Bridget said.

'Demographic?' Cole barked, ignoring her.

'Six men, one woman. The men range from thirty-six to eighty-four. The woman is thirty-seven.'

'Well, one woman is all you need. Looking for a mate before her eggs dry up. She'll stick with it long enough to become impregnated, and he'll be happy as long as she keeps providing intercourse. Pick the nearest match using the compatibility test, make sure he's young enough to seem reasonably fertile and move to phase two.'

'What the hell?' Bridget barked.

'With all due respect, Professor,' Cooper said at the same time.

Cole raised one eyebrow at Cooper to indicate he continue.

'That is a significant assumption to make...'

'Considering you haven't even read the application forms!' Bridget added, her face mottled with emotion.

'Considering my forty-one years at the forefront of world-renowned neuroscientific research and my position as head of this department, I'd consider myself more than qualified to draw a basic conclusion. Are you seriously questioning my direction, Dr Donovan? After coming in here with such an appalling lack of progress? Was I perhaps mistaken in thinking you'd advanced beyond this level of mediocrity?'

Cooper grabbed Bridget's elbow in time to stop her launching Cole's life-size, solid marble model of a brain across the desk.

'Professor,' he said, in a tone that was clearly intended to speak volumes to Bridget. 'What Dr Donovan is trying to convey is that we want this project to stand the best possible chance of success. Given what's at stake...' he paused to allow Cole to remember precisely what that was '... we suggest that another few weeks of sourcing the right subjects is going to be worth it if it means we can achieve the optimal outcome. We're confident that with a little more time we can come up with a pool of potential participants that will significantly strengthen the statistics. After all, the greater the pool from which we source compatibility, the more this showcases the accuracy of the Cole Compatibility Function.'

Bridget peeked at him out of the corner of her eye, and it was all Cooper could do to keep his face a cool mask as Cole nodded, pretending to consider Cooper's argument while actually picturing Ernestine Lavinski grudgingly admitting to the entire scientific community that the Cole Compatibility Function (which Cooper had made up on the spot) was flawless.

'Very well. You make a fair point. I'll give you until Easter. Another fortnight. However...' Cole leaned back in his chair, hands clasped across his bulging gut '... your funding runs out at the end of this academic year, Doctor. Don't let me down.'

'No, Professor.' Bridget and Cooper both stood to leave.

'And if that wasn't clear, if you mess this up you'll be out of a job.'

* * *

'Farts.' Bridget blew out a blustery sigh as she flopped into Cooper's office chair. 'I'm going to lose my job.'

Cooper's heart clenched at the wobble in her voice. 'If it comes to it, I'll take the fall. I'm project lead.'

Cooper should contact HR about Cole, file a report or something. Except that explaining to a research associate that her tenure might not be renewed if she failed to produce results was hardly grounds for involving HR. Especially considering the level of clout the professor held in the university. No, Cooper would have to wait until Cole really stepped over the line. If he tried something too soon, he'd be out of a job alongside Bridget.

But in the meantime, Cooper had one priority: how to ensure that the Cole Compatibility Function was a triumphant success.

And for that, all he had to do was find two people gullible or unhinged enough to marry a stranger on the basis of five random questions and a DNA test.

But Cooper would do it. Even if he had to apply himself.

It was Friday afternoon, and I was late. Which never happens, unless Nita keeps me waiting. But today, Nita was the one waiting while I faffed about looking for my keys, and then my coat, and then forgetting the invoice. And now we were stuck in Friday traffic, which was the whole reason I wanted to leave before three.

'Are you ill?' Nita asked, searching for an alternative route on her phone.

'I'm fine,' I said, in a far snappier tone than intended.

'Hmm. Pregnant?'

'As if!' I let out an involuntary snort, skidding through lights a microsecond before they switched to red.

'Hmm.' Nita didn't say any more, but I could feel her assessing me, even as I kept my eyes on the road ahead, dodging in and out of clogged lanes to try to defy the inevitable.

'I'm a bit... distracted. I'll be fine once this drop-off's over with.'

'Distracted by what? Right here.'

I waited until I'd safely turned before replying. 'I don't know. Bridget's wedding.'

'You love organising weddings.'

'Not the organising, just the whole... I don't know... everything changing again. First Dad got ill, turning Mum into a totally different person. Then Annie moved and Orla's found this whole new life for herself. Now Bridget's finally getting married and moving out. I don't know where I am any more. I feel like the earth around me is shifting. Every time I look up, old landmarks have moved or disappeared. I'm not sure where I fit. And at the same time, I'm going nowhere.'

'You're heading into the busiest month of orders since starting the business. Don't undersell what you've achieved in the past couple of years, Emma. Your focus has been in the right place.'

I stop-started down the ring road for another minute or so, pondering that truth. 'Maybe. No, definitely, you're right. Building the business has needed to be my priority, and I love it. But at the end of the day, I still feel a bit adrift. Unsettled.' I shook my head, in a vain attempt to shake off the weird mood that had been plaguing me recently. 'I'll be fine.'

'Why do I get the feeling there's something else you aren't telling me?' Nita pursed her lips. 'I won't ask about your love life, because I love you and I don't want to be another one of those irritating people who are plaguing you about how upsetting it must feel to be the last sister to get married. But could they be a tiny bit right? It might help to admit how you really feel about it.'

'I don't care about being the last sister to get married!' I blurted, frowning angrily at a sports car cutting into the queue ahead. 'This isn't *Pride and Prejudice*. But I am sick of going on crappy dates, and dates that in my opinion aren't that crappy, but end up going nowhere anyway. I haven't kissed a man in over two years, because I promised my loved-up sisters that I wouldn't kiss a man I didn't have genuine feelings for, and now I'm starting to think that I might never have a proper kiss ever again. I just want one proper, knee-trembling, heart-exploding, delicious kiss before I die! And I'm starting to wonder about doing something drastic to get it. I don't know if it's a great idea or the worst mistake of my life, and now I've had the thought I can't stop thinking about it and there's no room left in my brain for where's my keys and don't forget the invoice. So that's why I'm distracted, and thank goodness there's the hotel because I don't want to end up telling you because you'll probably think it's a terrible idea or even worse you might not and then I'll definitely end up doing it.'

I screeched into the car park and found a spot as near to the main entrance as possible. The wedding reception was due to start in under an hour, and we had four tiers of gluten-free scrumptiousness to assemble. We carried everything in – always the most nerve-wracking part of the procedure – and then Nita carefully constructed the cake, tucking icing miniatures of the bride and groom's six dogs, all dressed in doggy bridesmaid dresses, amongst the hundreds of tiny, sugary autumn leaves covering every tier in a dozen shades from dark chocolate, fading through oranges and reds to pale yellow.

While I was placing the last of the one hundred and forty bone-shaped wedding favours on the final table, I heard a voice from behind me. 'Hey, Old One. I thought I might find you here.'

I turned to find Sofia scrutinising one of the biscuits up close. 'Please put that back. They've been precisely positioned exactly two point five inches above each plate.'

'Why?' My sister looked at me, baffled.

'Because the bride asked us to.' I moved closer to kiss her cheek and simultaneously took the biscuit out of her hand, replacing it on the table.

'And was it her idea to give everyone a dog biscuit? Because that's bizarre even for my husband's family.' The bride was marrying Moses' cousin, Mervyn.

I shook my head at her. 'These are my finest vanilla spice crumble cookies. Wheat free, dairy free, egg free and organic.'

Sofia rolled her eyes. 'They probably cost as much as my whole wedding buffet.'

'Considerably more, actually. So please don't feed them to her dogs.'

Sofia grimaced. 'I can't believe the dogs are coming. I mean, I love a nice dog, I won't object to them joining the party if they're well trained and can behave themselves. But these are not those types of dog.'

'Tell me about it.' Nita came over, wiping her hands on a cloth. 'She insisted on bringing them all to the design room to model for the cake decorations. After fifteen minutes of pure pandemonium we were forced to abort, although it took another hour for her to round them all up. Which is nothing compared to how long it took me to clean up the mess and replace the eaten or damaged supplies.'

'They nearly ruined the ceremony. Barking and whining the whole way through. And Alia kept twisting round to check on them while saying her vows. I'm worried I've married her to a chihuahua. I thought I'd seen it all, but there's something wrong when a woman has dogs for her bridesmaids. Not even one token human to carry the poop bags.'

'I hope they've had a bath since they came to my design room,' Nita said.

'I can categorically state that they have not,' Sofia replied.

At this point, one of the hotel staff opened the main doors to let the rest of the guests in, proving Sofia right as the six dogs came scrabbling into the room in a flurry of tangled leads, yaps and slobber, pulling the bride behind them. They made a mass beeline straight for the cake, and it was only once Moses and three other men had intervened, dragging them over to the other side of the room and securing their leads to table legs, that Nita could breathe again.

'It's all right,' she wheezed. 'I don't blame the dogs. It is not their fault their owner is delusional.'

At that point Moses strolled up, the groom beside him. 'Ladies, this is my cousin Mervyn. Mervyn, this is Sofia's eldest sister, Emma, and her business partner, Nita.'

We exchanged congratulations and compliments about the cake, Mervyn not appearing to mind that the dogs had relegated him to the second tier.

'Alia's best friend from college is allergic to fur. She broke out in hives before the end of the first hymn, so her and her boyfriend had to leave,' he went on to say. 'If you want to stay in their place, you'd be more than welcome.'

'Well, yes,' Nita muttered. 'If it's between your best friend and six confused animals witnessing the most important day of your life, why wouldn't you choose the ones most likely to crap on the carpet?'

Mervyn pretended not to hear. 'It'd be a shame to let them go to waste.'

Nita shook her head. 'Thank you for the kind invite, but I cannot bear to witness the inevitable moment those dogs escape and my masterpiece is mauled to crumbs. I wish all eight of you a very happy life together, truly, but I'm going to get the bus into town and grab a drink with my husband.'

With that, she left.

'You'll stay, won't you, sis?' Moses asked. 'I want to introduce you to Mervyn's mate Rob.'

'No, you don't,' Sofia replied firmly. 'Emma's sitting with me, and you'll keep all potential set-ups well away.'

So, that was that. I found myself at a wedding where half the guests had only met me once before, at Sofia and Moses' wedding, the rest were complete strangers, and the six canine bridesmaids had stuck their noses into places that I didn't like to think about right then. Especially when I was trying to style-out chef's trousers and a black T-shirt smeared with icing sugar at a forty-thousand-pound wedding reception.

Sofia and I were shamelessly cliquey during the starters and main course, two sisters, heads tucked in close together, discussing whether Annie was brushing off our questions about how things were with Greg because we were worrying about nothing, or because the something we were worrying about was too big to admit via a screen, and whether we had the patience to wait until we saw them at Bridget's wedding in June to find out.

'I'm more worried about Orla,' Sofia admitted as Moses' niece toddled over and started patting her leg.

'Do you think it's more than letting off steam like she says?' I asked. 'Orla lived for going out and having a good time before Harry was born. I can't blame her for wanting to do a bit of making up for lost time.'

Sofia lifted the little girl up onto her lap and gave her fluff of baby hair a sniff, making my heart squeeze. 'No one picked the kids up last Thursday.'

That got my attention. 'Why? What happened?' Orla's three children all attended the after-school club that Sofia ran at her church.

'I couldn't get hold of Orla, so I drove them home myself. Sam arrived as I got there. He'd had parents' evening, and had no idea where Orla was. He seemed... not himself.'

'Tell me she wasn't with that guy from work.'

Sofia nodded grimly, before breaking into an enormous smile when she saw the baby on her lap frowning at her. 'She was though, wasn't she, Abigail?' Sofia cooed. 'She turned up a few minutes later and told us she was at the gym having a private one-on-one training session with Mr Gym Jiminy Jim, didn't she?'

'No wonder Sam isn't himself.'

'I had to break up their argument to suggest that maybe accusations about "all you care about now is your new job", and "well at least I care about something" were not helpful, given that right now their three children needed to know that what they cared most about was, despite the evening's actions to the contrary, them.'

'Crap.'

'I'm really worried about them. Orla's going through some sort of got-a-bit-of-my-life-back crisis, and she's lumping Sam in with all the negative things she's trying to leave behind in this quest to find herself.'

'He's not exactly helping matters by refusing to be part of it. Why don't they go out and have fun together? One of the reasons for living in Hatherstone was so Mum can babysit.'

'I texted her yesterday and offered to have the kids for a weekend so they could go away somewhere.' Sofia gave Abigail a kiss and let her wriggle to the ground, where she toddled off towards the next lucky relative. 'She said there's no point going away for a romantic weekend when Sam can't even be bothered to talk to her, let alone do anything romantic.'

We both let out a long sigh. There was a fine line between being a supportive sister and an interfering one. We all lived in slight fear of turning into our meddling mother, but could we really sit back and watch Orla teeter ever closer towards doing something that could destroy her family – presuming that she'd not already reached that far?

'We could visit this Jim who works at a gym. Run him off,' Sofia mused.

'We could. But if she found out then she'd totally shut us out, and we'd be even less able to help her. Or the kids.'

The waiters came round with goblets of chocolate mousse, and we moved the conversation onto other things. It was a wedding after all, we were meant to be celebrating.

'I'm presuming you don't want Moses to introduce you to his random single mates,' Sofia asked, her eyes dancing.

'You presumed right. If they are worth meeting, then I'll do it when I'm in a nice dress. Or at the very least a clean one. And my hair's been styled beyond "functional topknot".'

'Oh, so you are interested in meeting someone? I thought drunk neighbour might have put you off.'

'Drunk neighbour totally put me off. I'm definitely done with dating around. And all the new men I meet are planning their wedding.'

'What about him?' Sofia asked from behind her water glass, her eyes on the other side of the room where a photobooth had been set up.

'The photographer?' I swivelled my head round to look, taking in enough with my first sneaky glance to follow up with a second, more blatant one. 'He does look nice.'

And he did – coppery coloured hair framed an open, friendly face as he persuaded the two women now standing under the balloon arch to strike a pose.

'Nice? I was thinking more like pretty darn hot. Maybe we should join the queue.' Sofia grinned.

Before I could wriggle out of that suggestion, Mervyn's best man stood up and called for everyone's attention. Listening to all the speeches about how wonderful love is, and how amazing it is to find someone to love you for you, and how beautiful and special and magical it is when you have someone to share your life with, and how lucky they were, and how lucky Benji and Bramble and Carrots and Dink and Ms Sniffingtons and Lady Fluff were to have Mervyn as a step-doggie-dad, was not helpful.

As soon as the speeches were over, I kissed my sister and her lovely husband goodbye, gathered my stuff from where we'd hidden it behind the cake table, waved a thank you to Mervyn, and left, dragging my morose mood with me.

As I opened the door to the car park, an almighty screech echoed down the corridor from the direction of the reception room. A streak of fluff whizzed past, knocking me into the door frame as it galloped into the darkness beyond.

I stood holding the door open, unsure whether to go out after the dog myself, or leave it to someone who might stand a chance at catching it – someone who knew its name, for example, or at least knew anything about dogs at all. However, my agony of indecision lasted mere seconds, as a stampede of wedding guests, headed up by the bride, noticeably missing the groom, raced down the corridor, crushing me against the door frame as they spilled out into the car park.

A few steps behind them, looking decidedly less panicky, and quite possibly on the brink of bursting out laughing, came the Nice Photographer.

'She really loves her dogs,' I said, over the sound of the bride's hysterical wails of 'CARROTS!'

'Either that or Ms Sniffingtons stole her favourite carrot.'

'Carrots, plural,' I said, pointedly. 'Nobody has only one favourite carrot.'

He raised both eyebrows in amusement, his face breaking into a grin, and in an instant he transformed from being nice to being, well, as Sofia put it, pretty darn hot. I looked back at the crowd outside in an attempt to distract myself from how smoothly his black T-shirt fitted his torso and upper arms. Maybe if I stopped looking at him long enough, my heart would stop working overtime to pump all that extra blood to my flaming cheeks and I'd be able to stop my eyelids fluttering like some seventeenth-century damsel.

I took a deep breath, got a grip and wrestled back enough of my composure to focus on the real drama.

'Oh, no. they've gone totally the wrong way.' Despite all the evidence to the contrary, the gaggle of guests had presumed that the bride would know where Carrots had headed, and so instead of sensibly spreading out to cover the numerous potential hiding places where a part-Dobermann, part hound of the Baskervilles might have taken refuge, they'd all simply followed Alia in a jumbled herd towards a clump of trees at the far end of the car park.

'She ran behind the bins.' I winced as Alia let out another caustic screech. 'Maybe we should let her have a few minutes' peace before blowing her cover.'

'I'd be inclined to agree with you, if she hadn't taken the bride's wedding ring with her.'

'What?'

'She was showing her bridesmaids the ring.' He shrugged. Oh, dear. Even his shrug was lovely.

'A perfectly natural thing to do.'

'I guess Carrots wanted a closer look.' He went out of the door and started walking towards the bins.

'I'll go and tell Alia where she's hiding,' I called, but he turned round, shaking his head while still walking.

'Best if it's one person, rather than the whole crowd.' He gestured at the swarm of guests milling in the distance, some of them whacking the bushes with sticks.

Deciding that two people might be even better than one, I cautiously followed him to where a tiny stump of furry tail poked out from the side of the far bin. Getting down to a crouch, the photographer held out one hand, averted his eyes and started softly encouraging Carrots to come closer.

Unlike me, who found that gentle smile and warm words nigh-on irresistible, Carrots shuffled a few steps further behind the bin. Communicating with a series of random facial expressions, Hot Photographer managed to convey his new plan, and we swapped places before he slipped around the back of the bins. Once I'd given him enough time to get in place, I started edging closer towards Carrots, who, despite being the size of a small horse, was trembling.

I got to within a couple of metres before she turned and scrabbled away (which was the whole plan, after all – if I'd managed to get within touching distance I've no idea what I'd have done). Unfortunately, seeing a strange man with his arms outstretched to block her escape route made her even more frantic. In three swift moves, Carrots lunged from a discarded cardboard box, to a pile of crates, and straight into the open-topped, industrial-sized bin.

'Here, hold this.' Before I could blink in surprise, Hot Photographer had chucked me his jacket and vaulted in after her.

The bin was mostly full of packaging, but still, it was a *bin*. It smelt even worse than Carrots. Various giant plastic tubs and pieces of cellophane were still smeared with the remnants of soured sauces and other unidentifiable refuse that made my eyes water. Carrots was crouched in one corner while Photo Guy waded to reach her, cooing reassuringly in between the odd retch. He carefully steered himself close enough to take hold of her diamanté tiara, which was thankfully kept in place by a Velcro strap under her chin, and, using his body to hold her steady against the rusty side of the bin, attempted to prise open her jaws.

When he slipped in the pool of slime sloshing about on the bin floor for the second time, I knew the only thing to do was clamber in and join him. It took every effort on both our parts to keep Carrots still while Photo Guy opened her mouth wide enough to see the white-gold band glistening in the corner of one cheek.

'Can you reach in and pull it out?' he asked, breathless from the effort. I glanced at him, heart racing wildly, trying to assess the like-lihood of losing a hand.

'Don't take too long thinking about it!'

'Promise you'll not let go. I'm a baker and I really need both my hands.'

'Yes, I promise, whatever, just hurry up...'

Screwing my face up in horror, I tentatively started moving my hand towards the gaping cavern of enormous teeth.

And then before I could have a chance to prove how brave and awesome I was, Alia and her champagne-fuelled mob arrived, the tops of several heads poking above the top of the bin. Alia shrieked. Carrots jerked her head back, her colossal tongue filling her mouth as she swallowed, simultaneously rearing back so that both Photo Guy and I toppled into a pool of broken plastic and rancid slime.

'Carrots!' Alia cried. 'My baby! What have they done to you?'

The dog bounded out of the bin and straight into the arms of her demented mother.

The photographer, not looking quite as hot as he had done a few minutes ago, sat up, pulled me up to join him and flicked a clod of something brown and sticky off his other hand. 'She swallowed it, didn't she?'

I picked a string of green something off the side of my head, forcing down my gag reflex before replying. 'Is it wrong to feel some consolation knowing how Alia's going to get her ring back?'

'If that's wrong, then I don't want to be right.' He smiled again, and even lying in a pile of filth, smeared in bacteria-riddled food stains, it made my heart question the whole no-dating decision. I briefly considered Nita's three-point checklist for a successful marriage:

Chemistry – big fat yes.

Kindness – the way he'd murmured sweet nothings and tried so gently to open the dog's mouth, even after it'd led him into a swamp of rubbish, would surely indicate a good heart?

Commitment – going to all that trouble for a near stranger's ring – what feats would he take on for someone he loved?

'Yet one more reason to hate weddings.' He clambered to his feet, again offering his cleanest hand to help me do the same.

'You hate weddings? You're a wedding photographer!' The checklist disappeared in a puff of smoke.

He looked shifty, which wasn't difficult given the circumstances. 'It's a temporary stopgap.'

'How can you hate weddings?' I asked again, later, when we were waiting for the hotel staff to bring us out our things (for some reason, they didn't want us entering the hotel premises). 'Unless you hate beautiful decorations and delicious food and people having a great time and the whole idea of love and happy-ever-after.'

'I've been to enough weddings to know that hardly anyone has a great time. And the décor and the food and all those fancy little favours and choreographed dance routines are just a thin façade trying to help everyone forget the truth that happy-ever-after is a fantasy. Shackling yourself to one person in a futile attempt to pretend they'll be the answer to all your problems is only going to end badly. Either you both wise up, and spend another hideous amount of money trying to undo the mistake, screwing up any children you've had the misfortune to bring into the sorry mess in the process. Or, you remain too pig-headed, lazy or cowardly to do anything but wallow in the tepid remains of your noose-for-two for the rest of your pitiful lives.'

The door flew open. 'Is this all of it?'

Thank goodness! I virtually snatched my coat and boxes from the waiter's outstretched hands before Not-nearly-so-hot-now

Photographer could suck me any further into his vortex of despair. I nodded my thanks and started to head towards my car.

'Wait!' He caught up with me. 'Um, thanks again for the help.'

'You're welcome. Alia is married to my brother-in-law's cousin, so I kind of felt obliged.'

'Still, I'm not sure how many women – or men – this is totally unrelated to gender – would clamber into a skip so willingly.'

'I wasn't willing. But I couldn't stand there and watch you slip into that gloop one more time.' I reached my car, opening the boot and dumping my boxes inside. He didn't seem in a hurry to leave.

'Anyway... at least you were in your work clothes, and didn't ruin a nice dress.'

'Yep. Well, see you, then.'

He pushed his hands into his jeans pockets, rocking back on his heels. 'Would you like to have a drink with me some time, when we don't both stink of rotten mayonnaise?'

'Oh! Um...'

He smiled, face deceptively warm and affable considering the depths of bitterness that lay beneath. 'I promise I won't coerce you into a bin, or any other waste receptacles. No matter how huge the dog I'm chasing.'

I thought about it, for a whole three seconds. Were chemistry and kindness enough reason to go and have a drink with an attractive man, probably resulting in a lovely evening?

Then I thought about thirty-seven first dates in three years. About how I was so done with rehashing the getting-to-know-you chit-chat, the same old questions and big reveals, desperately pouncing on the tiniest scrap of common ground. And I made a decision. I wasn't going to go through the agonising wardrobe choices, the small talk, having to keep alert watching for any signs of weirdo/liar/creep, the awkward who's-going-to-pay moment, the fumbling half-hug, half-kiss goodbye, followed by the exhausting what to message, when to message, waiting for them to message, praying they won't message...

There was no way I was going through any of that again unless that commitment box was checked. And if I *knew* that the person asking, however kind and smiley he might be, considered commitment to be a noose-for-two? Well...

'Thanks for asking, but I don't think we're looking for the same thing.'

'Ah, okay.' He shrugged, looking sheepish, and so cute it danger-ously rattled my resolve.

'I guess it was the wedding speech. Probably should have saved that for the second date.'

'Don't worry, I'm sure you'll make someone else a very happy one-night stand.' I got in the car before I could change my mind and went home to use up all the hot water scrubbing the stink out of my hair, along with the whiff of lonely despair from my heart.

9

COOPER

On Tuesday, Cooper met his new housemate, Ben, in the Tav after work.

'Some things never change.' Ben laughed as they took their pints over to one corner. 'They've even got the same newspaper propping up the wonky table.'

'I think Scary Sue wore that exact same outfit the night she tried to seduce you in the men's.'

Ben nearly choked on his first sip. 'Ugh. Don't remind me.'

Never one for small talk, Cooper got straight to the point. 'I'm looking for someone to do some filming.'

'Oh?' Ben swallowed another mouthful of beer.

'It's fairly long-term, at least nine months, with a pretty intense first couple of weeks, then maybe one day a fortnight filming. And then we need everything edited.'

'What is it, a science project? Do you want me to film brains? This sounds like the opening scene in a horror movie.'

They sat back while Scary Sue slid a packet of Scampi Fries in front of Ben with a wink. 'On the house, for old times' sake.'

He managed a strangled approximation of thanks while Cooper stalled for time.

'You might prefer it to be a horror movie.'

'What, is it unethical? If it's experiments on animals then we can end the conversation here.'

'Nothing like that. The pay is crap though.'

'Honestly, mate, as long as it's not having to endure another twelve hours of wedding nausea, I'm probably up for it.'

'Yeah, so...'

Cooper told him about the project, waited out the initial deluge of scorn, bought another couple of drinks and wrote a figure on a piece of paper, sliding it across the table as big businessmen did in the films.

'It'll be easy money. You can film a wedding with your eyes closed, most of the rest is straight interviews.'

'Where's the honeymoon?'

'Where do you want it to be?'

Ben took a slow drink while he thought about it. 'Hawaii.'

'The entire project budget wouldn't cover that.'

'A May wedding? How about the Highlands. We can get some good shots in the mountains, messing about on a loch, cosying up in a log cabin.'

'This is documenting scientific research, not making a Netflix movie.'

'Mate, if I'm going to be shooting a nine-month wedding video, I'm going to make damn sure it's the last one I ever have to film. This'll be Oscar worthy by the time I'm finished with it. At the very least worth a late-night slot on Notts TV.'

'What, once you're a sought-after documentary filmmaker you won't do my wedding?'

Ben tipped back his head and full-on laughed at that. 'If you ever find someone gullible enough to marry you, I'll film it for free.'

* * *

Emma

By the middle of the week, I still hadn't shaken off my post-wedding blues. This was a tricky turn of events, given that I was supposed to be organising my own sister and housemate's wedding, and my job that week included meeting with and baking cakes for a whole range of people celebrating either their love and commitment, the tiny new people who existed as result of love and commitment, or how astoundingly long they'd ended up in love and still committed to each other. Love, marriage and happy-ever-afters seemed to be everywhere.

I dumped a stodgy lemon sponge in the bin, cleared up the mess and let Nita know that I was going out for lunch and might not be back for the rest of the day. She was lost in a world of lace gloves and hat pins; I'm not sure she even heard me.

Forty-five minutes later, I found my dad exactly where I expected him to be – sitting in his recliner chair by the fire, a rug across his knees, his walking stick propped against the coffee table.

He was fifty-six. My heart cracked every time I saw him.

'See that, Emma?' He pointed at the French windows, where on the other side a pair of rabbits were sitting on the lawn. 'Like your Candyfloss.'

I leant down to kiss his cheek, wincing at the recollection. 'What a terrible name for a pet.'

'Well, he was a pretty terrible pet, to be fair. Not that you can blame him!' Dad let out a hoarse wheeze of mirth.

'I can't believe you gave in and let me catch a wild rabbit.' I took a seat on the arm of his chair, leaning gently on his shoulder. I could fit my whole head on there with room to spare.

'After you'd spent nearly the whole summer trying to tame him, lying on the grass and feeding him dandelions before you lured him into that cardboard-box trap, I could hardly make all that work a waste of time, now, could I?'

'I'm not sure it was even the same rabbit.'

Dad full-on laughed at that, bouncing my head as his shoulders shook. 'You swore blue that you'd recognise him anywhere!'

'I'd have sworn every colour in the rainbow if it'd got me a pet.'

'Well, it certainly taught you some patience.'

'And that patience isn't always worth the wait. Not when it involves wild animals, anyway.'

We sat together and watched the rabbits wuffling through the wet grass. The only sound his steady breath, as I soaked up the unconditional love that remained strong and sure.

'I'll put the kettle on.'

'Grand. Your mamma won't be back for an hour.' Which really meant: *you can stay for an hour without risk of the grand inquisition*.

I brought the tea, strong and black how Dad liked it, and a plate of buttery raisin toast.

'I found a loaf in the dishwasher. I'm presuming it doesn't need a wash.'

Dad shook his head. 'Ah, yes. I wondered where that had got to. In the end I gave up and had a couple of oatcakes.'

'You hate oatcakes.' I sat on the nearest sofa, and handed him his mug.

'Well, I hate being hungry more and your mother had already left. It seemed the easiest option at the time.' He took a drink of tea and ate half a slice of toast in one mouthful. 'Now, do you want to tell me what has you floating about here in the middle of the day instead of building that business empire of yours? Mind, if your mother sent you over to babysit, it might be best not to tell me.'

He squinted at me, and before I could come up with an answer, my eyes were swimming with tears. Saying nothing, Dad handed me his neatly folded handkerchief.

'I don't know. I've been feeling a bit... lost. And at the same time, kind of stuck. I feel like I'm not going anywhere, but I don't know where to go.'

'Are you sure about that?' He gazed at me, steadily. 'Or do you know where you should go, but you're scared to go there?'

'The only place I can think of going is beyond crazy, Dad,' I whispered. 'Everyone, *everyone* would tell me not to go there.'

'Then the fact that you want to go anyway should say something.' He put down his cup so he could take hold of my hand, his rough work-worn fingers stroking my palm. 'If I was having this conversation with Annie, or Orla, I might give different advice. But the truth is, those madcap girls wouldn't ask, they'd just jump straight into it. You're a sensible woman, Emma. Too sensible sometimes. And more than that – you're wise. Trust that. Trust yourself.'

'I don't know if I can any more. My head's a mess from all the second-guessing.'

'Well, you can trust God. Ask him to show you the way.'

'Will you pray for me, Daddy?'

'Every day, my love. Every single day.'

After another precious silence, watching the fire crackle as we ate and drank, my dad spoke again.

'You know I married your mother on my twenty-first birthday?'

I nodded, leaning back into the cushions of the ancient sofa.

'Every day, from the morning after our wedding, I woke her with a cup of tea.' He shook his head, smiling. 'It was some time around our first anniversary that she confessed she'd hated tea. She was Italian, where was the morning espresso? But when I made her a coffee the next day, she wouldn't drink it. Said she'd grown used to the tea after all. And in all the pregnancies, all that morning sickness, I made her an apple and ginger. And the mornings I left at the crack of dawn, she'd still want her tea, so we could sit in bed and drink together before I left. Any time I was a little late, maybe having a lie-in after a wild one the night before, she'd ask me, "Do you not love me any more, Bear Donovan?" and that was my cue, up I'd jump and get the kettle on. This is how I loved her, you see. I'm not a man for the big fancy stuff. Flowers, or jewellery, romantic gestures. But this is how a nineteen and a twenty-one-year-old clue-less pair of skint eejits start building a thirty-five-year marriage. It's not about a few grand gestures, but the millions of tiny ones, every single day. It's making a choice, even the days you're knackered or feeling a bit selfish or lazy, or you're still smarting from a blazing row. It's rubbing her shoulders when she's had a hard day with five wee girlies. Sitting on the side of the sofa with the broken spring, so that she's comfortable. And it's how, when I couldn't get out of bed to make the tea, your mother fetched it for me. And has done every day since.

'I thank God I chose a woman I could love forever. But love is doing, more than feeling. Even when you can't do that much any more, the bit you can do counts. Maybe you're going to have to start doing before you know how you really feel about it.'

By the time I'd dried my eyes and blown my nose, he'd fallen asleep. I tucked a tartan blanket around his middle, tidied up the pots and closed the door on my way out.

* * *

That evening, the Donovan sisters convened in my apartment. I'd gone for a long run, followed by an even longer bath, but was still jittery and anxious and, as Orla put it, 'even more uptight than usual'. We sat reclining on the two sofas, heads back to stop our face-packs from slipping, drinking gin cocktails through paper straws.

'Oh, Bridget!' Orla suddenly sat up, causing the remains of her drink to slosh dangerously close to the rim of the glass. 'You'll never guess who I saw in town the other night! A right blast from the past.'

Bridget, lounging beside me on the other sofa, took a thoughtful slurp of Tom Collins. 'Was it Jake, crying into his pint about how every life decision he'd made since cheating on Emma had led him further into an abyss of premature middle-aged monotony?'

'Well, duh. If it was him I'd be asking Em to guess, not you.'

Sofia grabbed Orla's arm, jolting upright as she grinned so hard a blob of mask slowly slid off her face and down her jumper. 'Not Cooper!'

Orla gave her a triumphant high five.

'Oh, I *love* Cooper!' Sofia cooed. 'He's like the little brother we all thought Annie was going to be.'

'He's older than you!' Bridget retorted.

'Well, you know what I mean. And what was he doing in Nottingham? I thought he'd moved to Bristol. Did you know about this?'

Bridget glanced sideways at us. She was pretending to be relaxed about the whole thing, but really – *Cooper*? Her best friend was back in town and she wasn't excited about it?

'It was Cardiff. And I didn't at first. He's not exactly Mr Forthcoming, is he?'

'Have you *seen* him?' I asked, totally bemused that she hadn't mentioned this. Bridget had been bereft when Cooper moved away.

'He came to the awards dinner where Prof made the stupid bet.'

'*What?*'

'Actually, I don't know how this hasn't come up before... but Prof offered him a job and he's been working in the department for a month and managing the compatibility project,' she blurted out in one breath.

'Why wouldn't you mention this?' Orla screeched, leaning forwards in her chair.

'Are you still angry with him?' Sofia asked, face scrunched up in sympathy.

When Bridget had met Cooper I'd been living in self-imposed exile in Ireland under the guise of learning the trade at my aunt Mary's bakery, but I knew that the rest of the family loved him, and Bridget hadn't been the only one worried and upset when he'd disappeared from her life shortly after graduation.

Bridget shuffled on her seat. 'No, it's nothing like that. But after four years we aren't going to suddenly pick up where we left off. And things are different now. He's my supervisor, for one, and you know Paolo sometimes felt a bit unsure about Cooper.'

'If by a bit unsure, you mean insanely jealous,' Orla snarked.

Bridget shrugged. 'It wouldn't feel right having a friendship that close, now I'm getting married. I wouldn't want Paolo to have someone who he shared everything with, instead of me. Male or female. So, while it's lovely to have Cooper back, and it's brilliant to be working on this nightmare project with him, I'm happy keeping things chill. Friendly workmates.'

'Ooh, does he have a girlfriend?' Sofia asked.

'Or a boyfriend?' Orla added.

We had on more than one occasion discussed the potential of Cooper being gay. Personally, I subscribed to the Cooper Is In Love With Bridget And Always Has Been Theory. But, if he was in love with her, then he only really deserved her if he could pluck up the courage to tell her that, instead of running off to Wales.

'Not that I know of. He hasn't mentioned anyone. He's living with Ben, our housemate from third year.'

Sofia gave her cushion a squeeze. 'Aw, I loved how he was so shy, and would go all pink and nervous whenever we tried to talk to him. He was so *cute*.'

'That's one word to describe it,' Orla drawled. 'He did have that mysterious edge, though. Like, I'd have been mostly surprised to hear he was a secret serial killer, or Russian spy. But not *totally* surprised.' She looked thoughtful. 'It was quite sexy, really.'

'Ugh, Orla!' Sofia gasped. 'That's practically your brother you're talking about!'

'But he's not though, is he?' She shook her head in dismissal. 'A distant cousin at best.'

'Wait – I have another question!' Sofia said. 'Does Paolo know?'

Bridget didn't answer, but the look on her face as she buried it in her empty glass said it all. 'Right. It must be time to get these face packs off. Where's the wipes?'

'Bridget?' I asked, using my sternest Big Sister voice.

'All me and Paolo are talking about is the wedding!' she said, pretending to be exasperated. 'I barely think about Cooper outside work, there's so much to do.'

'Young One, if you don't tell him then when he finds out he'll think you kept it from him on purpose.'

'Which she did, so he'd be right,' Orla said.

'Fine, I'll tell him!' Bridget huffed. 'It's not that big a deal. Paolo and I trust each other. Now, can you please pass me the wipes and get your beaky nose back out of my business?'

'Have you got any further with the marriage project, now your old partner in crime is there to help?' Sofia asked Bridget, once our faces were all clean and smooth and we'd taste-tested my latest attempt at a gluten-free, sugar-free tiffin recipe (result: too claggy, way too sweet).

'Ugh!' Bridget thrust a cushion over her face. 'It's terrible. I'm going to lose my job and no credible research department will employ me ever again.'

She pulled the cushion back off. 'Can I come and bake cakes with you, Emma?'

'You cannot. But I'm always looking for someone to wash up and sweep the floors.'

'Who's the best candidate so far?' Sofia asked, always looking for a bright side.

'There's a couple of older men who don't seem completely terrible. We've still got male applications coming in though, so I'm less worried about that. But the women? You'd think there'd be loads of them hoping to find Mr Right. We've had two applicants. One of them insists on being matched to a *Lord of the Rings* fan. As in someone who spends his weekends dressed up as one of the characters, can speak Elvish, and preferably is called Aragorn.'

'Okay, so far so freaky. What about the other one?'

'She's sixty-four years old and still lives with both her ex-husbands. And I quote, "They'll move into the spare bedroom, we aren't peculiar or anything." She's looking for a man under the age of thirty-five with medical training. She didn't explain why and quite frankly I don't want to know.'

I took another swig of martini. Buzzing with nervous tension and the unspoken thoughts that had been bouncing about my brain for days now, I ate another piece of claggy tiffin in an attempt to stop some of the thoughts from spilling out. Then, as the others carried on the conversation without me, I started wondering whether maybe the only way to shut the thoughts up was to face the witheringly honest scrutiny of my sisters.

They were chatting about what kind of house Bridget was going to get with Paolo, and whether it would be nearer to Donovan's DIY, or where she lived now, when Sofia noticed that I'd been quiet for the past few minutes.

'So, Emma, are you going to carry on living here once Bridget's married, or find somewhere smaller?'

'I love our little flat, but I definitely don't want anywhere smaller.'

And then, I took a deep breath, and it suddenly all came tumbling out...

'I want a cottage in the woods with three bedrooms and a garden, and lots of pairs of tiny shoes and Munch Bunch yogurts in the fridge and chaos and noise and a hamster. A house like ours used to be. And I want someone to buy it with who'll never get married to someone else and move out, because wherever I am is their home. I made a sixtieth anniversary cake last week for Moses' Uncle Henry and Aunt Ruby. Sixty years! They invited me to stay for the party, and when I saw them together, how he still looked at her like she was his dream come true, and how she leant on his shoulder like she'd found the answer to all the problems of the universe... To each other, they're everything. I want to be someone's everything.

'And in answer to the question everyone keeps asking, no, of course I don't mind that Bridget's finally getting married, and I'm genuinely 100 per cent happy for her. But yes, I do want that too, before it's too late for Munch Bunch yogurts. And. So.' I took another deep breath... *here goes...* 'I've decided to apply for the compatibility project.'

Stunned silence.

'You're our everything, Emma. You really don't need to do this,' Bridget said, her voice a mixture of panic and bewilderment.

'That doesn't count – you all have other people who matter more.'

'Yes, and the reason they matter so much is because we fell in love with them. We specifically chose them, knowing them well enough to know we could stand living with them for the rest of our lives,' Orla practically shouted.

'Really? Is that really the main reason you got married at nineteen, Orla? It was nothing to do with the fact that you were pregnant, and Mum and Dad were fuming at your no-good wastrel boyfriend, until Sam proposed? Isn't it commitment, tons of effort and sheer good fortune that meant it worked in the long run?'

'Get lost! Getting pregnant was the excuse, not the reason. I'd hardly let that happen with a man I wasn't in it for life with! Give me some credit!'

'Well, that's by the by – you were pregnant, Annie would never have married Greg so soon if she hadn't needed the visa. And we all know Sofia got married at twenty-one after her three-month engagement because she couldn't wait any longer to have sex, and her preacher man wasn't putting out without a ring on it.'

'Excuse me!' Sofia tried to look offended, but she couldn't hide her enormous grin. 'I wasn't putting out, as you so nicely put it, either! Waiting was a joint decision!'

'Either way, only Bridget is getting married for normal reasons. And I tried the normal route. Had the amazing proposal from the love of my life, who I'd known forever, and after promising me everything he left me with nothing. So, none of you can judge me.'

'We aren't judging you,' Orla said, taking an angry swig of her drink.

'What's the worst that can happen, if Bridge finds me someone with integrity and morals and the same values and life goals as me? How can it be worse than sitting at home on a Saturday night, with a meal for one, a glass of wine that should probably be for two, watching brain-shrivelling TV with no one to moan about it with or laugh at my jokes? I want someone who'll notice if I wear a stunning dress or get my hair done.'

'Babe, don't get married then!' Orla laughed. '"What's the worst that can happen?" Piles of disgusting boxers left on the floor, never getting a decent night's sleep because of having to lie next to a snoring rhinoceros. Arguing about stupid crap like whose turn it is to empty the bin.

'Feeling alone because you're on your own is one thing. Feeling lonely when there's a man who promised to cherish and honour you sat on the other sofa, crisp crumbs on his old T-shirt, eyes glued to the rugby, completely ignoring your existence, let alone your new hairdo, that's lonely.'

'Orla, are you and Sam doing okay? Do you want Moses to take him out for another drink and a "wise up" chat, like last time?' Sofia asked, frowning.

'Maybe. I dunno. I'll think about it. Right now, we're trying to save Em from making the biggest mistake of her life.'

'But what if it isn't?' I said. 'What if this feels right?'

'A lot of people get married because it feels right, and find themselves divorced.'

'Yes, when the feelings are based on lust and romance. I've made a rational decision to commit myself to someone who'll be a good match for me. None of those people have the benefit of an amazing neuroscientist setting them up.'

'Emma, I told you the test is a load of crap.' Bridget looked stricken. I was ignoring her. I'd felt like that, too, when I first had the idea. But once I'd had time to get used to it, I'd realised it solved everything.

'Well, either way, I trust you to find me a good match.'

'Have you been listening? You'd find a better pool of potential matches on Tinder.'

'You said the men weren't that bad!'

'I'm not marrying my sister to a man who isn't that bad!'

'Then don't match me!' I sighed, putting down my drink. 'Look. I promise that if you can't find me a brilliant husband, one that you think I could want to marry if I met him the normal way, like through work or at a party or on Tinder, I won't do it.'

Bridget sat back, breathing out a giant sigh of relief. 'Well, that's fine, then. Because the statistical probability of that happening is zero.'

'But if someone like that *does* apply, and we end up being the most compatible pair, you have to support me in going through with it.'

'Deal.'

There was a lull in conversation while we all had another drink, and I suspect everyone else tried to pretend that conversation had never happened.

'Have you prayed about it?' Sofia asked, breaking the silence.

'Of course! I've been praying for this since Jake married Helen Richards.'

'What if Bridget finds someone who's right on paper, but you don't find him attractive?'

'Maybe I'll find his heart attractive, his brain. Looks fade, character lasts.'

'Yes, but you can't blame us for wanting our sister to have a guy who takes her breath away,' Sofia continued.

'Who she feels blessed to call her partner,' Bridget said, enjoying the conversation now that she was sure it was all purely theoretical.

'Who she can't wait to get home to at the end of the day,' Orla said, frowning as she added, 'while still maintaining a reasonable life of her own, and also enjoying time with her friends, sisters, and by herself.'

'Isn't fancying him the extra icing on the cake? Not what makes a marriage work?' I thought about Nita's theory of chemistry, compatibility and kindness. But that was only one person's opinion.

'It's not what makes a marriage work, but it can certainly help. Especially when other, deeply handsome, toned and charming fitness instructors start making it clear they'd be very happy to ice your cake,' Sofia said, pointedly not looking at Orla. 'The odds are that one day you'll meet a man who makes your heart go boom, and then you'll wonder what if.'

'Honestly,' Bridget said around the last piece of tiffin, 'you don't need to worry. This is never going to happen.'

'Okay, how about this? If once I see him, there's no potential for him being "the one", I won't go ahead with it. I'll simply say, "I don't". Bridget – can you make that part of my contract?'

'I might go for slightly more scientific language, but, yes, if we get that far, which we definitely won't, I'll add in whatever you want.'

So that was how I decided to marry a man I'd never met.

10

COOPER

Patrick Charles Cooper was not nearly as drunk as he wanted to be. Three beers in, and he was feeling too depressed to bother pushing through the Tav's evening crowd to reach the bar and order another one. But as he was about to give up and go home, Ben finally arrived.

'Good day?' He pulled up a stool and raised his eyebrows at the row of glasses on the table between them.

'No.' Before Cooper even had a chance to ask Ben what he wanted, Scary Sue appeared out of nowhere and dropped two more pints on the table.

'Don't worry, I've stuck these on the tab. We can figure out payment later.' She winked at Ben, and disappeared as quickly as she'd arrived.

'You're paying, then?' Ben grimaced.

Cooper only grunted in response.

'So, are you going to tell me about it, or are we just sitting here in silence?'

Cooper sighed, taking another half-hearted sip before reaching into his pocket to pull out a crumpled card and handing it to Ben. Ben opened it up, nodding as he read the invitation inside.

'Well, it was going to happen at some point.'

'Yeah. But knowing about it and being invited to watch it are two different things.'

Cooper appreciated that Ben didn't pretend to be surprised at Cooper's reaction to Bridget's wedding invitation, or make a big thing about him indirectly confessing how he felt about her.

'You have to go.'

'I know.' Cooper rubbed his hand through his hair. It still felt as though someone had jammed a screwdriver into his skull.

'And you're going to have to move on. You can't spend the rest of your life drowning your sorrows in the Tav.' He paused, looking off to the side as he casually added, 'Unless you want to fight for her.'

Cooper jerked his head up. It wasn't as if he'd never thought about it, before he'd moved. But he'd thought about it enough to know he couldn't do that to her.

'She's been with him since they were kids. She stayed in Nottingham working for a sexist troll to be near him. He runs her dad's shop. Bridget's future's all sorted, and it's a good one. Even if I did want to fight for her, I know I couldn't win. Bridget deserves better than me. I moved away because I loved her enough to let her have it.'

Ben rolled his eyes. 'Honestly, mate. You know my opinion on marriage. I wouldn't wish it on my worst enemy. But I always thought that if anyone stood a chance at happy-ever-after, that minuscule anomaly of couples that actually end up not loathing the crap out of each other, it would be you two.'

'Not a helpful thing to say given the circumstances.'

'Then fight for her.'

Cooper shook his head. 'No.'

He put down his glass with a decisive slam. 'No. I've spent

enough time wallowing over Bridget Donovan. I don't need to waste any more of my life pining after someone who doesn't want me. Which means I need to get over her. Now. Or at least before I go into work tomorrow and she asks me to be her best man or something. Time to man up and move on.' He paused. Rubbed his chin. Squinted up at his new best mate. 'Any ideas about how the hell I do it?'

'You could always find someone else.'

Cooper shrugged. 'And how am I meant to do that? My track record isn't great.'

'Aren't you supposed to be a leading expert on compatibility? If anyone can find someone, you should be able to.'

That gave Cooper an idea that he'd definitely not have had if he hadn't chugged four beers on an empty stomach.

And by the time he'd chased the beers with two double whiskeys and some other drinks Scary Sue brought over that he couldn't be bothered to identify, he could almost convince himself that having the added bonus of being able to save the woman he loved from losing her job had nothing to do with it.

So, with clumsy fingers and unusually carefree abandon, once back home, Cooper completed the totally biased, non-impartial and clearly inadmissible application to get himself a wife and forget about Bridget Donovan once and for all.

* * *

It felt as though he'd barely closed his eyes before the alarm was going off. And, *ugh*, the hangover…

Three glasses of water, one mistaken mouthful of coffee and a scalding shower later, he braved the ten-minute tram journey from Ben's flat near the station out to the medical school.

It was only once the tram had started moving that he remembered.

A blinding flash of horror and disbelief, followed by a rumbling thunder of regret and panic that caused his stomach to flip almost inside out. A woman on the seat opposite glanced up, saw the look on his face and then switched to another spot further down the tram.

Okay. Think about this, Cooper. Take a couple of breaths.

It was fine.

Easily sorted.

No one even had to know.

The applications were anonymous. So, even if Bridget hadn't slept in, and she'd already read the form, all he had to do was send another anonymous email to explain he'd changed his mind and he could go back to breathing properly again.

He hurried up the steps into the medical school building, as fast as he could without having to heave into a bin, and took the lift up to his office. Even as he willed himself not to, he felt too tired and wretched to resist glancing in the lab door as he scuttled past.

'Cooper!' Bridget called out from her usual perch.

'Give me ten minutes,' he croaked without slowing.

There was a two-second pause before he heard her scurrying after him. She caught up as he unlocked the office door.

'Are you ill? You sounded terrible. Ugh! You look even worse.'

He went inside and flicked on the coffee machine. Even if he couldn't face it, Bridget would want one.

'I didn't get much sleep last night. You don't look too great yourself.'

'Something awful has happened. It can't wait ten minutes.' Bridget sat in one of the office chairs, but her knee jiggled up and down like a pneumatic drill, and she was chewing fretfully on a nail.

He filled up two mugs with coffee, adding milk and three sugars to the one without the chip in the rim and waiting for Bridget to put down the folder she was carrying before handing it to her.

'Are you going to tell me what it is?' He didn't want to sound unsympathetic, but he had an email to send.

'Emma's applied to the project.'

'*What?* Your sister Emma?'

'Well, it's hardly going to be Emma Watson. *Yes, my sister Emma!* She'd talked about it, but I never thought she'd genuinely go through with it. Cooper, you've seen the men who've applied. I cannot marry my sister off to one of them.'

'So don't. None of those men could be compatible with Emma, even using the Cole Compatibility Function of Stupidity.' Cooper managed a sip of coffee. The hangover retreated a millimetre or two.

Bridget picked the folder back off his desk and opened it. On top of a printout of one of the applications was a handwritten note in the prof's familiar scrawl:

This is a good one. Use her.

'He's right. It is a good one,' Bridget said glumly. 'I can't believe he decided this was the time to look through the applications.'

'You're sure it's her?'

She nodded. 'I compared the DNA sample to one of mine. Unless I have a secret sister out there somewhere, it's Emma.'

'Then you can't use her. It wouldn't be an impartial selection.'

'I tried that. He said that seeing as he made the selection, it is. He also said that if for any reason she happened to change her mind, he'd assume it was down to my interference. I'd be fired for fixing the outcome of the study.'

Bridget tugged at her hair in exasperation. 'I almost don't care if

I get fired for this. I love my research but Prof is getting worse and it barely seems worth it any more. But I need the salary so that Paolo and I can buy the shop off Dad. I know the stress of the business makes him worse. How can I choose between Dad's health and letting my sister marry the wrong person? So then I think, well, she could just get divorced if it doesn't work out. But there's no "just" about having to go through a sham marriage, and then a divorce. And I'll have betrayed her, because she said she'll only do it if I can find her someone nice. I can't let her choose a dress and have all our family and friends come and watch her marry someone who's been married four times before, or is twice her age. I mean, if she was in love with them and everything, then I could. But she doesn't even know what she's letting herself in for.'

She burst into tears. 'Either way, I'm ruining Emma's life, or my parents'. How am I supposed to make that choice? How did this nightmare even happen? I can't believe Emma did this.'

'Bridget, Emma is an adult. She can make her own decisions. You need to tell Emma that Prof is insisting you pick her no matter how compatible the match, and then she can pull out. And your dad's health doesn't hang on whether Paolo buys the shop. You know that's not how ME works. Even if it did, they'll figure something out.'

Bridget was crying too hard to hear him.

'Maybe it's time we took the whole situation to the vice chancellor.'

Screw professional boundaries about supervisors and their staff. He wrapped his arms around Bridget and pulled her tightly against his chest. After a moment she returned the hug, leaning against him as her jagged breaths began to steady.

And he realised that Bridget Donovan was the only person he'd hugged in years. And before then, her bonkers mamma, Gabriella Donovan, and her soft-spoken, warm-hearted bear of a dad had hugged him every time he'd visited. Sofia and Orla had always hugged him too, ruffling his hair and calling him 'Little Brother'. Annie used to tuck her arm through his on nights out, grabbing his hand whenever she had a point to make, which was often.

For three incredible years, the Donovan family had welcomed him into its loving and strong arms, and he had known what it was like to have a family. To very nearly belong.

And as he held onto Bridget, it was as though the box in his brain where he locked away all the memories – all the *feelings* – sprang open, and along with it came pouring out an overpowering rush of loneliness.

He'd tried to ignore it, to pretend he was fine. But whether it was sudden or had been building for years, he wasn't fine any more.

Suddenly the thought of going back home to an empty flat night after night was unbearable. The abandoned teenager still hiding under his lab coat flashed back to what it had been like, always being hungry, freezing cold in winter, choosing between luxuries like toiletries or washing his clothes. He'd survived it, but the survivor in him knew he'd do anything not to go back.

He surreptitiously wiped his eyes on his jumper sleeve, and gave her one last squeeze before pulling away (literally a goodbye squeeze, if he was about to do what he was about to do, goodbye to the woman he'd been utterly in love with).

'You don't have to do anything today. We've had a steady stream of reasonable applications from men. You never know, something incredible might happen. You Donovans believe in miracles, don't you? Maybe this is going to be the most romantic ending to a neuro-scientific study ever.'

Bridget blew her nose, pulling a watery smile.

'Now, don't you have some brain samples to study or something?' Cooper resisted the urge to tuck the stray lock of hair back off her face. Those days were done now.

'Yeah. See you at lunch later?'

Cooper shrugged, picking up the folder and casually dropping it onto his desk. 'Maybe. But I need to speak to one of my students about their assignment at some point, so don't wait for me.'

As soon as she left he opened up his laptop and clicked through to the online portal they'd created so people could submit anonymous applications.

Bridget cared more about her family than her career, but, at the same time, Cooper knew how much she loved her job. And if she and Paolo really were saving up to buy Donovan's DIY from Bear, it would crush her if that could no longer happen.

He thought about what he knew about Emma. They'd met a couple of times, when she'd come home for Christmas. She'd spent four years living in Ireland after breaking up with her fiancé. She was a few years older than him, but that hardly mattered; Cooper had grown up pretty fast. She looked lovely. Not like Bridget, but he could definitely find her attractive. She was kind, and had started her own business from nothing, which he respected, and could relate to.

Could he grow to love her, as she deserved?

More to the point – could she love him?

The rest of the Donovans had managed it easily enough.

He considered life with Bear and Gabriella as his dad and mum. Belonging to a family of sisters and brothers-in-law ('brothers-in-love' as Gabriella insisted on calling them), of nieces and nephews and family Sunday lunches, Christmas in the farmhouse, summer barbeques in the garden. The laughter and the love. Sharing the heartbreaks and the hard times.

A happy ending all round.

Before he knew it, Cooper was the one crying. He swiped at his eyes a few times, before giving up and letting the tears come. They'd been held back in there long enough.

Then, he opened the folder to Emma's application, clicked open his own and for the first time in his life prepared to fix a scientific study.

'Oh, come off it,' he mumbled as he adjusted all his answers to make sure they matched perfectly with Emma's. 'This is not scientific research, it's a stupid bet. No ethics or morals required.'

Except for the part about marrying his best friend's sister, of course.

* * *

He managed to spend nearly the whole day hiding in his office pretending to do work while actually veering between complete panic and full-on freaking out, but at five twenty-nine, Bridget threw open his office door.

'Oops!' She laughed, before shutting the door again and knocking on it several times in rapid succession.

After about twenty seconds of knocking she cracked open the door and poked her head in the gap. 'Why aren't you asking me to come in?'

He couldn't help smiling. 'I did. You'd have heard me if you'd stopped thumping the door and waited for a reply.'

'So, I can come in?'

He pushed out a chair from under the table with one foot and Bridget bounded in and plonked herself down in it.

'Why didn't you tell me about that new application?' she demanded. 'I don't know when you snuck out to run the DNA test, but the match is virtually perfect. With the questions, it's a compatibility of 94 per cent! *Ninety-four!* The DNA markers were uncanny! I checked them three times to make sure it wasn't a mistake.'

She glanced at the open door, got up, closed it, and sat back down, huddled forward so she could whisper. 'I even used Prof

Love's compatibility test, as best I could given the limited information, and the initial indicators were "excellent potential for compatibility". I'm gobsmacked.'

She pressed both hands to her cheeks, shaking her head in wonder. 'On the one hand, I can't believe it. I mean, compatibility tests are one thing, but reading about this guy in the additional information section, he seems like everything that Emma wants. But then, how much can you tell from a few questions? There could be hundreds of reasons why he'd be terrible. But, I don't know... this genuinely could be a miracle! I've been going back and forth and round and round, wondering what to do, wanting to ask you about it. But as project supervisor I know you have to tell me to follow the protocol. So, I'm going to give him a follow-up call, as listed in the project plan. That way, at least I'll know if he's serious. He could have filled the form in for a joke. Or when he was drunk and feeling lonely. I can find out if he sounds weird. And I can speak to his references, do some online stalking...'

She looked up. 'Am I a horrible person for even thinking about going ahead with this?'

'What would Emma say?' Cooper couldn't believe how normal he sounded, given that his heart rate was approaching warp speed.

'She'd say shut up and do your job, Young One.' Bridget gaped at him, eyes shining. 'I can't believe I'm going to do this!'

Then, before he could suddenly dash off on urgent business, or find his phone underneath the piles of student papers and switch it off, she whipped out her phone and pressed call having obviously had the number typed in and waiting to go.

Cooper's work phone rang several times before Bridget nodded at him to answer it, her own phone pressed to one ear.

Unable to think of any way to avoid this, especially given that he had a recorded answer-phone message, and he could hardly keep his phone switched off indefinitely, Cooper slowly picked up his phone and answered it.

'Hello?'

Bridget's eyes widened with excitement, and she pointed to her phone as she spun the chair to face the wall in order to hear better. 'Hello? Um, this is Dr Bridget Donovan. I'm calling from the Nottingham University Neuroscience Department. You completed an application and submitted a DNA test for a study we're conducting?'

'Yep.'

'Well, I'm very pleased to say that we are interested in taking you through to the next stage of the study. Is that something you'd still be prepared to consider?'

'Yes.'

Bridget spun back around and gave Cooper a thumbs-up. He stared at her, holding the phone, eyebrows raised as he waited for her to connect the dots.

'Would it be possible to have your full name, please?' Bridget asked slowly, her tone turning from friendly to decidedly stern as she stared back.

'Patrick Charles Cooper.'

'*WHAT THE HELL ARE YOU DOING?*'

'That's hardly an appropriate way to address your supervisor,' Cooper said, once they'd both hung up. 'Or a potential research candidate.'

'How about addressing my friend, who seems to temporarily have lost his mind?'

'Really? Have you got any evidence to back that statement up?' Cooper tried to keep his voice calm, even as the blood careened through his veins.

'Why else would you complete the form? Was this some bizarre way to make me feel better? Or a sick joke? How far were you planning to go along with it? Emma's already been left standing at the altar once before. The whole point of her taking part in this was to prevent it happening again. I don't understand why you would do this!'

'Really?'

'Well, I know you don't want to marry my sister!'

'How do you know?'

'Why would you?' Bridget was pink with indignation.

'Well, if she's anything like the rest of your family, she'd be an amazing wife!' Cooper said, sounding strangely angry considering it was one of the nicest things he'd ever said to her.

All Bridget's bluster deflated in an instant. She sank into the chair, hands covering her face while Cooper waited.

'I didn't know you wanted to get married,' she mumbled through her fingers.

'I didn't either. And then I did.'

'I'd be so happy for you if you had someone.' She dropped her hands. 'And, honestly, Cooper, while we're being nice to each other, I couldn't choose anyone better to marry my sister.'

Cooper quickly shut down the stab of pain that she'd be happy about it, rather than ripe with jealousy, as if the prospect of him marrying Emma would make her suddenly realise that she was the Donovan sister he should be with.

'But you couldn't run away again,' she said, her voice tight with anxiety.

'I didn't run away. I relocated for work.'

'And you'd have to try really hard at expressing your feelings, and being vulnerable. Are you sure you can do that?'

'I manage it with you, don't I?' Some of his feelings, anyway.

She nodded, thoughtfully. 'Are you really, really sure?'

'I think I can make her happy, if she's up for it.'

'Emma's not very good at failing.'

Cooper grinned. 'Well, that's sorted, then, because neither am I.'

'It'd be strange. You being hers, not mine any more.'

He gripped the seat with both hands to stop them ripping the application form out of her hands and shredding it.

'How the hell am I going to keep this a secret from her?' She laughed, although at the same time a tear spilled out of one eye and ran down her cheek.

'We'll make it a short engagement.'

'Shall I tell my family? It'll stop them worrying once Emma tells them that she's having a blind-date wedding.'

'Can you wait a week or so first? I have a couple of things I need to do.'

Bridget took a deep breath. 'This is the maddest day in my family's mad history. I think I need to go home and stare into space for a few days.' She got up to leave. 'Oh! But, hang on! I'd almost forgotten this was Prof's stupid work project and not just two people deciding to spend the rest of their lives together under the bizarrest circumstances ever. How can you do this if you're the project supervisor? That's totally against protocol.'

'One, this project is outside any protocol. Two, as of this lunchtime I'm no longer working on the compatibility project. From now on, you're on your own.'

'Okay. Well. I'd best get on with it, then, hadn't I?'

11

EMMA

As soon as I'd got home that evening, I'd known something was up. It had been a fairly standard Thursday – baking fifty cupcakes for a bridal shower, meeting a woman whose daughter was allergic to strawberries but somehow wanted me to come up with a straw-berry-flavoured gateau for her eighteenth birthday party. I'd caught up on some admin, been wowed by Nita's wedding cake ideas for a couple who had met at a medieval re-enactment society, then caught the bus home to collapse on the sofa with a reheated bowl of lentil stew.

Bridget was already home, which wasn't that unusual. But she'd cooked dinner, which started my suspicions humming. She'd also opened a bottle of wine, which never happened on a Thursday.

'Is Paolo coming over?' I asked, dumping my bag as I eyed up the carefully laid table.

'No, it's for you.' Bridget smiled, but the way she wrung her hands together at the same time cancelled the smile out.

'Okay... should I be worried?'

'Definitely not!'

Unconvinced, I sat down and accepted a glass of wine and a portion of pasta bake.

'Aren't you going to eat it?' Bridget asked a few minutes later, somewhat hypocritically given that all she'd done was push a few pieces of penne about with her fork.

'I'm not going to be able to eat anything until you tell me what's going on.' I did, however, manage a slow sip of wine.

'I found you a match.'

'Oh.'

Oh.

I put the glass back on the table with a clonk. Then changed my mind, picked it up and took another swig.

'It's a 94 per cent compatibility. He's the right age, has a brilliant personality, a good job. His moral values are in line with yours, and he wants the same sort of things in life. Plus, he loves cake. And, not that it matters according to your application, but he's also not bad-looking.'

I sat back. Never mind butterflies, my insides felt as though there were a turkey flapping around in there. 'You got all that from his application?'

'I did some follow-up investigations. Maybe not strictly in line with the project remit, but, given that we'd already decided you were the most compatible pair, it seemed okay to do some off-the-record research.'

'Well. Wow.' I poured out another half-glass of wine, my hand shaking. 'Is it too late to ask if we can go on a couple of dates first?'

'You can back out whenever you like. But I won't be able to give you any of his details if you do.'

'Have you met him?'

Bridget's cheeks coloured slightly, a chunk of pasta halfway to her mouth.

'Yes.' She sighed. 'I'm not going to let you marry someone

unless I'm sure that you've got as good a chance as possible that it might come to something.'

I nodded.

My trust in my sister was absolute. She knew me better than anyone, and I knew that if she had doubts about this guy then she'd tell me. I reminded myself of my own track record in finding a partner. I'd made my mind up. I wanted to get married, and have a family, and, while not ideal, this was the best option I'd got. Who was I kidding? This was the only option!

'Great. What do I have to do next?'

What I had to do next, it turned out, was plan a wedding in three weeks. With work commitments and the groom's schedule, it was three weeks or wait until the wedding season was over, and there was no way I could hang about in limbo land until then. That was fine, the groom was happy to keep it simple, and I was very happy to be on maximum organisational duties between now and then, as a way of avoiding thinking too hard about what it was I was organising.

But before all that could begin, I had to face telling my family. Thank goodness Bridget agreed to let me get the Easter weekend out of the way first.

* * *

Cooper

For the second time in as many months, Cooper donned his suit, made the best of his hair and polished his one smart pair of shoes.

He'd thought that looking the part might help, but as he drove out of the city along the familiar winding roads that led towards Sherwood Forest, he faced the stomach-twisting reality that a smart tie and clean shave weren't going to do anything to lessen the impact of what he was about to do. Even with the air-con on its highest setting, he was still sweating.

All too soon, he reached the farmhouse driveway, pulling to a stop before taking a long moment to get his breathing under control. He tried to remember what he'd planned on saying. It had managed to sound half reasonable the countless times he'd practised during the long Easter weekend, but now the snatches that came back to him seemed hollow and pathetic.

He asked himself for the millionth time what he was doing.

Just being back here, seeing the rambling house – starting to look a little rough around the edges, but still like something out of a cosy TV drama – remembering the warmth and the welcome that lay behind the red front door, the longing to truly belong here was a physical ache in his chest. The chance to be a part of a family – *this* family – was beyond anything he'd hoped for.

No, the problem wasn't whether he wanted to do this.

The problem was that he knew he didn't really deserve it.

As if the only way he could become one of the Donovans was to sneak in undercover. He could argue that he had to do it this way to avoid Bridget losing her job, and screwing up the finance to buy the shop. But he knew that part of the reason was because he didn't really believe that someone like Emma would ever choose him, if she had the choice.

So, what kind of man did that make him, given that he'd manipulated things so that she ended up with him anyway?

One who is going to step up, do what it takes and figure out how to be the best husband she could have. One that, in time, she'd be able to say that she would have chosen.

So that was why he was here, wiping the perspiration off his forehead and plucking up the courage to get out of the car and make the first step towards being the kind of man she deserved.

He knocked, and then pushed open the door, calling out a hello.

Bridget had told him that Gabriella would be out and it was best not to make her dad have to get up.

'In here!' Bear's voice echoed through from the living room.

Cooper was there in three strides, trying to hide his shock at how frail Bear looked compared to four years ago. He was sitting with his feet propped up on a stool, his legs covered in a tartan blanket. Seeing who it was, once the fog cleared from his eyes, Bear made to stand up, a huge smile breaking across his face. Cooper was quick to move over to him, intending to shake his hand but instead finding himself pulled into a giant hug.

Tears welled up in his eyes for the second time in a week as he felt the once-strong arms embrace him.

'Cooper. You're home!' Bear gave him another squeeze before letting go. 'Kill the fatted calf! Or, at the very least, stick the kettle on. My long-lost son has returned.'

'I brought you this.' Cooper held out a bottle of one of Ireland's finest whiskies. 'If it isn't too early?'

'Ha! I'd say it's about four years too late! Fetch a couple of glasses, and tell me what's the craic.'

They spent far longer than Cooper had expected talking about what he'd been up to for the past few years, and what led him to come back to Nottingham. At first he'd felt awkward, chatting away with such a bombshell waiting to be detonated. But, on the other hand, Bear was genuinely interested, and if Cooper didn't seem like such a stranger, then surely that could only help.

After asking about the business, and the wider family, noting that Bear refused to go near the topic of his health, Cooper knew they'd finally reached that point in the conversation he had been dreading.

'Now, what brings you here in the middle of a Tuesday afternoon? I know it's not because you got a sudden urge to ask me how I was faring.'

Cooper put down his whisky glass and smoothed his hair back one more time. *Here goes.*

'I've come to ask for your blessing. To marry your daughter.'

Bear narrowed his kind eyes. 'Ah, son. How do you expect me to respond to that, given that Paolo was here asking me the same question only a couple of months since? Are you maybe jumping the gun a bit? Or, more to the point, missed the boat altogether? Unless Bridget's had a grand change of heart and the news hasn't got around to me yet.'

'No. Not Bridget.' He swallowed. 'I want to marry Emma.'

'*Emma?*' Bear pulled his head back in surprise, mental cogs grinding. 'But wasn't she away with my sister when you used to hang about here? I didn't know you even knew her.'

Cooper coughed; the collar on his shirt seemed to have shrunk inches in the past ten seconds. 'I don't. It's quite a long story, if you'll allow me to explain.'

Bear's eyes narrowed. 'I think you better had.'

And so, Cooper left the farmhouse a long while later, leaving his remarkable father-in-law-to-be snoring, and taking with him several meandering tales of Irish love and courtship, a lifetime's advice on the mysterious ways of women, numerous heartfelt promises made through a veil of manly tears, and the blessing of Bear Donovan to wed his eldest daughter.

He also left with a full heart and the absolute certainty that he'd made the right decision.

And if spotting Gabriella skidding into the driveway as he left made him press his foot down on the accelerator, ensuring he had gone before she had the chance to flag him down and sow a seed of doubt in his mind, well – one step at a time. He was still pretty new to all this sharing and caring family stuff.

* * *

Emma

'Your father told me you've got news to share.' Mum plonked a huge plate of roast potatoes down, right in front of me, and, with one satisfied scan of the table to check all was present and correct, took her seat at the far end, opposite Dad.

'Are you going to tell us, or do we need to say grace first?' she asked, eyebrows arched.

I gave Bridget a side glance, expressing what I felt about her dobbing me in to Dad. She only shrugged in reply, pulling a face to let me know that she'd not said anything.

'It can wait until we've eaten.'

'No, it can't. We fill our plates, then you talk while we eat.'

We passed the plates of food around, my family barely noticing what they were dumping on their plates in their hurry to get to the gossip. Moses said a quick prayer of thanks, and, instead of the usual diving in, no one so much as picked up a fork. Eleven pairs of eyes were on me.

Bridget offered a smile of encouragement, but before I could put them out of their misery, Mum pointed at Sam.

'Sam, why is your plate empty? What is happening?'

Sam shrugged, as all eyes swivelled to him. 'It's not empty. Look, I've got everything apart from sweetcorn. You know I hate sweetcorn.'

'Well! I did not know that. Do you also now hate chicken parmigiana, and potatoes and carrots? Or is it only *my* food that you now dislike so much you are eating less than your eight-year-old daughter?'

'Mamma, you know I love your cooking. I'm sorry, I don't have much of an appetite at the moment.'

'Are you unwell?' Mum gave Dad a worried glance. 'Have you been to the doctor about this? You won't recover if you don't eat.'

'He's not ill,' Orla snapped. 'That's plenty of food for an energy output of practically zero. Jim says that once you slump into a rut, your body feels tired all the time because it's on snooze mode. Nothing that getting up off your backside and doing something productive won't fix.'

'Orla, do not say backside at the dinner table!' Mum said.

'Who's Jim?' Paolo asked.

'Good question,' Bridget said.

'Being a teacher is a full-on job,' Sofia said. 'Every teacher I know is exhausted most of the time. Maybe if you worked together to support each other through the recent changes in your lifestyle—'

'Oh, please. Don't start pastoring us.' Orla rolled her eyes. 'If we want a counselling session we'll book one in. With someone else.'

'If you don't have an appetite and feel more tired than normal, maybe you should see a doctor?' Bridget asked, her face pinched with worry. 'Best to check it out, just in case.'

I was worried, too. But what concerned me more than Sam's grey face was that he couldn't be bothered to handle Orla. Normally he'd speak up when she crossed the line into rude.

'Daddy, are you poorly?' Oscar asked, while trying to stab a floppy carrot baton.

'I'm fine, sweetheart.' Sam looked up at his kids. Lottie was watching him with round eyes, while Harry stared moodily at his plate. 'I'm *fine*. It's been a busy year, and I'm ready for the summer holidays. Auntie Sofia's right, all teachers get tired. That's why we're allowed weeks off to recover.'

'Maybe you should—'

'I said I'm fine,' Sam said, in his no-arguments teacher voice. 'Didn't Emma have some news?'

Thankfully, my news had to wait even longer as at that point Annie video-called. We spent another ten minutes catching up on not-a-lot-since-last-week, Mum filling Annie in on the food she'd cooked while the rest of us ate. 'Yes, Mamma, the focaccia looks lovely. I can't wait to be home to try some.'

Bridget and Paolo updated her on the wedding plans, now the invitations were out so it was official. 'So, have you booked flights yet?' Bridget asked. 'I want to make sure I've got time to see you before I go off on honeymoon.'

'I'm landing the Saturday before, and staying for two weeks.' Annie grinned. 'My clients will have to manage without me.'

'How lovely that Greg will be finally taking some time off!' Mum beamed. 'That man works too hard,' she said to Moses, as if she didn't say the same thing every week.

'Oh, no, Greg will join us the day before the wedding,' Annie said, inspecting her perfectly polished nails. 'He can't get two weeks off that time of year. Or any time of year, to be honest. And I don't want him getting in the way of my sister time.'

'What? Is this normal in New York, for wives to gallivant across the world on holiday without their husband?' Mum was indignant. 'What will he eat?'

'Whatever he cooks!'

'Mum, it's perfectly normal for people to visit their family while their husband or wife has to work. He's joining her later. It's fine,' I said, patting her hand. I wasn't at all sure it was fine, but there was no point worrying about it until Annie got here. Or at least until Wednesday Wine, when we stood a better chance of getting her to open up.

'Ah, yes!' Mum exclaimed, gripping my wrist. 'Emma has news to share! Do it now, while Annie is here.'

I braced myself, knowing that I had to tell them sometime, and it might as well be now.

'I applied to the compatibility study that Bridget's doing at work and it turns out I'm the best match so the wedding is in two weeks, on May eleventh. A Saturday. Sorry, Annie, I know that's another plane ticket, and it's really short notice so I'll completely understand if you can't make it. It's going to be really small and low-key, you won't be missing much.'

'Wow! Well. That is news. But as for missing my big sister's big day? I wouldn't dream of it. I also might have to come over in good time to SHAKE SOME SENSE BACK INTO YOU! What the hell are you thinking?' Annie shrieked. 'And more to the point: Bridget! What the hell are YOU thinking? Emma's in a vulnerable state right now. I can't believe you'd take advantage of that to drag her into your insane work project. We're talking about marrying a STRANGER! Can somebody who is actually there please stop this insanity from going any further? Why is nobody else saying anything?'

'Excuse me, what is this? I don't understand. What stranger? Who's getting married? Emma, are you making a cake for strangers to get married?'

'No, Mum. That's not it.'

By the time everything had been explained, the remaining food was congealing on our plates. Annie hung up after another frustrated rant, and Sofia and Moses brought out dessert and coffee. We always handled things better with a proper cappuccino and a bowl of homemade mint ice cream.

Dad carefully hauled himself up from the table, reaching for his stick. 'Thank you for a lovely dinner, Gabriella. But I'll take my dessert later. I need a wee lie-down.'

'Excuse me?' Mum was indignant. 'Do you have nothing to say on this matter, Bear Donovan?'

In answer, Dad plodded around the table until he reached me. He bent down, kissed the top of my head and straightened up again. 'Do you think that Emma would do this lightly, without considering what she's letting herself in for?'

'Up until today I wouldn't have believed she'd do it at all! But she is broken-hearted. First Jake and Helen Richards, then Orla and Sofia and Annie and now Bridget. She's a desperate woman, and desperate women do stupid, desperate things. They forget their heads, listen only to their hearts. And hers is broken.'

'And is that such a bad thing, listening to your heart?' Bear asked. 'Did we listen to our heads, thirty-five years ago? Come now, woman, the moment I saw you I'd lost my head. I gave up looking for it decades ago.'

'This is different! We must stop her making this mistake! How can you even consider letting her do this?'

'We can't stop her. She's a grown woman,' Dad replied, gently. 'Emma, are you sure?'

'Yes, Daddy.'

'Then I'm sure too. We've raised some fine, wee girls, Gabriella. They know what's what. Trust in that, trust Bridget. Trust Emma. Like we trusted Orla to raise a wean with Sam, and trusted that Sofia knew what she was doing at twenty-one when she gave up her nice, cosy future to take care of the downtrodden. And we trusted Annie, didn't we? To marry some old fella she barely knew, on the other side of the world? Trust that there is more to this than you know.'

'Will you trust this strange man with our daughter?'

Dad winked at Bridget. 'I will.'

And on that note, I decided it was time to go home so I could stress about the whole thing in peace.

It was very noble and touching that my dad had such absolute faith in me. Right then, and for about a zillion more moments over the next few weeks, I really wasn't sure I trusted myself.

Sunday morning, Ben and Cooper headed out along the river Trent for an eight-mile run, stopping to grab a bacon cob from a café on the way back.

Cooper almost felt like a normal person. It was as they stood eating, watching a clutch of ducks bobbing about on the river in what Cooper hoped was a companionable silence, that he decided to go for it.

'I took your advice.'

'Which bit?' Ben's mouth creased up. 'I hand out so much, I lose track of it all.'

'About finding someone else.'

Ben turned round to look at him properly, taking another bite of bacon cob. 'That was quick. Have you found someone you like, or just decided to start looking?'

Cooper swallowed the last mouthful of bread, screwing up the wrapper and throwing it into the nearby bin. 'It's a bit more serious than that.'

'What? How serious can it be in less than two weeks?'

'I'm getting married on the 11th May. Providing you're free to film it, of course.'

Ben stared at him, mouth open. 'You've signed up to your own experiment. Even knowing it's a pile of crap. Must have been some woman who applied.'

'Yeah.' Cooper nudged a stone on the gravel footpath with his toe. 'Bridget's sister.'

Every trace of amusement dropped off Ben's face. 'Man. That is... are you sure? In what universe can marrying the sister of the woman you've been in love with for years be a good idea? Let alone when you're not even in a relationship with the sister. And haven't met her. Have you met her?'

Cooper nodded. 'A couple of times. She's... great.' He looked up at the clear April sky. 'And I've not been in love with Bridget for years. I've not *seen* her in years. Besides, according to your great theory on love and marriage, no one's in love with the same person forever. This is me moving on to someone else. I'm happy about it.'

'Does Bridget know?'

'Yes.'

'She's happy about it?'

'Why wouldn't she be? Her friend marries her sister. She marries Paolo. Happy-ever-after all round.'

They turned to start walking home. After a while Ben said, 'Well, I think you're insane to even think about it, but I wish you well, mate.'

'In that case, I have a couple of things to ask you,' Cooper replied.

Ben glanced at him. 'You're not going to ask me to be your best man?'

Cooper returned the look.

'Aren't I meant to be filming the wedding? How am I supposed to do both?'

Cooper shrugged. 'You only need to record the actual ceremony, and then maybe a couple of interviews afterwards.'

Ben sighed. 'You haven't got anyone else to ask, have you?' He shook his head. 'No stag do though. And no speech.'

'Believe me, I think one of your speeches on marriage is the last thing anyone wants. Cheers though, honestly. It might help make me appear a bit more normal.'

They reached the pedestrian crossing in front of the apartment block, and stood waiting for the lights to change.

'What was the other one?' Ben asked. 'You said a couple of things.'

'Oh, well. Given that you're planning on travelling for work a fair bit over the next few months, I was wondering how you felt about my new wife moving in?'

* * *

Emma

Monday, I spent deciding what sort of wedding I wanted, given I had twelve days to arrange it. Every time Bridget messaged or called to update me on the groom's reply, it hit me a little harder that this was a Real Life Man, who I would soon be living with, and trying to learn how to love – calling him the groom might distract from the fact that he'd soon be my husband, but it didn't make it any less true. Anyway, he was happy to let me plan the whole event, and in return he'd sort us a short honeymoon and buy me a ring. He was bringing one guest, his best man, due to his family living abroad. I wondered if the lack of relatives nearby might explain why he was prepared to marry a stranger. And better absent in-laws than nightmare ones, I supposed.

When I sent Bridget a frantic text asking why he only had one friend, she replied that he only had one friend *coming to a last-minute wedding*, with next to no budget, under circumstances that a lot of friends would find hard to get their heads round. And then she asked me how many friends I was bringing. Answer: Nita and Vik.

I had sisters to stand with me and support me, so I didn't need many friends.

Annie was coming, although she'd be travelling alone as Greg had a work thing in Baltimore. So, with the sisters and brothers-in-love, my parents and nieces and nephew, plus the groom, his only real friend, and my only real friend and her husband, there would be seventeen of us.

I dithered about whether to book a venue somewhere, but I was worried about how Dad would cope with a whole day out. He'd had a tough week, including six days without leaving the house, and three crashed in bed. Certain that I wouldn't be able to get through the day without him (and Mum definitely wouldn't), and even more determined to give him the gift of being able to walk me down the (very short) aisle, I decided to bring the wedding to him.

With some sisterly support, I could empty out the back barn. It needed sorting out for the pop-up tea room in a month's time anyway. And once I'd draped sheets around the walls, filled it with flowers and fairy lights, I wouldn't be ashamed to show my future kids the wedding photos. Nita would cater, Sofia would perform the ceremony, and while we couldn't legally get married without a venue licence, Moses would whizz us over to New Life church to complete the paperwork.

All I needed was something to wear and I had organised myself a wedding.

If only I was half this good at being married, things might actually turn out okay...

* * *

A few days later, I woke up with a jolt, my heart pounding, skin slick with sweat. At some point during a night of anxiety dreams and fitful twisting myself up in my duvet, a thought that had been hiding somewhere in the depths of my subconscious had floated to the surface.

After running to work, I spent a fretful couple of hours baking a batch of cookies, trying to ignore how, instead of dissipating with my dreams, my panic had only grown sharper. By ten-thirty I was done. I cleared up, ditched my apron and hastily filled my travel mug with chamomile tea in the vain hope that swigging it while scurrying the one and a half miles through the rain to Sofia's church might help calm me down. I barrelled through the doors, even more dishevelled than I had been when I woke up that morning, somewhat startled to find the hall jam-packed with babies and the various people responsible for them. They were all sitting on blankets in a giant semicircle, holding balloons and listening in entranced silence to my sister, her hand encased in a giant sock puppet.

'Wet lady!' A toddler pointed, laughing. 'Funny hair!'

'Where wet lady funny hair?' a few more chorused in response, craning their necks to ogle, while their assorted adults all followed suit. Three children got up and tottered over, coming to stand about six inches in front of my squelching boots.

A little girl cried out, 'Scary lady, I don't like her! She looks like a monster!' and squeezed her balloon so tightly that it popped with a bang, causing several babies to start wailing. Most of the older children immediately starting squealing in response, getting up and running off in about thirty different directions, tripping over toys, adult's legs, discarded balloons and each other as they went.

The parents and carers scrambled after them, their calls to come and sit down adding to the staggeringly loud ruckus.

I backed a few steps away towards the door, my retreat hampered due to one child having decided to wrap their arms around my soggy jeans.

Giving up, I took in the carnage and wondered why anyone would choose to work with pre-school children in such large quantities. Sofia then expertly dodged through the marauding toddlers like a soldier under fire, racing to the sound desk at the back of the room. Suddenly, the opening notes of S Club's 'Reach for the Stars' started booming through the speakers. Every child froze. Even the babies were startled into silence. The parents who hadn't yet managed to catch their errant offspring (which was all of them except for two) stopped mid-stride and visibly sagged with relief. When the S Club lead singer began reassuring us how we can count on her, nearly every single child in the room who was able to walk independently, and some of them who were still at the crawling stage, started calmly picking up toys and depositing them into the stack of toy boxes in one corner.

By the time that rainbow was shining over us for the last time, the entire room had been cleared of toys. The music stopped, and Sofia called out, 'Story time part two!' while doing a funny half-jig, half-walk over to where the sock puppet sat quietly waiting. As if she were a mummy duck and they her brood, the children obediently followed behind, finding a place on the blankets once they'd reached their destination, the adults meekly joining them.

'Are you going to sit on the blanket with everybody else?' I said quietly to the limpet on my leg.

'You come too,' she mumbled into my knee.

'I don't think that's a good idea.'

'Stay here, then.'

So we did, as Sofia redonned the puppet and finished her story about a lost sheep, everyone behaving as if nothing had ever happened.

Once story time was over, followed by several songs about animals, everyone started getting ready to go home. A man whose bedraggled T-shirt bore more than a few face-smears came over, carrying a baby. 'Come on, Macey, let the lady go now.'

Macey wound her arms around me tighter, burying her face into the wet leg of my jeans.

'I'm really sorry.' The man winced. 'She's been like this with women ever since Kez left. Think she's trying to find a new mum. I've not adapted that well, to be honest, so I can't blame her. I'd be clinging to women's legs too if it didn't get me arrested.' He paused then, and looked more carefully at me, hiking the baby a little higher on his hip. 'I don't suppose there's any chance you're single? You could maybe come round sometime, meet the other kids. I make a mean fish finger sandwich.'

I answered automatically, without thinking about it. 'Um, no, sorry. I'm already seeing someone.'

And then, when I realised a split second later that this was true, only the person I was seeing I hadn't actually even *seen* – as if I hadn't caused enough of a scene already, I promptly burst into tears.

The man looked stricken. 'Wow, I'm really sorry. I didn't mean to offend you.'

'Macey, it's home time.' Sofia came over and bent down to stroke the little girl's head. 'I heard Daddy say he's got fish fingers for lunch. That's your favourite, isn't it?'

Macey twisted her head round to peep one eye at my sister.

'With yummy soft bread. And ketchup. And maybe some carrot sticks? What do you think? Does that sound like a nice lunch?'

Macey nodded her head about half a millimetre. She released

her grip on my leg and went to pull her dad's trousers instead. 'Daddy, can I go home have lunch now?'

'Please do,' Sofia muttered, winking up at me. She shooed the last of the stragglers out of the hall, then locked up and led me to the office she shared with Moses. The space wasn't huge, but they made the most of it. Matching desks and associated paraphernalia like filing cabinets, bookshelves and a giant noticeboard were squeezed into one half, while the other was taken up with two fat armchairs, a stripy rug, a coffee table and an enormous potted plant. It was one of those days where it never quite managed to get light, and Sofia clicked on the desk lamps, adding a cosy glow.

She fetched herself a coffee, and opened up a plastic tub containing a home-made wrap.

'Are you sure you don't mind me eating while we do this?'

Sofia had an hour to spare between the toddler group and visiting the nearby care home. She'd then race back to oversee the preparation for the Friday youth club.

I didn't mind.

Especially if eating left less time to ask questions.

'You were awesome with those kids, Sofia. Like magic. You are so good at your job.'

'Thank you. It helps that I love doing it.'

'Have you thought about adoption?'

She crinkled her eyes. 'I don't think Macey's dad is that bad.'

'You know what I mean.'

She picked at the corner of her wrap. 'I've thought about it, obviously. But it's felt like too big a step to seriously consider. Like it would be shutting a door on ever getting pregnant. I don't know how Moses'd feel about having a child that isn't biologically his. I don't know if he'd be ready to consider that as an option. Being a father, passing on the family line, is a big deal in his family.'

'Urr, hello? He's been bringing home children – and adults – in need of a family the whole time you've known him. If it was still in the days when you could simply decide to adopt someone and that was that, you'd have collected dozens of children by now. If you're not ready, or it doesn't feel right for you, then fair enough. But don't decide Moses' no for him. You can at least start a conversation.'

She took a thoughtful bite of her sandwich. 'To be honest, we've not really talked about it at all lately. It's so big and the grief is so painful. There are times I feel completely crushed by the weight of it all, and the only way I can keep going is to put it to one side, try to get on with things.'

'And is that helping?'

She furrowed her brow. 'Not really.'

'Do you think adoption might be worth considering, then? Because if you do, you should talk about it.'

'I guess so. I'll definitely have a think and a pray. Now.' She put her lunchbox to one side and straightened her shoulders. 'No more deflecting by talking about my problems! We're here to talk about you. And Mr X. I have to say, I've done a fair number of marriage preparation classes over the past seven years. This is the first one I've done without the groom.'

'Is he doing one too?'

'Moses met him last night.'

I sucked in a deep breath. 'Oh, my goodness.' I flapped one hand in front of my face. 'Did Moses tell you what he said, what he was like?'

Sofia shook her head. 'No. But the fact that Moses is still happy to go ahead and marry you says more than enough.'

'Really?' My voice was trembling. 'Moses likes him? Thinks that I'll like him? Enough to get married! Oh, that's such a relief.'

Only, I didn't feel relieved. I felt as if I'd spent the night in a tumble drier. The reason for my morning's panic came bouncing back into my head, and before I knew it I was sobbing again.

Sofia said nothing, coming to kneel by my chair so she could put her arm around me as she let me cry.

'I bet you've never had a bride-to-be cry in marriage preparation classes, either.' I gulped, trying to get a grip on myself.

'Oh, no, that's a common one. Stress about the wedding, pressure from relatives, money issues. Worrying about the practical stuff. Sometimes they're just overwhelmed and need to let out some pent-up emotions. When it's tears about who they're marrying, that's when we get serious. So. Do we need to get serious?'

I sat up straighter, pushed my hair back off my face and tried to appear as if I weren't freaking out.

'I'm okay about getting married. So many things are making me feel like this is the right decision. If Bridget and Moses think it's not a terrible mistake, that's really encouraging. And Dad's reaction totally surprised me. I can't explain why, but it feels right.'

Sofia nodded. 'You have peace about it.'

'Yes. And haven't Mum and Dad always told us to trust that?'

'So why the tears?' She got up and took a seat in the free chair.

I shrugged, smiling ruefully. 'Oh, a dozen reasons, probably. I didn't think I'd mind not going through the whole wedding-planning palaver this time. Been there, done that, learnt that it's meaningless. But having to plan it all by myself is lonelier than I expected. Even though Jake wasn't that bothered about where we held the reception, or what colour the flowers were, I always thought that when I did it again it'd be with a man who cared enough to make those decisions with me. Or would at least be there to nod and smile and then go along with whatever I wanted. And I'm sad that I'll be moving out. I know there's not enough room in the flat for a married couple trying to get to know each other and Bridget, but living with Bridget is lovely and the idea of living with a strange man is terrifying. The only man I've lived with is Daddy. Will we be sleeping in the same bed? Will he expect sex on the wedding night? Will he leave the toilet seat up and his shaving dregs in the sink and his sweaty gym clothes on the floor – I don't even know if he goes to the gym! Or shaves!'

'I guess a lot of things you figure out the same way you figured out living with Bridget, or with Aunt Mary in Cork. But as for the big stuff, bedroom stuff, I can tell you that you don't need to worry. Your husband will be unswervingly respectful, and considerate. Without going into details, I can tell you that much.'

'Thank you.' I narrowed my eyes at her. 'Have you met him too?'

Sofia screwed her face up. 'Please don't ask me that.'

'Has everyone met my husband apart from me?'

'I can't say anything. But I promise you'll understand once you meet him.'

'Crap – he's not famous, is he?'

'Stop asking questions about him!'

'Wow.'

Sofia gave me a moment to process that non-information before leaning forwards, scrutinising my face. 'There's something else.'

I avoided her gaze, shrugging as if to pretend I didn't know what she was talking about. Sofia ate some of her wrap and waited. It was her genius counselling technique and it worked every time.

'What if he doesn't like me?' I asked, my voice breaking on the words.

Sofia put her wrap down.

'What if he thinks I'm boring, and overly controlling, or not smiley enough? Or just... not attractive? What if he likes me, but doesn't love me? Bridget keeps telling me how wonderful he is, and now Moses thinks so too, and you and probably Dad and that's why he was so chilled about it, but what about me? If he's so wonderful, then he deserves a wonderful wife. Not someone who's been rejected after nearly all her first dates. Not someone whose fiancé thinks she's worth cheating on. Not an Emmapotamus. Not even someone who feels like an Emmapotamus, even if she isn't any more. Jake knew me, and he didn't want me. What if this person wants a wife who's confident and funny and who knows who she is, instead of flailing around so lost and disappointed with her life that she's prepared to marry a stranger?'

'Oh, Emma.' Sofia wiped her eyes. 'I wish you could see yourself how we see you. Jake was young and stupid. None of us thought he was good enough for you. We hoped he'd step up, once he grew up, but the problem there wasn't you. If he was a decent man he'd have broken things off, not let himself get caught fumbling about with your worst enemy.

'And I promise you, if Bridget thought this man wasn't going to fall head-over-heels for you, she'd never have matched you. How many of those first dates did you think were the right person for you? How many of them were so ready to make a relationship work, they'd make a legally binding commitment to stick with it?

'You are an amazing woman. Beautiful inside and outside and from every which side you look at it. Bridget, who is one of the top people ever, is gutted that she won't get to live with you any more. We all know you're her best friend as well as her sister. And that's saying something, considering she's a twin. If someone as lovely as Bridget loves you that much, then this guy can love you, no problem. All you need to do is be you, and you're better at that than anyone else.'

I nodded, feebly.

'Or, don't. Rip up the contract and walk away. Start dating again, or embrace being single. It's your life, Emma. You have to live with it. I don't know if what Dad says is true, that you should listen to your heart and forget your head. But what I do know is that you shouldn't listen to your fear.

'Now, how about we whizz through this lovely marriage-preparation booklet that my own gorgeous husband prepared, and see if that helps?'

It did. And it didn't. But by the end of my solo marriage-preparation class I had accepted that I could either spend the next week flapping about, freaking out over every possible thing that could go wrong, or I could learn to live with the not knowing.

Which, it turned out, was not an easy thing to do.

* * *

The next day, I left the house early to deliver a five-tier vanilla sponge cake plus gluten-free doughnut wall to a wedding. A few minutes after I'd arrived home, my neighbour, the delightful when not drunken Ralph Hutchens, knocked on my door.

'This came for you.' He held out a parcel.

'Thanks.' I tried to take it, but he kept holding onto the box.

'Um, I wanted to say sorry again about our date.'

'Right.' Ralph had sent me a couple of messages after the terrible date, apologising for actions he couldn't remember, but assumed weren't great. I hadn't bothered to reply.

'No hard feelings? I wouldn't want there to be any awkwardness between us, given that we're neighbours. And friends. At least, I hope we're still friends.'

'It's fine. Thanks for bringing the parcel.'

'I mean, we could try it again sometime? When I haven't got a work thing on first. And I've been thinking hard about cutting down on the booze, anyway. That evening was a wake-up call, to be honest. I'd hate for one night of fun with the lads to ruin things between us.'

'Um, I don't think so, but thanks anyway.' I managed to tug the small box out of his hand.

'Maybe breakfast, tomorrow? Or next weekend? Some people

say you haven't lived until you've tried my scrambled eggs.' He grinned. 'Well, my mother does, anyway.'

'I'm a vegan.' I stepped back, swinging the door shut as I added, 'And I'm getting married next weekend.'

'Ugh, thank you whoever you are for saving me from any more encounters with people like Ralph Hutchens,' I muttered, ripping open the parcel as I wandered back into the kitchen.

Inside was a velvet box.

Inside the box was a ring. A white gold Claddagh ring, with a heart diamond in the centre. A lot of the Claddagh rings I'd seen were verging on tacky, or were chunky and dated. This was stunning. Delicate, with clean, flowing lines. It must have cost a fortune.

There was also a note:

I know this isn't how it's meant to be done. And it's too late for me to ask you to do me the honour of being my wife, seeing as we've already signed a contract. But although you've had to miss out on a proposal, I hope you will accept this ring as an indication of my commitment to becoming your husband, and to doing my best to make the unconventional start worth it. I intend to make sure that you never have to miss out on anything else as a result of choosing me to be the man you spend your life with.

While I don't even know if you're someone who likes jewellery, let alone what type of ring you might want, I'm looking forward to discovering this, along with everything else about you. But in the meantime, the Claddagh ring seemed like an appropriate symbol for the adventure we are about to begin together:

The crown is my promise of loyalty.

The clasped hands are my offer of friendship.

The heart is my hope of love.

It goes without saying that I can't wait to meet you on the 11th. It probably also goes without saying that I'm scared witless.

But as a wise man I know always says, 'If you're scared as shite, then something serious is at stake.'

I hope this allays any fears you might have about how serious I am when it comes to making this work. Truth be told, I am very much looking forward to falling in love with you.

See you soon,

X

I was still sitting at the kitchen table staring at it when Bridget came home from talking to Paolo's parents about their guest list.

'Oh, is that from Mr X?' She dumped her bags on the worktop and came to have a look. 'He asked the project team if we'd post it on to you, but I didn't know what it was.'

'Couldn't you have just brought it home?'

'Well, where's the romance in that?' She picked up the box and flipped it open. 'Oh, wow. That is gorgeous!'

'Wait till you read the note.' I pushed it across the table towards her.

It took about three seconds for her to burst into tears. 'Now do you see what I mean?' She sobbed. 'If he can come up with a proposal like this, when he isn't even here, what else will he do to make you fall in love with him?'

'Should I be concerned that you seem more touched by my non-proposal that you did about your actual proposal?'

Bridget wiped away her tears with both hands, grabbed a biscuit from the cupboard and sat down. 'No. I'm fine. I'm feeling very emotional about the whole thing, that's all. I know I was only a stroppy teenager who had to find out about Helen Richards by earwigging through the crack in the floorboards, but I wasn't quite so self-absorbed that I didn't notice your broken heart. And years later it's still not completely fixed. I think this man might be able to fix it. I can't believe that what looked like a disastrous work project has turned out to be the best thing ever.'

'It might not turn out to be the best thing ever, Bridget. There's a lot could go wrong. And the chances are it will.'

'Emma, I know who you're marrying. I'm confident this is your happy-ever-after.'

'What does Dad say? "No happy-ever-after happens without hard work."'

Bridget grinned, leaning over to take my hand and push the ring onto my finger. 'Well, that's perfect, then, isn't it? Hard work is your favourite thing.'

13

On Monday afternoon, I drove out to Hatherstone to investigate further. Sunday lunch had not been what I'd expected. I don't know what Dad, or one of my sisters, had said to Mum, but instead of spending the whole time agonising about my terrible decision, or using the full force of her emotional blackmail arsenal to try to stop the wedding, she had asked me a few polite questions about the practical details and then moved on to outlining her latest plans for the new and improved pop-up tea room (bouncy castle, face-painting, pony rides...).

I was initially staggered. Then increasingly suspicious.

Even Annie smiled sweetly and asked about bridesmaid dresses and whether we were having a hen do (not unless a quiet night in with my sisters counted).

So on Monday afternoon, once Dad and I were settled with tea and some taster samples of my wedding cake, I asked him what was going on.

'I'm starting to wonder if, not only does everyone know who it is I'm getting married to, you all must know him personally. Otherwise, why aren't you all continuing the campaign to stop this from happening? Unless you have something else up your sleeve? Are you going to kidnap me the night before and put me on an aeroplane to Alaska?'

Dad smiled. 'Maybe your mother listened to me. She does, you know, every decade or so. It was my idea to paint the front door red.'

'Well, what about this, then?' I showed him the ring, which still felt alien and awkward on my finger. I'd had to take it off to bake the cake samples that morning, and it had taken a lot of mental effort to put it on again.

'Ah, now, isn't that lovely? That's a grand wee ring. I've not seen one like that before.'

'Bit of a coincidence, though, giving me an Irish ring.'

'Ah, come on, now, a coincidence, or could it be a sign to ease your jitters? That's not a cheap bit of tat there, love. He's showing you already that he's willing to invest in this marriage.'

I shook my head, exasperated. 'This is ridiculous. My mind is completely boggled at how my family have fallen in love with this complete stranger, and suddenly seem so sure he's going to be amazing. Were you all really that desperate to see me married off?'

Dad looked crestfallen. 'That's not it at all! But the signs are good so far.'

'Daddy, be honest. You know who it is, don't you?'

Dad said nothing, coincidentally choosing to stuff in a whole cake sample in that moment.

'It's one of Moses' relatives, isn't it?'

Dad swallowed, took a mouthful of tea and sat back, relief all over his face. 'Not that I know of. Now, I have something to show you. Can you fetch over that package over there?'

It took me a minute hunting through the assorted debris in the corner of the living room until I found the right box. As soon as I saw it, I knew.

Carefully opening it up, I found a wedding dress inside.

'Oh, Daddy.'

'It was my mother's. Auntie Mary sent it over.'

I was too choked up to reply. Lifting it gently out, I unfolded a calf-length, sleeveless white dress with a simple lace bodice and scoop neck.

'I know I've said this before, but you're more the spit of her every year, so I reckoned it would suit you. And you know, fashions and that tend to go round in circles, so I thought it might do. I didn't think you'd want something all flounces and sparkles.'

I stroked the soft fabric, blinking hard so a tear didn't plop onto the lace and leave a mark. Dad lost his mother when he was nineteen. When I first moved to Ireland, every person over sixty told me how much I looked like her.

'She made it herself, so it'll be top quality. Love and care in every stitch. But if you don't like it, or you've already chosen your own dress, something modern, I'll understand. It's your day, and it's not as though it cost me anything.'

'I'll try it on.'

I had been considering wearing one of my old bridesmaid's dresses rather than return to the bridal shop in town. But part of me wanted to look like a traditional bride – a return gesture to show Mr X that I was serious about this, too. And, of course, that included looking my best, in the hope that he wouldn't be disappointed when he finally saw me.

This dress was perfect.

It fitted as if it were made for me, and, most importantly, when I wore it I *felt* like me. Wearing my grandmother's dress, with my dad's blessing, helped soothe some of the fraught nerves with a warm glow of hope. For a while there, I felt like a bride-to-be.

* * *

Cooper

Cooper had planned out the morning of his wedding day with scientific precision. That plan nearly went dangerously awry when he was woken up with a man leaning over his bed, flicking his nerves instantly into fight-or-flight mode. Thankfully, in the second it took him to blink the sleep from his eyes, the man came into focus, saving a potential trip to hospital to get his best man patched up, and the need to answer some very awkward questions.

'Man. You scared the life out of me. What the hell are you doing?'

'My job. Which you hired me to do.' Ben spoke from behind the camera. 'Getting some rough footage, off-the-cuff reactions.'

Cooper ran a hand through his hair, dreading to think what he'd look like after such a pathetic amount of sleep. 'Get lost. I'll talk to you when I've had coffee. And I'm dressed.'

Ben pointed to a steaming mug on the bedside table. 'Restless night?'

'Yes.' Cooper attempted to clear his throat. He had a feeling this interview was happening whether he liked it or not. He might as well try to appear cooperative, pretend he wasn't such a grumpy old fart.

'Up all hours looking at Mrs Cooper on social media?'

'If that comment ends up in the final cut, you're not getting paid.'

Ben grinned from behind his camera.

'And how are you feeling about getting married today?'

Cooper paused, waded through the fog in his head to see if he could uncover the truth about that before deciding whether to lie or not. Surprised when he came across the answer. 'I feel ready.'

'No regrets at this stage? Last-minute nerves? Cold feet?'

'Nope.'

'Still denying the many levels of absurdity that constitute this entire farce?'

Cooper swallowed a mouthful of scalding coffee. 'Acknowledging them, and choosing to go ahead anyway.'

Ben dropped the camera. 'Seriously, mate. The project is one thing, marrying a stranger. As if marrying someone you know isn't a big enough risk. But you aren't marrying a stranger. It's Bridget's sister. Are you sure?'

Cooper had another sip. *Could anyone be sure, really?*

'I'm sure that I want to do this. That I'm going to do everything I can to make it work. Isn't that all any of us can do, at the end of the day?'

'Which is one of the reasons putting yourself into a position where your time, money, living arrangements, mental health, heart, soul and about 90 per cent of every decision you make are dependent on the actions and feelings of one single other person never makes logical sense.'

'Thanks for the pep talk. You've clearly been reading up on how to be a best man.'

'Yeah, well. I thought you might be more in need of a best mate.'

'We're not such good mates that I'm prepared to let you stand there with a camera while I get dressed.'

'Fair point. I'll be warming up outside.'

The pair of them smashed out ten miles before stopping at their regular café for a jumbo fry-up, and then returning home to get ready. And once Cooper had put on his new suit and tie, pinned a white rose to his lapel, and placed a box containing two rings in his pocket, he was ready to face what was going to be either one of the best or the worst things he'd ever do.

Ben drove them out to Hatherstone. He'd leave the car at the farmhouse overnight, and pick it up in the morning. A room had been booked in a nearby B & B for Emma and Cooper's wedding night. Cooper's phone beeped as they left the city:

She's all ready to go. Hope you're not feeling too nervous! And for the record, I give my full neuroscientific endorsement to the Cole Compatibility Function. You guys are going to make the best couple.

Widget x

He was about to reply when she messaged again:

Okay, so don't freak out, but I have some bad news.

Cooper stared at the three dots on his phone for an agonising length of time until the next message came through.

'What's happened?' Ben asked, trying to be subtle as he switched on his camera.

'I don't know. Bridget says it's bad news.'

'She's changed her mind?'

Cooper shook his head, distracted. 'No, she said Emma was ready to go. I hope it's not her dad.'

Cole called
Asking to confirm the venue address
Couldn't think of how to fob him off in time
Sorry

Initially, Cooper was so relieved that it wasn't anything terrible, it took him a moment to consider that having Professor Cole standing about throwing out smug comments at his wedding was terrible enough. He knew from hanging around the family as a student that they all thought Bridget's boss was an arrogant prig. He also knew that those Donovans wouldn't allow any priggish comments to go unchallenged. Especially today.

Would Emma rather he be the kind of man who stood up and called his boss out, defending their honour and refusing to allow him to ruin the day by asking him to leave, even though he'd then end up unemployable (to anyone who wanted a reference), meaning he'd have to rely on his new wife to pay for the room he rented off his old uni friend?

Or would she rather he swallowed his pride, kept his head cool, his mouth shut and let Prof have his fun, potentially ruining their wedding for the sake of the marriage that came after?

'Everything all right, mate?' Ben asked, jolting him out of his spiral of doom.

'Well, actually...'

14

It was my wedding day.

For real this time.

After three weeks of feeling as though a swarm of ants were living under my skin, today I woke up feeling...

Serene.

Or, to put it less optimistically, numb.

I skipped breakfast as usual, had a bowl of Mamma's minestrone soup for lunch, followed by a bath, and two hours under the attention of my sister Annie, while the rest of my sisters sat around laughing, applying their own make-up, topping up our Buck's Fizz glasses and asking me for the hundredth time if I was okay.

The day before, Annie had painted all our nails, waged war against any unwanted hairs and applied various treatments to my skin that were guaranteed to make me gorgeous for my big day. We'd decamped to the farmhouse straight after picking her up from the airport, having cancelled all other commitments for some much-needed sister time.

Annie had been trying her best to show us how happy and excited she was – happy to be home, if still not 100 per cent convinced about the reason she was here. But we knew our sister, and we were watching closely. We all caught the unguarded moments when her smile faded to reveal the underlying sadness. And while happy to talk about her beauty therapy business, her new friends, the differences of life in the big city compared to a sleepy Sherwood Forest village, we noticed how she deftly detoured any conversation away from the merest cursory remarks about Greg.

In the end, when ten o'clock was approaching and Mum had trudged up the stairs after pointing out how even daughters as gorgeous as hers needed their beauty sleep, as we snuggled up on the sofas in the safety of our childhood duvets, Sofia just came out with it.

'How are things with you and Greg?'

Annie buried her face in her hot-chocolate mug for a moment, until she had to acknowledge that we were all waiting for an answer. 'Oh, you know, it's Greg, he's stupidly busy, but at least he enjoys the work. They've promised him a new assistant soon, so hopefully things will ease off a bit.'

'That's not what I asked.'

Annie pursed her lips. 'Well, that's how I answered it.'

'Then I think that's answer enough.'

'Annie, you know you can talk to us,' Bridget said, her voice tight with worry.

Annie rolled her eyes. 'Well, if you must poke and pry into none of your business, we had an argument before I came, so I'm mad at him. It's nothing, we'll sort it when I get back. End of. And I don't want to waste any of the four days I'm here thinking about it, discussing it, hearing you all dissect it or being given advice about it. So, can we please move on now?'

'Are you arguing a lot?' Bridget asked.

'No!' She wriggled down deeper into her duvet. 'We argue about the same thing, lots of times. But no couple agrees on everything. Apart from maybe Pastor Perfect and her perfect pastor husband. You know me, you know I argue. It's fine.'

It so wasn't fine. Annie did argue, often, with the rest of us when she'd lived at home. All of us apart from Bridget, who would simply give in to Annie's point of view straight away. But if Annie was secure in her marriage, she'd have happily spent some time telling us how wrong Greg was about something, eager to hear our assertions of why she was right, and what she should do about it.

'Married couples fight, Bridget,' Orla said, putting down her phone. 'You might have glided along with Paolo for hundreds of years, but you've not had to deal with the irritating day-to-day crap that goes on when you live in each other's pockets.'

'Or make any big decisions, beyond saying yes. Have you even decided where you'll be living yet?' Annie asked.

'Don't make this about me!' Bridget said, her face crumpling.

'You're right, this weekend is about Emma. Not me, and not Greg. So, as I requested, move on.'

* * *

We had an afternoon ceremony planned, so that Dad could rest all morning, and by three o'clock the barn was transformed, Nita's three-course banquet was prepped to perfection and my sisters and mother were dressed, styled and only a little bit squiffy.

I was as beautiful as I was ever going to be, which, if I say so myself, felt beautiful enough.

A car had pulled into the driveway about half an hour earlier, sending my sisters into fits of squeals as they grabbed each other's arms and formed a human barrier to prevent me from getting near the bedroom window.

I took it from this that the groom was ready, too.

'Come on now, girls,' Mum called from the bottom of the stairs. 'Time for a quick prayer before we go.'

* * *

'Well, God. Here we are, finally, so many, many years later than we initially planned, we thank you that you have intervened with a miracle and eventually after all this time blessed Emma with a man who stuck around until the wedding day. We trust in you, God, that this will work and she will not become biggest joke in the village, whatever Janet Patterson might think. After all, she is divorced three times so what does she know about it?'

'I forgot something,' I blurted, catapulting myself off the sofa, and pushing my way through the huddle.

'But I haven't said amen yet!' Mum said, opening her eyes to glare at me.

'No one's saying amen to that, Mamma,' Orla replied. 'Come and sit back down, Ems. Sofia will pray instead.'

'No, I mean it. I need to get something. It won't take a minute. You can finish off without me.'

'What did you forget?' Annie asked, eyes narrowed. 'If you're doing a runner, then tell us. We'll be happy to help.'

'I'll fetch it for you,' Bridget said. 'I'm chief bridesmaid, it's my job. You wait here, don't mess your hair up.'

'I'm not doing a runner!'

Probably.

I seemed to have forgotten how to breathe, and I wasn't sure Bridget could help me with that. I'd also forgotten all the many reasons I'd come up with to convince myself that this was a splendid idea.

What I needed was a minute to ask myself, one last time, what the hell I thought I was doing.

Then I'd decide whether I was doing a runner or not.

'Give me one minute.' I held up one perfectly manicured finger, picked up the soft, lace skirts of my grandmother's wedding dress and whisked myself out of the living room, down the flag-stoned corridor and through the creaky old door into the kitchen.

Opening the kitchen door into the back garden, as stealthily as possible to prevent my sisters from assuming the worst, I stepped outside into the blustery May air.

Maybe a smack in the face from the wind would head off my panic attack. I turned my face into the breeze, and then – *oh*.

A man.

At the edge of the house.

Standing with his hands in his pockets, his face frowning in concentration.

In a suit, and a tie, a white rose in his lapel.

The groom.

And I'd met him before.

Oscar, my four-year-old nephew, was with him. I took a tiny step closer, leaning forwards in the hope that those extra three inches would allow me to hear them.

'I'm did running away,' Oscar announced.

Oh, so that makes two of us, then. Maybe we could team up, scarper together.

'Why are you running away?' The man tilted his head to one side, as if considering the matter. 'That's a big, brave decision to make.'

'Cos I don't want to carry the stupid rings cos I got a stupid baby walk and everyone will laugh and then I'll fall over and drop the rings and Auntie Emma can't married and it alls my fault and I don't get any cake.'

'Right.' He rubbed his jaw, thoughtfully. 'I'm guessing that maybe someone else dissed your walk?'

'Lottie said I look like a baby rangtang.'

'Okay. And if you don't carry the rings, does Lottie get to do it?'

'Yep.' Oscar sniffed, swiping a tear away. My heart squeezed, for a whole lot of reasons.

'Do you think that Lottie could have said that about your walk because then she can carry the rings?'

Oscar thought about this.

'Do you think that your lovely aunties and uncles and grandparents will laugh at your walk? Have they ever laughed at you before?'

'Only when I did tell a funny joke.'

'There you are, then. She's jealous. I'm willing to bet this Lottie is your big sister, isn't she?'

'YES!'

'What normally happens if you fall over?'

'Mummy gives me a cuddle better, and says, "Come on, soldier, up you get".'

'She doesn't say you can't have any cake?'

'No! If I hurt myself, I do get cake!'

My groom shrugged his shoulders. 'There you go, then.'

'Lottie did lying?' Oscar didn't sound convinced.

'Hey, why don't you show me your ring-bearer walk, and I'll tell you what I think?'

Oscar ducked his head, smearing at his runny nose with both hands, one after the other. 'You might laugh.'

The groom crouched down, gently took hold of Oscar's snotty hand and shook it, looking him right in the eyes. 'I won't. Here, I've shaken on it. And a real man never goes back on his handshake.'

He stood up again. 'Come on, we've both got very important jobs to do in a few minutes, and they can't start without us. Let's see you walk to that bush and back.'

'I don't have a ring to practise with. When I practised at home I was holding Lottie's ring.' Another swipe of his nose and eyes.

'Well, that's easily solved.' The man reached in his pocket, opened what could only have been the wedding-ring box, and carefully placed the contents in Oscar's trembling hand. 'Might as well practise with the real thing. Oh – hang on a minute though, got to look the part even when you practise.' He whipped the forest-green pocket square out of his jacket and bent down to give Oscar's disgusting face a careful wipe. 'There. Now you're ready to rock.'

As Oscar began his ring-bearer walk to the holly bush, a smile broke out on my future husband's lovely face, and in that moment, my doubts and fears dissolved into insignificance.

If a man was prepared to put his about-to-be-wedding ring into the snotty, grubby, trembling hands of a boy he'd only just met, and send him off across the garden while smiling, that told me all I needed to know.

So, yes, he had told me at a wedding only weeks before that marriage was a 'noose for two'. But at the same time, he'd voluntarily climbed in a bin to prise a wedding ring from a dog's drooling jaws.

And people could change their minds, couldn't they?

In that moment, mine was definitely made up.

I was getting married to Hot Photographer.

I was getting married!

In about fifteen minutes!

Except I really needed a wee first...

'Perfect!' I heard him call out as I ducked back inside.

I couldn't agree more...

No wonder we matched so highly on the compatibility test, I marvelled while readjusting my dress in the downstairs cloakroom. Both in the celebration industry. Both self-employed. Both loved children. Both... lived in Nottinghamshire. I presumed.

I found everyone hovering nervously in the corridor, trying to pretend they weren't organising my search party.

'Ready?' Bridget asked, as if she didn't want to hear the answer.

'Yep. Ready to rock.'

Everyone released their breaths in one relieved puff.

'Well, actually. Can you wait here a minute?' Sofia asked. 'Let me get in position.'

'I need to round the kids up, too,' Orla said, hurrying out of the front door behind Sofia.

'Yeah, I'm going to check on the groom,' Bridget added.

'Well, looks like it's just us, then.' My mamma clutched her hands to the bodice of her gold sequinned dress. 'I can finish the prayer while we wait for the minute.'

'Actually, Mamma,' Annie interjected. 'I think someone else wants to escort Emma to her wedding.'

She grabbed Mum's hand and dragged her out of the door and halfway across the yard before Mum had time to protest. Heading over in the opposite direction, taking slow, careful steps without his stick, came my father.

With a few metres left to go, he took his eyes off the uneven gravel and looked up. As he caught me there in the doorway, his face transformed from that of a weighed-down, weary old man, wracked with pain, into a face shining with love and unadulterated pride. He stopped, wobbling on his feet for a moment, and I hurried out to join him.

'Darling, your shoes!' he chided as I linked my arm through his, giving the impression that he would be the one helping me to the barn.

'Ah, it's only a bit of mud. It'll wipe off later.'

'Now wait a wee moment, let me get a proper look at you.'

I dutifully took a step back and let him look.

He breathed out a long, slow sigh and reached for my fingers, bringing them to his lips, even as the tears leaked out of the corners of his eyes.

'You were the most precious thing I'd ever seen, from the moment I first saw you. Even red, bald and wrinkly, you stole my heart with a glance. I'd never known a feeling like it. Emma Maraid Donovan. My firstborn. I know it's considered silly and old-fashioned and anti-feminist and whatever to be giving you away. As if something so priceless could ever be owned in the first place. But today I give away the joy of holding first place in your heart to another, trusting that soon enough you'll be the first in his. And for that I'm full of delight even as my heart breaks a little. You know I could not love you more, no matter what you did, and I'm so blessed to see the woman you are. God bless you with a man who is worthy of you. And now let's get on because it's feckin' freezing out here. Stop crying or you'll be messing all that lovely make-up and making Annie cross.'

And so my father, the first man in my heart, led me off to meet the man who we all hoped, prayed, dreamed, would take his place.

15

COOPER

'Mr Cooper, kindly explain what's going on.'

Cooper was in trouble. There aren't many situations where the term *Mr* is an insult. But here it was a calculated reminder that Cooper's title wasn't Dr, or Professor. That his position in the Nottingham University Neuroscience Department depended on, first and foremost, keeping in his boss's good graces. 'I'm not sure what you mean.'

All Cooper wanted to be doing was focussing on what was about to happen, while trying to keep reasonably calm and not come across as a total idiot. And instead he had to stand here underneath an archway of white flowers and fairy lights while enduring a grilling from Professor Cole, who had already established that everyone present was related to the bride, not him.

'Well, they seem to all know you.' Cole raised his straggled eyebrows, rocking back on his heels as he smirked. Orla, Sofia and Annie had each given him a hug and a kiss when they'd arrived in the barn. Gabriella had nearly broken a couple of ribs as she'd flung her arms around him, swiping fat tears from her heavily pencilled eyes. Even Bear had shaken his hand, calling him 'son' as he'd asked how he was holding up. 'And not just the family. The vicar is clearly a close acquaintance.'

'Actually, I've not seen any of them in years.' Well, apart from Bear. And that was hardly worth mentioning.

'But you do know them.'

'Yes. But I don't know the bride.'

'Although you know who she is.'

'I don't think having known her relatives a few years ago could constitute me knowing her.'

'Oh, come off it, Cooper. This is Dr Donovan's family!' Cole gestured at Bridget with his chin, sending his jowls jiggling. 'I cannot fathom how you hypothesised that the lead researcher's sister could pass as a valid test subject.'

Cooper took a deep breath, reminded himself that this was meant to be a celebration, and that he really needed to not lose his job today. Then he thought, *Screw it.*

'She's the woman who's about to become my wife. She's not a test subject.'

Cole interrupted him with a loud guffaw. 'Well, *Mr* Cooper, I think you'll find that today those are mutually inclusive. The overlap of the Venn diagram, as it were.'

'Look, with all due respect, Professor, this might be a little side project for you, to win a bet and save you a bit of pride. This is my *wedding day*. I'm about to turn my whole life upside down, and commit to this woman for better or worse. You signed off on me leaving the project in order to become one of the *test subjects*. Bridget handled every step of the anonymous process to match the two most compatible people taking part. That happened to be me, and her sister. At this point in the project, if you really want to end it now, and trash all those weeks of work, meaning you're the one who'll have to explain what happened to the funding that was supposed to be spent on a new centrifuge, let alone look Ernestine

Lavinski in the face and tell her that your couple didn't even make it to the vows, then there's a specific moment during the service when you can officially object. If you'd rather make the best of the situation, and graciously accept Prof Love's award from her bitter hands, then let's get on with it, shall we?'

Before Professor Cole could let him know which of those options he was going for, Bridget burst through the door at the back of the barn, and for a split second Cooper couldn't think about anything else.

She wore a deep red dress, one of those 1950s styles with a square neckline and a full skirt, highlighting the curve of her hips. Her hair was curled into soft waves and she wore lipstick to match the dress. She was smiling, but he knew full well that this particular smile was as fake as her new nails.

Then she saw him, and as their eyes met Bridget's real smile burst out across her whole face. He had the three seconds it took her to race up the makeshift aisle to pull himself together.

'Looking good,' he said, giving her a brotherly peck on the cheek. Bridget was about to reply, when she noticed Professor Cole standing there.

'Oh! Hello, Professor. This is an... unexpected... pleasure. How lovely of you to come.'

'Purely for scientific reasons. Making sure nothing happens without my knowledge, which may then go on to invalidate the project.'

'Right. Of course. I'll find you a seat, shall I? We're about to start.' She led Cole off to a folding chair beside Sam, Orla's husband. Cooper had helped babysit Sam and Orla's son Harry a few times with Bridget, and from what he could remember Sam was only a year or so older than him. The years had not been kind. He looked closer to forty than thirty. And a knackered, lost-the-will-to-live forty at that.

He hoped that was down to three kids, a stressful job in teaching and bad genes.

Not a result of ten years being a Donovan-in-law.

Either way, Cooper was glad when Ben came in, camera on, and strode up to join him.

'Did you get something?' Cooper asked. Ben had gone to record some footage of the bride.

He took a moment to answer. 'Um, yeah.' Ben paused, then nodded firmly. 'Yeah... I didn't interview her, but I got what I needed.'

'And?'

Ben wasn't listening.

'Ben? How was she?' He gave his best man a nudge.

'What? Oh, yeah, she was great.' He nodded again, causing the camera to bob up and down. 'Really great. You know what I think about all this, but if you're going to legally chain yourself to an unknown woman, with the extreme likelihood of weeks of awkward, increasingly desperate attempts to manufacture feelings that don't exist, followed by months of disappointment as you try to undo the almighty mess you made, she looks like the woman to do it with.'

'Thanks. I appreciate that.'

'No, seriously, mate. Watching her with her dad just now... I almost... Well. She almost had me revising the Ben Baxter theory on why long-term commitment is an inherently flawed social construct. Good luck to you. You might not need as much as I thought. Think I might have to edit my speech.'

'You said no speech!'

But before they could argue about that, Sofia gave Cooper a pat on the shoulder and whispered, 'Positions, please, gentlemen. Now, this is a bizarre situation for all of us, but whatever you do, keep smiling.'

Everyone else had already taken their seats, on two rows lined up neatly to form the shortest aisle ever. As 'I Can't Help Falling in Love with You' by Elvis started playing, they all turned to see Bridget's niece start slowly walking towards the front, chucking white rose petals in every direction, her nephew striding confidently behind her holding the ring box. He was followed by Bridget, clutching a bouquet of roses to match her dress, tears unashamedly streaming down her face. And then, before Cooper had a chance to steel his shoulders, or take a much-needed breath, Emma walked through the barn door, the May light casting a soft yellow glow behind her. It seemed like forever as she led her father the few metres down the aisle, and if Cooper had wondered if she might have guessed it was him – or whether Bridget or one of her other sisters had given it away – he knew even Professor Cole couldn't deny the pure shock on her face as she glided closer.

'Hi,' she said, once she'd come to a stop and gently helped Bear take his seat beside Gabriella. Emma glanced at Ben, filming away, before looking back at Cooper again.

'Hi.' He hoped his smiled seemed genuine, not the nervous grimace he feared it probably was.

'You're Cooper.'

'I am.' He cleared his throat. 'It's very nice to meet you properly at last.'

'I'm Emma. But I guess you knew that?'

'I do now.' Cooper leant forwards as if to kiss her hello, and muttered, 'Prof is here, so if we can play down our link to Bridget, she'll really appreciate it.'

He sensed the warmth radiating from the skin beneath her ear, caught the gentle vanilla of her perfume, and felt an automatic prickle of awareness that he was millimetres away from a beautiful woman.

Phew.

Emma looked him directly in the eyes as he straightened up, and nodded, the corners of her mouth creasing in a conspiratorial smile.

Several dozen of Cooper's muscles that he hadn't realised he was clenching unclenched in that moment.

Maybe this wasn't going to be a complete disaster, after all.

* * *

Emma

What? What the...?

I had confidently arrived at my wedding, feeling a million times better now that I knew who would be waiting for me there. But while, yes, Hot Photographer was indeed standing at the front and grinning at me in a suit and tie, he was most definitely occupying the position of photographer – from behind a video camera.

And directly in front of me, in what I knew from the mini-rehearsal the day before was the designated groom's position, was who I was pretty darn sure was Bridget's long-lost best friend, now colleague, Cooper.

A thousand thoughts whizzed through my brain like sparks running up a dynamite fuse as I continued walking, only a small part of my brain able to appreciate the comfort of Daddy's arm in mine, the smiles of my family and Nita, the voice of Elvis in the background.

No wonder Bridget was so keen for this to happen.

And Dad – he must have known.

They all knew.

Moses did marriage prep with him!

Oh – and the engagement ring – not an amazing sign that we're meant to be together!

He knew.

He KNEW.

Was I the only person in this family who didn't know?

But he knew – and he chose to marry me anyway.

A man CHOSE to marry me.

He's been to Sunday lunch with my family – he's been to CHRISTMAS DAY with my family, and still hasn't been put off.

He's not at all bad-looking, either.

Phew.

Maybe this isn't going to be a complete disaster, after all.

*   *   *

To be honest, the rest of the ceremony was something of a blur. Which, according to my sisters, is perfectly normal even if you have met the person you're marrying more than a handful of times before.

However, the unusually tense moment when Sofia asked people to speak now or forever hold their peace did stick in my mind. Especially when Oscar called out, 'Can I hold a piece? Is it cake time now?'

As did my uncontrollable giggles when reciting my vows. Sofia had avoided the usual lines, coming up with alternatives that would mean I wouldn't be going back on them before we'd reached the toasts. It's probably a bad thing to not remember the vows you made to your husband, but I made a note to ask her for a copy at some point.

Cooper didn't laugh, but he seemed relieved and amused that I did, as if he'd been expecting me to scream and run off once I saw who it was. Knowing what I knew about his background, that seemed fair enough. His background also offered a solid explanation for why he had no family here. I remembered that he'd been on his own since his aunt emigrated, and even if his dad was still somehow miraculously alive he'd be the last person Cooper would want at his wedding (followed closely by Professor Cole, who was lurking in the corner for some reason, glaring at us as if we were misbehaving laboratory specimens).

Another sticky moment was when Sofia pronounced us husband and wife (*HUSBAND! AND WIFE!*). She raised her eyebrows at Cooper and said, 'So, this is the part where I'd normally announce that you can now kiss your bride. Given the circumstances, I think we'll check if she's okay with it first. Emma? How do you feel about a first kiss?'

I didn't admit that I'd sort of stopped feeling anything about three vows ago. Instead, I managed a shrug, and enough of a smile that Cooper smiled back, leant in and gently pecked my lips.

I met his eyes once more, and amongst the deep, dark blue I saw kindness there.

Cooper took my hand as we walked down the aisle accompanied by The Monkees' 'I'm a Believer', and it felt safe there. Whatever happened in the long run, right then I felt a distinct twinge of cautious optimism that maybe I could live with Patrick Charles Cooper. I was certainly open to the possibility of falling in love with him.

In the meantime, I really needed some of Nita's vegan vol-au-vents and a large glass of something fizzy.

* * *

Cooper

To Cooper's astonishment, things seemed to be going okay. The Donovan family were everything he'd remembered, and more – in numbers, and in love, laughter, liveliness and a whole lot of other good things that he'd heard that families were meant to be.

After the ceremony, Moses, who unlike Sam seemed exactly the same as he had been four years ago, had driven them over to his church, then ushered the newly-weds into his office to sign the register. Most of the other family members had come along for the ride, with Orla and Annie acting as witnesses while the rest hung about in the main hall. Bridget also came in to ensure authentication for the project, Professor Cole having made a swift retreat straight after the ceremony.

Cooper declined Moses' invitation to add his father's name and occupation to the marriage certificate. 'Is it legitimate if I don't?'

Moses' gaze was steady. 'It's totally up to you.'

While he knew his father's name – hard to forget when it was identical to his – Cooper had no idea what he'd put for his occupation. Professional waster? Sleazebag? Child beater? Sociopath?

Hopefully it was 'inmate'.

'I'll pass.' He noticed Emma's face, creased with concern beneath her veil. One more thing he would have to explain to her at some point. She reached out to squeeze his hand, and as she held on the twang of bleak loneliness that always accompanied any thoughts about his family faded into the background.

A loud thud on the door was accompanied by, 'Are you finished in there cos Nonna says we can't go and eat until you come out and I'm so-o-o-o-o-o hungry I'm starving!'

'Oscar, you just had an apple and a massive oatmeal cookie, you'll survive twenty more minutes!' Orla yelled at the door.

'Twenty more minutes? That's to-o-o-o-o long. I can't wait twenty whole minutes, I'm a growing boy and I'm so hungry I think I'm shrinking instead! Help, Mummy, help, now I'm as small as a dog! Now I'm as small as a worm! Now I'm as—'

'Well, now I'm busy so you'd better wriggle off and tell your dad before somebody steps on you. SAM? CAN YOU PLEASE PARENT YOUR YOUNGEST CHILD SO EMMA AND COOPER CAN GET MARRIED? Ugh.' Orla rolled her eyes. 'Enjoy the honeymoon period, guys. Won't be long before it's a distant memory you get confused with a romantic film you once saw.'

Cooper took the pen Moses offered him with a grin and signed on the dotted line. Sofia had spoken briefly at the ceremony about how Cooper wasn't simply marrying Emma, he was now joining their family, and while on the one hand their unswerving commitment to doing life together with in-your-face honesty felt akin to jumping out of an aeroplane blindfolded, he figured that if he was going to start learning how to be part of a family, he could do a lot worse than this one.

'Right, all done.'

They moved out of the way to allow Ben, who had done that documentary-maker's trick of slipping in unnoticed, to take a close-up shot of the certificate, and then Moses tore off the top sheet and gave Cooper a copy.

'There you go, bro. Welcome to the Donovan clan. First things first, let's get you and Mrs Cooper back to the farm before Oscar disappears altogether.'

'Mrs Donovan,' Cooper replied, looking at Emma before she had a chance to object. 'I really don't expect you to take my name.'

'You should take hers,' Annie said as they all trooped back out to join the others. 'Cooper Donovan. Might be a whole lot less confusing. And you can ditch your secret first name for good.'

So, it would appear that Cooper was a fully fledged Donovan now.

He wondered how long it would be, if ever, before he could really believe it.

After the food, and the drinks, and Bear's brief speech before he went up to bed, while most of the family lounged on sofas or played

Uno with Orla and Sam's kids at the dining-room table, Cooper ducked outside to grab some fresh air, and a chance to process some of the dozen thoughts whirling through his head.

He wandered over to a neighbouring sheep field, and leant his arms on the wooden boundary fence, deciding to start by simply breathing for a while.

It took about four breaths before he saw a pair of coat sleeves leaning on the fence beside him.

'Thought I might find you out here.' Bridget stopped and reconsidered. 'Well, I thought I might find you lurking somewhere on your lonesome, and so I looked out every window until I spotted you.'

Cooper continued to breathe for another minute or so, sifting through everything he wanted to say.

'Is Emma okay? I mean, about it being me. About you *knowing* it was me. I'm guessing from the look on her face that you hadn't told her.'

'Hardest secret I've ever had to keep.'

'*Only* secret you've ever managed to keep from your sisters, more like.'

Bridget turned to face him, waiting until he moved to look at her.

'How could she not be okay? Of all the men in the world I could have fixed her up with, she's got you. One of the loveliest, kindest, most interesting people a woman could hope to end up with. Not to mention you're also not completely ugly. I know you'll do whatever it takes to make this work, and that means everything. To her, and me.'

'I will.' Cooper nodded, in that moment absolutely sure he meant it. 'And thanks, that was actually quite nice. But don't let Paolo hear you saying it. Now I'm married to your sister I was kind of hoping he might stop looking like he's permanently deciding whether or not to punch me.'

Bridget rolled her eyes. 'Well, Paolo does have lots of other qualities that you can't claim.'

'Really? Am I going to be last in the pecking order of Donovans-in-law, then? What does Paolo have that I don't?'

'Well, me, for starters.' Bridget laughed.

Well, obviously. Once, that comment would have felt like a scalpel jammed between his ribs. Today? More of a hard poke. He was getting there. Not where he should have been, given the circumstances, but this whole thing was going to take time. Emma would understand that.

'Let me see, what else?' Bridget pretended to think about it as they walked back to the house. 'Oh, how about the ability to change a car battery? Or brew his own cider? Hmm, what else...? Paolo has a brilliant business mind, he's most certainly never been forced to resign because everyone in his company hates him. In fact, he is eminently likeable. Not moody or withdrawn or prone to disappearing on me because a fancy job turns up in Cardiff. I always know where I stand with Paolo.' She grinned, eyes dancing.

'You always know where you stand with me, Widget,' Cooper replied, his voice soft and serious. 'The only difference now is, you're officially family as well as my friend.'

Bridget stopped walking then, as they reached the farmhouse door. 'Well, as your friend, and your sister, I'm here for you with all the Donovan family inside info and advice you might need. I know it's not the best chance, statistically, despite you scoring 94 per cent in the compatibility test. But I'm hoping and praying with all I've got that you'll be happy. I don't know anyone who deserves it more than you two do.'

'Thank you. But you're involved enough in my marriage as it is, thanks. I think me and Emma are best figuring it out on our own.'

'Fair enough.' Bridget opened the door. 'I guess you're on your own, then.'

But for the first time since he was five years old, he wasn't, Cooper thought as he stepped back into the hubbub of the farmhouse. Wasn't that the whole point of marriage, after all?

Okay, so the time had come. We'd put it off long enough, with chit-chat, cups of tea and yet more wedding cake. It was now pushing nine o'clock, Orla and Sam were ready to get the kids to bed, the guys had helped Nita and Vik clean up the kitchen, Dad wouldn't be resurfacing until the morning and everyone else had had enough of my mother for one weekend.

Ben would also be joining us, having spent the day using his wily documentary skills to extract juicy information from each family member, most of them without even realising. I was slightly relieved to have the extra person, partly because it delayed the moment when Cooper and I would be alone, and partly because he had that photographer's knack of breaking awkward tension and helping people relax. Putting his good looks to one side, he was easy company, and it was becoming clear that neither the bride nor groom was that.

I ignored the questioning prickle that hinted maybe Ben would have been an easier blind-date husband. He might have been easier while riding along in the taxi to our B & B, but who knows what he would have expected once we got to the honeymoon suite? Or for the days, weeks and years we were stuck together afterwards. A noose for two, if my memory was still functioning correctly after three too many glasses of Prosecco and a shot of finest Irish whiskey to calm my nerves.

Ben filmed Cooper opening the taxi door for me, and carrying our overnight bags into the cottage where we were staying. The owner of the B & B, a friend of Mum's and therefore someone who knew my romantic history in excruciating detail, signed us in with a wink and showed us to our room. She opened the door before turning to Ben, hands on generous hips.

'I have welcomed a lot of newly-weds to Lavender Cottage, and, I must say, these are the first who've brought the videographer with them. Sir, are you planning on filming the whole night? Because we are not that sort of establishment, and I don't believe that Bear and Gabriella's eldest daughter is that sort of woman. If you would kindly turn off the camera, I will escort you to your room.'

Ben grinned from behind the lens. 'Sorry, I've been paid to do a job. You'll have to take that up with my client.'

The proprietor let out a harrumph. 'I'll rephrase, for clarity. You shall turn off the camera, and allow me to escort you to your room, or else I shall call the police, and allow them to escort you to the police station.'

'Boss?' Ben asked.

'Ben's filming a documentary, Mrs Lavender,' I said. 'He's conducting a short interview with us, and then returning to his own room.'

'Oh,' Mrs Lavender said, one hand flying up to preen her hair as her face assumed a glinty smile. 'Is it going to be on television?'

'No!' I practically shouted, the very thought curdling the whiskey in my stomach.

'You never know!' Ben replied at the same time.

'Yes, we do know. It is definitely not going to be on television.'

Cooper glared at Ben, nodded politely at Mrs Lavender and, before I had a chance to breathe a sigh of relief, scooped me up and carried me over the threshold.

I liked how he had asserted himself over Ben. I also liked the feel of his arms cradling my shoulders, and how I felt snug, pressed against his chest... but I don't think either of us knew what to do next.

'You can put me down now,' I whispered.

'Right.' Cooper glanced around, as if looking for a suitable place to deposit me. The large room had been honeymooned-up, with several vases of white roses to match my bouquet, and petals scattered across the enormous bed. There was champagne on ice, and a box of fancy vegan chocolates. Panic fluttered in my chest when I saw the tiny silk robe hanging outside the bathroom door. If it had been a proper robe size, it might have covered the sheer pane of glass taking up most of the door. The panic morphed into a deranged flapping when I realised it gave a direct view to the toilet.

I hadn't allowed any of my family to share a bathroom with me since I hit puberty. Jake hadn't seen me in such a compromising position, and we'd been together for six years. Maybe that was part of the problem. Maybe Helen Richards wasn't uptight about that sort of thing. Either way, that was irrelevant, because I didn't want a man I barely knew but needed to impress and earn the respect of watching me wee. Could I hold my bladder until morning?

'Right here is fine,' I croaked.

Cooper gently placed me on the patterned rug. We stood next to each other for a moment, trying to look calm and as if we were having a nice time.

'Lovely room,' he said, nodding his head.

'Yes, and the flowers are beautiful.'

Another lingering silence.

'I wonder what the view's like,' my husband said.

'It's probably amazing.'

Ugh. I glanced surreptitiously at Ben, telepathically begging him to ask us a question, make a joke or say anything to break this horrible tension.

'Would you like a chocolate?' Cooper asked.

'Oh, um, yes, please.' We made a great show of opening the box, studying the little piece of paper identifying the chocolates, managed to kill another drawn-out minute discussing which one we wanted.

'That's so perfect that you hate the coffee ones, and they're my favourites! And it wasn't even a question in the compatibility test, ha, ha!'

'Any caramels in there?' Ben balanced the camera in one hand, holding out the other.

'You can have one once you've finished doing whatever it is you're here to do,' Cooper replied, opening the champagne with a pop.

'Right, well, let's have the two of you sat on the bed.'

'We're fine in the chairs.' Cooper poured us both a glass, and we took our seats.

'So, how are you feeling?' Ben began.

'Tired, relieved, looking forward to some time alone with my wife.'

'Emma?'

'Um, I'm feeling... a bit surreal, to be honest. I don't think it's sunk in yet.'

'Okay, so how do you feel about Cooper being your husband? Are you sensing a connection yet?'

'Oh, well, I can't help but feel a connection, given that he's known my sister—'

'Let's edit that out,' Cooper interrupted, before turning to me, his face creased in concern. 'Sorry, I think it's best that we don't refer to the Bridget link unless we have to.'

'Right, of course. Sorry. Um, yes, there's a connection. I feel really positive about having married Cooper, and I'm looking forward to getting to know him better.'

Ben waited, until I found myself elaborating. It was probably the alcohol, the tiredness, the sheer discombobulation, but I figured I might as well start by being honest.

'I feel safe with him. And like I can trust him. Which is a very high priority for me in a relationship.'

'Do you think you'll consummate the marriage tonight?'

Cooper shot up off his chair. 'Right, that's enough for today. We'll see you at breakfast.'

'Chill out, mate, I'm just doing my job!'

Cooper waited until a shamefaced Ben had left before slumping back onto the chair, head down, both hands running through his hair. 'I'm really sorry about that.'

'No, it's fine. I can understand why he'd ask.' I ate another chocolate. 'They always talk about it on the TV show.'

'Maybe. But you signed up for a serious scientific study, not a TV show. Perhaps hiring Ben was a bad idea.'

'No, it's fine, honestly. If he asks anything I don't want to answer I'll just say, "no comment". And I like Ben – he does a good job of lightening the mood.'

Cooper took a long drink of champagne. 'To be clear... about the question... I'm not expecting anything. At all. I'm very happy to sleep on the sofa.'

I thought about that. It wasn't even really a proper sofa. More like a chaise longue. I didn't think a man Cooper's size could sit on it comfortably, let alone sleep.

'No, it's a massive bed. I'm so tired I'll not notice you're there. I mean, you have got pyjamas, haven't you?' I peeked at him, smiling to show I was retaining a sense of humour about the whole thing.

'I have indeed. Well, a pair of jogging bottoms and a T-shirt.'

'Great.'

We sat in companionable silence for a while, sipping our drinks.

'What the hell is that bathroom door, though?' Cooper said, grimacing. 'Maybe we could drape a sheet over it or something?'

Phew.

I really did think this might turn out okay.

* * *

Cooper

Cooper lay in bed counting the number of times he'd shared a bed with a woman for the whole night. It didn't take long. He might be twenty-nine, but his longest relationship had been weeks, and one-night stands had never appealed. Never mind the awkwardness of exposing himself like that to a stranger, coupled with the fact that he was far too busy putting distance between him and his past to think about luxuries like love and dating.

He checked the time. Two minutes later than last time he checked. Was five fifty-eight too early to get up and have a shower?

Glancing over at Emma, he felt another wave of mild panic that she was there, churned with relief that she was comfortable enough to sleep. Unless she was pretending. Feigning sleep to avoid more awkward small talk before breakfast. Cooper leant a little closer to her half of the giant bed to check, but then she let out a tiny snore-snort and rolled over, so he carefully edged away again, smiling.

Emma awake had struggled to relax. She'd tried to be friendly but there was a wall of awkwardness that verged on stiff at times.

He wondered if she was shy. He hoped she wasn't regretting her marriage before they'd even set off on honeymoon.

Emma asleep was... well... adorable.

Other men might feel relieved that their blind-date wife turned out to be gorgeous, even with tangled hair splayed across her face and yesterday's make-up smudged around her eyes.

Cooper felt totally out of his league.

No change there, then.

* * *

Emma

I woke up at six-thirty on the dot, as always. Cooper pretended to have scarcely woken up himself, but no one wakes up with eyes that clear.

Ugh – had he been watching me sleep? Been awake all night, wondering how it was possible to plunge into oblivion five seconds after hitting the pillow, with a stranger less than three feet away?

I wiped my face, in case there was any trace of drool. It seemed okay, but when I scurried into the bathroom, the mirror revealed that drool was the least of my worries.

Ouch.

I looked like a poster girl for the morning after the night before.

Oh, well. If Cooper had been horrified, he'd hidden it well. And if this marriage was going to work, he'd have to get used to the real, make-up-streaked, gravity-defying-haired, bloodshot-eyed, slightly stale-smelling me.

I wanted the sort of husband who loved me at my worst. Or at the very least wasn't repulsed. Although, in an ideal marriage, I would have gradually eased him into my worst over time.

Half an hour later, I emerged from the bathroom, dignity reapplied and heart rate under control. I'd even compiled a list of questions to ask over breakfast, so that we could move past the stilted getting-to-know-you talk into couple mode as soon as possible.

Cooper smiled at me in the exact same way he'd done when I first woke up.

I liked that.

So far, I liked Cooper.

* * *

The rest of the day went... well... better than I'd feared. After breakfast in the B & B dining room, where I broke my golden liquid-only-breakfast rule as Ben hovered surreptitiously in the background, Cooper drove Ben's car up to the farmhouse in the Peak District that he'd hired for the next three days (again, Ben in the back seat, camera on: 'Pretend I'm not here!') We went on what should have been a three-hour hike, but turned into nearly twice that long due to mostly consisting of trying not to slip over in the drizzle, interspersed with half-conversations that never went on long enough to get anywhere. It was memorable, though, trudging through the terrible weather. And making some memories felt almost as important as getting to know each other. Wasn't that what a marriage was – thousands of shared experiences, all adding up to a life together?

Once warm, dry and clean again, we wandered down a country lane to the enticing lights of an old pub, where we found perfect, cosy seats in front of a crackling fire. While Cooper went to fetch us drinks from the crowded bar, I insisted Ben put down his camera and join us.

'Come on, you've got more than enough footage for one day.'

'It's the crucial first date. There's a lot to capture.'

I stepped right up to him, close enough to press my hand over the camera lens, and pulled my fiercest face. 'You've trailed behind us up and down miles of massive hills in the rain. I think not giving you a dinner break would be in breach of employment law.'

'I'm not about to double gooseberry. Me and my zoom lens are sitting right over there.'

'Double gooseberry?'

'The guy who years later becomes a dinner-party story about how he gate-crashed your first date and honeymoon in one. I'm already wandering dangerously close to my moral boundaries, just by taking this job.'

'Okay, how about I swear never to twist this into anything other than me badgering you into eating with us?' I took my hand off the lens, but leant closer so I could keep my voice down. Not that Cooper could hear me while trapped in the bar crush. 'I've spent a whole day with a stranger who I'm now linked to for life. Spending this much time with someone I don't know is probably a record for me, and would be intense enough whoever it was. But this is Cooper. You've probably gathered that I'm about as easy-breezy as he is. Please sit with us and make light-hearted conversation peppered with stupid jokes and amusing anecdotes and whatever other magic photographer tricks you've mastered which can make even oddly intense people like me feel relaxed and comfortable.'

'I make you feel relaxed and comfortable?' Ben lowered the camera and raised one eyebrow.

Woah. I pulled my eyes away from Ben's enquiring gaze and fixed them firmly on my 94-per-cent-compatible partner-for-life.

Thirty-seven first dates had proved that a zip of chemistry was next to nowhere on my list of priorities. A man who had chosen to commit himself to me? A good, kind, very nice-looking man?

'Yeah, on second thoughts, that table in the corner looks perfect for you.'

'The one covered in dirty plates?' Ben grinned.

'Yes. That one.'

'Well, I'll take a seat, then. Enjoy your dinner.'

'I will!'

I turned away, brusquely. Ben was a *rogue*. And I was done with rogues. Along with charmers and smooth-talkers and anyone who thought marriage was a noose for two.

Right.

Here was Cooper with my craft gin and organic tonic. Perfect timing. I gave him a peck on the cheek, and sat down, turning my seat firmly away from the poky corner table covered in dirty plates.

'Okay?' my gorgeous husband asked, eyes full of nervous hope.

'Yes.' I smiled back, reaching out and brazenly squeezing his hand for a brief second. 'I'm very okay.'

I remained that way for most of the evening. The more Cooper and I talked, the more I was able to ignore Ben's camera prickling the centre of my back.

And we really talked, this time. The kind of conversations I had always dreamt of having on a first date, without any of the fear of seeming too keen or too much of an organisational control-freak who had succeeded in planning out her whole life while simultaneously failing to achieve most of it.

We covered our romantic history (in the few short minutes before ordering food), our work, my time in Ireland and Cooper's sad, lonely existence in Cardiff. He listened with furrowed brow as I told him about Dad, trying to describe the anguish of seeing my larger-than-life father withering away before our eyes. The stress of dealing with a bureaucracy that seemed stacked against the most vulnerable in society at every turn.

And when I'd finished wiping my eyes, and ordered another drink plus mango sorbet for dessert and decided that it was probably time to change the subject to something not quite so heartbreakingly depressing, given the occasion, and given how I was trying to make a good impression, Cooper then started talking about his own family.

Now *that* was heartbreakingly depressing.

My dad was ill, and had been forced to give up running the business he loved about two decades earlier than planned. He wasn't able to romance his wife, dance with his daughters or kick a football with his grandchildren.

But he was there.

And his love for us continued to be the life and soul of the Donovan family, as it had been for thirty-five years. Cooper's dad? He was about as opposite as it was possible to get. Bridget had told me he was a lousy cockroach undeserving of the filthiest crack to creep about in. But hearing first-hand how he had treated Cooper, after Cooper's mother died when he was four and he reluctantly agreed to take in the son he'd barely met. How he had left his son, ripped away from everything he'd ever known and dumped in hell, to scavenge for scraps from bins, wear newspaper under his jumper because he didn't have a coat and he was so skinny that even in the summer months he froze. How he had kicked Cooper out of the way after his tiny, skeletal body had collapsed with hunger and a raging fever on the living-room floor. And how he had laughed about it. Well. That left me wondering if Bridget's comparison was an insult to cockroaches.

After six months of his shocking neglect and drug-fuelled abuse, Cooper's teacher had finally woken up to the fact that his haunting silence and shrunken cheeks weren't simply due to the grief of losing his mother, but the horror of gaining a father. He'd been rehomed with his dad's sister, daring to allow himself a twinge of hope when he saw the clean bed linen, and the full kitchen cupboards. But while Aunt Louisa could provide him with his basic physical needs (all those except warmth or affection), she resented every moment spent in her nephew's company. As though it were his fault his mother died and his dad was an evil monster.

It was those first four years that saved him, he concluded when reading up on childhood trauma as a teenager, desperate to find some answers about whether he was ever going to become a normal person. Those vital, early years had been jam-packed with a mother's love strong enough to last through all the very deep crap he'd had to battle through since.

So, yes, I ended up blubbering again on my first-date-honeymoon.

'Was your dad's name Patrick?' I asked, dessert long since cleared away and replaced by decaffeinated coffees.

Cooper looked at me in surprise. 'Yes. Though most people called him Paddy.' He paused, pulling a wry grimace. 'Or arsehole. He probably got called that most. That and Total Prick.'

'What did you call him?'

Cooper fiddled with his mug, his gaze twenty-five years away. 'Him. It. The Man. If I avoided giving him a name, it made him less real, somehow. And I wasn't ever going to call him "Dad".'

'Thank you for sharing that. I'm guessing you've not told many other people.'

We got up, shrugging into our coats.

Cooper looked at me as we walked to the door. 'Just one.'

I thought as much.

Maybe it was a bad sign that I didn't feel more jealous of my husband's friendship with my little sister. Maybe I was a fool not to.

We were halfway back to the cottage when I stumbled on a wonky paving slab, and Cooper grabbed my hand, gently helping me upright so that we were standing face to face in the darkness.

He took hold of my other hand, tugging me two steps into the shelter of a nearby wall.

'Okay?' His voice was warm and as soft as the night air.

'I'm very okay,' I whispered back, tilting my head up in answer to his unspoken question.

'Good.' Cooper bent his face to meet mine, as cautiously and carefully as he probably approached a brain sample to examine, his eyes not breaking my gaze until our lips met, when he closed them. The kiss was tender, and sweet. Still slightly hesitant, but carrying more than enough promise of deeper, wilder kisses to follow. He pulled his mouth away, letting out a faint sigh as we rested our foreheads against each other.

I smiled. 'Sigh of disappointment?'

I felt rather than saw him smile. 'No.'

'Phew.'

Phew!

And then my phone rang.

'Who is this?' Emma retook Cooper's hand, gripping it tightly as her face froze. 'Grandad won't get up? Your *DAD*? Where's your mum? Have you tried ringing her...? Well done, you did the right thing. The paramedics will know what to do. Okay, I'm going to hang up in a moment, and call Sofia and Annie and Bridget. I'm quite far away, with Cooper, remember? But Annie is at Nonna and Grandad's house, she'll be there in five minutes, ten at the most. Okay, that's brilliant. You're doing great. I love you, Harry. Bye... Bye.'

Emma turned to Cooper, eyes wide with shock and horror. 'Sam's fallen down the stairs and won't wake up. Harry couldn't sleep and heard him. It sounds like he's hit his head.' She broke off in a sob, before visibly pulling herself together. 'Harry's called 999, an ambulance is on its way, but Orla's out and she left her phone at home.'

'Where is she?'

'At eleven on a Sunday night? Who knows the hell where she is? Probably pumping weights with Jim.' Emma was trying to scroll through her numbers, but her hand shook too hard and she was still gripping his with her other one. '*Shit, Orla.* What the hell are you playing at?'

Cooper took the phone from her, making sure Sofia's phone was ringing before handing it back.

'Sofia,' Emma gasped. 'Sam's fallen down the stairs and is unconscious. Harry's called an ambulance.' She filled her in, then silently waited while Cooper called Annie, and once again handed the phone back.

'Annie? Are you at home? Oh, thank God…'

Once Sofia was on her way to Sam, with Annie and Bridget close behind, Emma finally let go of his hand.

'I'll drive.' Ben had at some point in the scramble of the past few minutes come to stand beside them. 'I've only had one beer.'

'You don't have to do that,' Emma said. 'I can get a taxi. Or we could wait until morning. My sisters are on their way. I'm sure Orla will be home soon. There's no need to ruin everyone's holiday. I'm sure it'll turn out to be nothing. Just a nasty scare for Harry. Sam'll be fine…'

'Come on.' Cooper put one arm around her, steering her back up the lane. 'I'll pack while you change into something more comfortable. We'll be home within a couple of hours.'

* * *

Emma

Ben dropped me off at Orla's around one. Cooper had sat in the back and held my hand the whole time. I told him not to bother coming in. Sam had been taken to A & E at the hospital in Mansfield, and Bridget and Sofia were there waiting for any updates. Annie was with Harry, and Lottie and Oscar were fast asleep.

'Call me if you need anything.' Cooper had unloaded my bag

and carried it into Orla's house for me, in case I wanted a change of clothes or my toothbrush. 'Anything at all. Or just to talk.' He pressed a kiss to the top of my head, and I ached with the unfamiliar comfort of knowing someone had made me their priority.

'Thanks. I'll keep you updated.'

'Please do. Even if it's still the middle of the night.'

It was after two when Orla stumbled through the front door. Annie was dozing on the sofa with Harry's head on one shoulder, so I jumped up to intercept.

'Orla!' I whispered as she tried to yank off her ankle boot.

'What the hell?' She spun around, hand pressed to her chest. 'Bloody hell, Emma, you scared the life out of me. What are you doing here?'

Then she saw the look on my face.

'What's happened?' She froze, one boot still on.

'If you had your phone with you, I'd have been able to tell you.'

Her eyes darted away, the guilt rippling across her face. 'I forgot it. Sam and I had a row and I left in a hurry. You know what he's like at the moment.'

'At the moment he's in King's Mill A & E.'

She whipped her head back to look at me, as her features crumpled. 'What?' She began trying to shove her boot back on, instead succeeding in toppling into the coat rack.

'Come on, let's sit in the kitchen and I'll tell you what's happened.'

'Screw the kitchen! I need to get to the hospital! I need to be with Sam. Oh, no. No, no, no, no, no. Is he okay? He's not okay. I knew something was wrong. I knew he wasn't himself. Dammit. I need to get there. DAMMIT! WILL SOMEBODY DRIVE ME TO THE HOSPITAL, PLEASE?'

'Orla. ORLA!' I gripped both her hands, pulling them against my chest so she had to pay attention to my face, right in front of hers. 'Harry's in the living room. Keep your voice down. He's upset enough without hearing his mum freaking out.'

'Did he see it? Did he see Sam? What happened?' Orla managed to pull herself together enough to stop shouting and sit down on the kitchen bench. I told her what had happened, including about the empty bottle of vodka and blood all over the hall floor, pulling her up against my shoulder so Harry wouldn't hear her wail.

'I was with Jim. I was with Jim, dancing and laughing and letting him put his hands around my waist, and my Sam was lying on the hall floor. Oh, Sam. Can we go now? Will you drive me? Will you take me to Sam?'

Knowing that my earlier two drinks would be well clear of my system by now, I drove Orla's car the fifteen minutes to the hospital. I dropped her off with Sofia and Bridget, who hustled her towards the A & E bay where Sam lay, still unconscious.

Annie would need at least one extra pair of hands in the morning, so I left my sisters to it and sped back to Hatherstone, praying the whole way.

* * *

The verdict was concussion, three snapped knee ligaments, a broken collarbone, and enough alcohol churning in Sam's veins to have potentially caused lasting damage.

If Harry hadn't still been awake worrying about his parents' argument, and heard the fall, it could have been far worse.

As it was, the doctors were hopeful Sam would recover physically. They pieced his knee back together with metal screws, the incision running from mid-shin up to his thigh. A sling, painkillers and weeks of rest would sort his collarbone. The concussion would take as much rest as it took. And as for his mental state, well, that remained to be seen. Sam hadn't told Orla that he'd been taking antidepressants. Or that he'd been put into probation at school due to underperforming for the first time in eight years of teaching, and was starting to crumble under the stress and the secrets.

We didn't ask our sister what had happened that evening before she left to go dancing and flirting with another man. It wasn't our business what words had passed between them, or what had led Sam to go drinking himself half to death.

Annie postponed her flight home to look after the kids, with the rest of us chipping in around our own work schedules at crunch times like breakfast and early evening and dinner time and bedtime and, well, any time they weren't in school. Three stressed, scared and energetic kids were harder work than I'd have thought. For someone who prided herself on being organised and efficient, I was doing a pathetic job of helping Annie keep on top of everything. How could every item of school uniform get so filthy every single day? Then for each child, on a different day they needed PE kits, which might be the standard school kit or might happen to be the football strip, or swimming costume. Let alone prepping three totally different lunches, and not running out of after-school snacks or bedtime drinks or breaktime snacks, of which the primary school only allowed a specific list, none of which were found in the late-night-opening supermarket. Forms filled in, spellings learnt, reading done, homework completed, piano practised, hamster fed, rooms kept below nuclear-disaster levels of chaos...

My respect for Orla expanded exponentially. I could see how a job coupled with some positive attention and a new, vibrant social life had seemed appealing compared to a distant, uninterested husband on top of answering ten thousand impossible questions per day, along with dealing with one child who refused to eat anything green, brown or yellow and another who had taken it upon himself to become the local single-use-plastic police.

Cooper was brilliant. He drove over after work each day with

Bridget, played Xbox with Harry, listened to Lottie's recorder practice, read Shirley Hughes stories to Oscar until they both knew them off by heart. He made hot drinks, poured the odd glass of something stronger and even brought me snacks.

And at the end of each day, he wrapped his arms around me and rested his head against mine for a long, slow minute before kissing me goodnight, not a murmur of complaint that I was dumping my new husband to take care of my shattered sister and her kids. He never once suggested that I had a night off and let the others manage without me. Cooper understood that we Donovans were there for each other, and that, as the only two who were self-employed, Annie and I were there when the others couldn't be. Bridget, being the one most likely to understand the medical gobbledegook, spent most evenings at the hospital with Orla. Sam's mum also drove down from Newcastle for a couple of days, before returning to care for his grandmother. Sofia did what she could, but with Eli still staying with them, and a dozen other crises kicking off every time she checked her phone, her capacity was limited.

But was I also making excuses for my sisters because it was kind of an awkward time to be moving in with a man I still barely knew?

Did they figure this out for themselves, and tactfully refrain from insisting that they take their share of night duty, giving me a perfect reason to postpone the scariness of moving into my new home?

That would be a yes.

I did love those sisters of mine.

* * *

After a week in hospital, the decision had to be made about what would happen next. As predicted, Sam's body would make a full physical recovery. Unfortunately, his concussed brain controlled his body, and that was going to take much longer. He would be on crutches for months as his leg healed, but add to this shaky coordination, and frequent bouts of feeling dazed and confused interspersed with violent headaches and nausea, and things were extra-complicated.

'I strongly advise that Sam spend some time in Meadow House,' Dr Farouk explained to a haggard, wretched Orla. 'It is an excellent facility. They take a lot of younger patients, who generally do very well, and they'll be able to support his physical rehabilitation as well as carefully monitoring his brain function.'

'How long would he be there for?' Annie asked, given that Orla seemed to be ignoring him.

Dr Farouk frowned. 'It's very difficult to say at this point. Anything from two weeks to a few months. It's only once we can assess the rate and extent of recovery that these kinds of decisions can be made. But the aim will be to get him home as soon as possible.'

'Where is it?' I asked.

'On the outskirts of Birmingham.' The doctor frowned in sympathy. 'I'm sorry there were no places available any nearer. This was the best we could do.'

Bridget glanced at me. 'That'll be, what, over an hour's drive?'

'Far longer in rush hour. But don't worry.' I reached across Annie to touch Orla's knee. 'We'll help with the kids and everything.'

'No.' Orla shook her head, weakly at first, and then increasingly determined. 'No.'

'We will!' Bridget said, her distress clear. 'I have holiday I can use, and Sofia's working to offload some of her other commitments—'

'No, he's not going.' Orla glanced in the direction of the ward, where she'd left Sam sleeping. 'He's coming home.'

'Orla, have you thought about this?' I asked. 'If Dr Farouk thinks Sam needs specialist care—'

'It's not his decision!' she barked at me. 'Right now, Sam needs to be with me so we can work through this together. It's called in sickness and in health.'

'But what about your job?' Bridget said, tentatively.

'I quit my job at eight a.m. last Monday morning! Right after deleting Jim's number from my phone.' Orla's eyes darted between her three sisters, and it looked as though something had broken in their watery depths. 'My husband nearly died, while I was out farting about pretending I was young, and carefree, and that it mattered if a fit bloke thought I was special. My child found his dad sprawled on the floor, his head stuck there with his own blood. His aunties had to step in because his mother was out getting off her face on two-for-one cocktails and compliments. I'd never have got over losing Sam. But given that he's still here, I've got the rest of our precious lives to make it up to both of them. And that starts by taking Sam home, to be with his kids and feeble excuse for a wife.'

'With all due respect, Mrs Peterson, your husband had consumed an extremely worrying amount of alcohol. We need to establish whether—'

Orla stood up. 'With all due respect, Doctor, my very depressed husband was having a very bad day, and, being a vocally repressed personality type who thinks that real men don't talk about their feelings, he dealt with feeling that his life was drowning at the bottom of a cesspit by getting off his head on vodka. Once.' She bent closer, looking him right in the eye. To his credit, Dr Farouk did not shrink back. 'He needed me, and I wasn't there for him. That's not going to be happening any more. If you can look me in the eye and tell me you never drowned your sorrows with a few drinks and ended up taking it too far, then I'll gladly wave him off to this rehab place myself.'

'Mrs Peterson, a place at an establishment like Meadow House doesn't come up every day. Brain injuries are very complicated matters. Add to that his physical injuries and I'm sure that you would agree that we need to put your husband's needs first, rather than prioritising assuaging your guilt for not being there.'

'She *is* putting him first!' Annie said, taking hold of Orla's hand. Partly to offer her solidarity, partly to stop Orla committing physical abuse towards a member of hospital staff, which the signs assured us would not be tolerated under any circumstances. 'Surely he'll recover better if he's at home, surrounded by his family. Who love him.'

'We can arrange for him to receive treatment as an outpatient; however, it is essential that you are aware that his state of mind is extremely fragile. And if there has been an underlying issue with alcohol dependency, then you need to be prepared to deal with potential mood swings, difficult behaviour, poor choices regarding his self-care—'

'What, and he didn't have to deal with all that from me through three nightmare pregnancies?' Orla was practically yelling now.

'Mrs Peterson, I appreciate that you want to do whatever you can for your husband, but we must stick to reality. Your husband has experienced a period of extreme mental distress.'

'Well, that makes two of us, then. And sticking to reality is exactly what I'm doing. The reality is, I vowed for better or worse. He's coming home with me.'

'Well,' said the either very brave or slightly stupid doctor, 'I will bear your input in mind, but perhaps we allow Mr Peterson to make the final decision.'

* * *

That evening the Donovan sisters gathered in a pub a short walk from the hospital for an impromptu Non-Wednesday Wine. Sofia had joined us, leaving Moses and Paolo babysitting the kids. Mum had offered to watch them, but she was exhausted enough from having to do without our help for a week, and we didn't want Dad left alone for the evening with all this going on.

'Fill me in on the meeting,' Sofia said, squashed up on a padded bench beside Annie and Bridget.

'Orla ignored the doctor's advice and said she's taking Sam home instead of letting him go to a rehab place,' Bridget replied, her sisterly solidarity somewhat lessened now we were alone.

'I'm *not* not letting him go!' snapped Orla, who like Sofia had chosen Coke instead of wine. 'But him being off in some facility in Birmingham isn't going to help. Sam got drunk and fell because we had a fight about me going out and I dangled in his face who I was going out with. He was depressed and stressed and I didn't know, so I made it tons worse. The reason for the fight is over; he's taking a break from work. I've searched the house and there's no evidence of any hidden alcohol stash. It was us not facing things together that caused this. I'm not going to let that happen again.'

We filled Sofia in on the rest of the meeting, including Annie's startling admission about sticking around, which it turned out even her twin had known nothing about.

'Is everyone just resigning from their jobs?' Sofia asked, somewhat exasperated. 'How's that going to work out long-term?'

'I'm self-employed,' Annie huffed back. 'It'll take no time at all to build up the business again once I'm back. Besides, my husband is loaded, remember? The bills'll still get paid.'

'And what does Greg think about you ditching everything and turning a week-long visit into an indefinite one?'

Annie shifted on the bench, her elbow knocking into Bridget. 'He knows how important my family are to me.'

'You haven't told him.' I gaped.

Annie grew very engrossed in faffing with her fringe for a moment. 'He's currently working on a thing at the Singapore office. I'll tell him once he's back, and we know a bit more about what's happening.'

'How long is the thing?' Bridget asked, frowning as a message pinged through to her phone. 'I have to go,' she said, tapping off a quick reply. 'A lab emergency.'

'Ooh, is it a radioactive leak?' Sofia wondered. 'Or a massive explosion?'

'More likely the rats have escaped,' Annie said.

'Prof's forgotten to tell anyone that the funding donors are visiting first thing tomorrow. There's no way they can see the labs in their current state. The mess is one thing, but the ceiling tiles hanging off and the defaced health and safety posters don't quite say "successful neuroscientific research laboratory".'

'So, Emma.' Annie turned pointedly to me as soon as Bridget had left. 'How's married life? Spent one night with Cooper and then decided to move into Orla's? That must have been a night to remember.'

'That's not fair,' Sofia warned.

'Well, that appears to be no longer a problem, seeing as you've offered to move in. I'll let Cooper know I'll be home later tonight.' I took a defiant swig of wine.

Only, in the end I completely forgot about messaging Cooper, as to all of our astonishment, our mother suddenly barrelled through the pub door.

'What is this?' she asked, assessing the evidence. 'A family gathering without me?'

'No, Mother, that would never happen,' Annie muttered under her breath.

'We were all here for the meeting with the doctor, and thought

Orla could use a breather,' Sofia added, ever the peacemaker.

'Hmm.' Mum eyed the glasses of wine, as if mentally filing away which of her wild daughters were chocking back booze on a weeknight within a stone's throw of a hospital. 'Well. I heard about your crazy plan, Orla, and I decided it was time we have a talk.'

'Mamma, I'm really not in the mood.' Orla folded her arms and leant back on the bench. 'Let's talk another time.'

'What, like once Sam is home, and the rehab place given to someone else, who doesn't have a wife and three children to support?'

Orla shrugged.

'Orla Peterson, you are not going to make this decision without hearing first-hand what it is like to take care of a proud, stubborn man when some days he hates that he can't take care of himself so much, he acts like he hates you. Everything your man thinks makes him a proper man has vanished. You want to hear how you can show him what being a man really is, even when he can't wash his own backside? Or you want to stick your nose in the air at your silly old fool of a mother who has been married all these years, who knows better than all you girls put together what better or worse, sickness and health really means? Don't be ridiculous, child. Get up, we're going for a walk.'

Orla got up, and went.

The rest of us spent the hour and a half while we waited for them to come back discussing our relief at her removal of all things gym/Jim related from her life, our concern about how the challenges ahead would impact our niece and nephews, and how, in an odd way, something so terrible might have saved Sam and Orla's marriage.

Then Sofia tossed us a complete humdinger.

'Sam had been reading her messages.'

'Jim messages?' Annie sat back, mouth open, before deciding to pour herself another glass of wine. 'Well, that maybe explains some of his behaviour lately.'

Sofia nodded, wincing. 'He told Moses at the wedding.'

'How bad were they? I mean, don't give us details or anything.' I was horrified.

'Moses didn't give *me* details. Sam deduced they hadn't crossed over into anything physical yet, but they were definitely heading that way. He was contemplating paying Jim a visit.'

'Jim would have beaten him to a pulp,' Annie said.

'Not if Sam ran him over first.'

'Well, thank goodness Moses talked him out of it!' I shuddered to think what might have happened otherwise.

'Oh, he didn't,' Sofia replied. 'Moses offered to go with him. Only then, well, the accident.'

'Orla doesn't know,' Annie said. 'She feels terrible enough already. It would devastate her.'

'Should we tell her?' I asked my younger, more-experienced-in-marriage-matters sisters.

'Maybe we should wait and see if Sam says anything.' Sofia shook her head, eyeing us gravely. 'It's not really our place. I think they have more than enough to deal with right now, without this knowledge of an almost-affair on top of it.'

'Yes, but both of them already have knowledge of the almost-affair, they just don't know the other one has it,' I said. 'Are secrets ever a good thing in a relationship? Don't they inevitably create a wall between you? If Sam won't let her know, should we step in? Let them start again with a clean slate?'

'It's not our secret to share,' Annie pronounced, finishing off her wine with a grimace and starting to gather her things together.

Maybe not. That had never been a reason to stop us sharing, all the same.

Once upon a time it hadn't anyway.

18

Moses and Sofia gave me a lift to Ben and Cooper's – now my – home. It was nearly eleven by the time I'd swapped the bedding on Orla's futon ready for Annie, gathered my stuff together and made the journey into the city. The decision had been made that I'd move in with Cooper as I considered it too weird for all of us to be living with Bridget, especially given that she knew both Cooper and I better than we did each other. Ben wouldn't be around much as he travelled a lot for his work, which was a plus, and when he was home he'd be on hand to do more filming for the research project. Which was a big fat minus.

Once Bridget was married in June, we'd look at moving into my apartment in Sherwood. Or, with two incomes, maybe even consider buying a house together. Providing the very thought of such a long-term commitment had stopped causing me stomach cramps by then.

I let myself into the flat, using my shiny new key. I'd messaged Cooper to let him know I'd be coming home, but had no response. Of course, I didn't know what time he usually went to bed – perhaps he'd already been asleep? The lights were off in the kitchen and living room, and I had no idea which was my bedroom. Dumping my bags in the hallway, I sent Cooper another quick message.

Three minutes later I still had no response, so I tried calling. No answer. What if he was a really heavy sleeper? Should I try a door anyway? There was a fifty-fifty chance it would be Cooper's bedroom, rather than Ben's. I could try to get comfortable on the sofa. But then I'd feel awkward in the morning about being too embarrassed to find my own bedroom. Which would mean a night of fretful sleep as I counted down until the inevitable humiliation.

Come on. Start acting your age and knock on a door. What's the worst that can happen?

I gently tapped on the nearest door. The worst happened, when, instead of anyone responding to my tap, the door swung wide open. Straight ahead of me, duvet crumpled to one side, lay a naked man, face pressed into the pillow, back and legs and everything else swathed in shadow from the light of the hallway behind me.

Was it my husband?

I might be the only wife in the world who couldn't recognise her own husband's body.

I didn't think that staring at it any longer would help me work it out. Although, it had to be said, it was very nice to stare at. I'd married a beautiful-looking man.

Phew.

Right, Emma, stop ogling and do something. You've got two options.

Either I ran back to the sofa and pretended this never happened, or risked this being Cooper, and slipped into the other side of the bed.

Either way I wouldn't be getting any sleep that night.

Of course, I ran away.

Except that in order to ensure he didn't know I'd seen him naked, I had to step into the room to pull the door closed again.

And, perhaps inevitably, that was the moment he decided to wake up.

Wake up, spring out of bed like a ninja, grab a cricket bat from the floor by his bed and thrust it at me.

'It's me!' I squeaked, flapping my arm in a cross between a deranged hello and an attempt to stop him charging me.

'Eh?' the man mumbled, peering at me through the semi-darkness of his bedroom. 'Emma?'

He took a step closer, bringing his face and all other body parts into the light, some of which he swiftly covered with the bat, thank goodness.

Oh, great.

I threw both hands over my face and spun around, but not too late to see the enormous grin break out on Ben's face.

'Can I help you at all?'

'I was looking for Cooper. He didn't answer his phone.'

'He's doing an all-nighter in the lab. Prof called with some emergency.'

'Oh. He never told me.' *That he was working all night with Bridget.*

More to the point, Bridget never mentioned that she'd be with Cooper. For maybe the first time since getting married, I felt a flash of jealousy about my sister's friendship. I hadn't thought it would matter. If anything, it would be a positive. But having my sister like my husband was one thing. Her spending all day and all night with him and me not knowing about it, that was different.

'Well, I guess you never told him you were moving in tonight,' Ben said.

'Fair enough.'

'Maybe you both need to learn to be accountable to someone else.'

'If it helps avoid moments like this one, then definitely.'

'You can turn around now.'

'I'm not sure I want to.'

'Don't worry, it's all good.'

'And by that you mean you're fully dressed?'

'A vision of respectability.' Giving up waiting for me to brave dropping my hands from my eyes and turning round, Ben nudged past me and walked towards the kitchen. 'I don't know about you, but after a shock like that I need a drink.'

'*You* were shocked!' I followed him in.

'You looked like something out of a horror film, standing there, your face all in shadow. I was ready to call your sister to perform an exorcism.'

'Thanks a lot!' I shook my head as Ben held up a whisky bottle. 'I'm baking four hundred chocca mocha caramel muffins tomorrow, followed by the joy of Lottie's recorder recital. I don't need any other reason for a sore head. But I will have a chamomile tea.' I found my handbag on the floor and pulled out a teabag.

'You carry tea in your handbag?' Ben flicked the kettle on.

'I didn't think you two were chamomile-tea-in-the-cupboards kind of guys.'

'Fair enough.'

* * *

We settled on the sofas, me with tea, Ben with a beer. I tried to stuff the image of him a few minutes ago to the back of my brain. I should have felt mortified. I was the kind of woman who felt uncomfortable even talking about body parts, let alone seeing them. But Ben made it impossible to feel self-conscious. He cracked a couple of jokes about getting me to sign a flat-share agreement that included not barging into each other's bedrooms in the middle of the night along with, 'You know, the basic stuff like flushing the toilet after a number two and not borrowing each other's toothbrush. I mean, I thought they were the basics, but I guess it's safer to be explicit.'

He paused.

'And by explicit, I mean clear and unambiguous. Not... naked.'

'Does the agreement include not bringing up embarrassing incidents ever again, especially in front of other people such as flatmate's sisters or parents?'

Ben paused again, face solemn, dark eyes dancing. 'It does now.'

'Can I please say sorry one more time?' I asked.

'I think the flat-share agreement says that you can't, as that would require bringing up the incident.'

'Okay, so can I say sorry about this whole thing, then? Cooper's only been living with you for a few months, and now he's moved his new wife in. It will only be for a few weeks, and I promise I'll be a perfect flatmate. I'm really tidy, and love cleaning. I'm often out working at the weekends, and I make the best cakes, doughnuts, bread, pizza... anything really.'

'What makes you think I mind you being here?'

I sat back, surprised. 'Well. Living with a newly-wed couple is not what most people would choose.'

He shrugged. 'I've lived with a lot worse. A couple who've been married for years and descended into bitterness and loathing, for example. A couple where both parties used to sneak lovers into the house and expect me to cover for them. And, ah, yes, the couple who alternated between screaming abuse at each other and gag-inducing PDAs on the kitchen table. They were possibly the worst.'

'That's horrible. I hope you booted them all out for wanton violations of the flatmates' agreement.'

'Given that it was my parents plus assorted step-parents – five, if we're counting – and their houses not mine, I hunkered down until I was old enough to boot myself out.'

'Is that why you hate marriage?'

Ben took a slow swig of beer. 'I don't hate marriage. In principle.'

'At Alia and Mervyn's wedding you called it a noose for two!'

Ben burst out laughing. 'Did I really say that?' He shook his head. 'In my defence, I had spent the day with a nightmare bride, been slobbered on and gnawed at by her monstrous bridesmaids and then scrabbled around in a skip. I wasn't in the best of moods.'

'So, what *do* you think about it?'

He took another drink while he thought about it. 'I think the very rare occasions it ends up working well in comparison to the hassle and the devastation when it doesn't make it a completely illogical option.'

'Since when did logic come into it? Marriage is based on love, not logic.'

'Yours isn't.'

I nearly choked on my tea. For a moment there, I'd forgotten I was no longer single.

Ben stood up, draining the last of his beer. 'Which is why I'm giving you and Cooper better odds than most. His bedroom's at the end of the corridor. The door to the left is the bathroom. If you need clean sheets then, well, next time tell your husband you're coming.' And with a wink, he left me to it.

* * *

Cooper

Thank goodness he'd changed the sheets that weekend.

Not getting home until six in the morning had been brutal. Seeing Emma curled up in his duvet like a dormouse made resisting the urge to climb into bed next to her only harder. Instead he backed out of the bedroom and went to turn on the coffee maker. The donors would be arriving at ten, and he had to get some sort of presentation set up that Prof would consider sufficiently impressive.

Coffee brewed, porridge steaming hot, he poked his head back into his bedroom door.

'Hey.'

'Hey.' Emma was sitting up in bed, scrolling through her phone, her blonde hair sticking out in several different directions.

'Welcome to my humble abode.'

She looked up, squinting. 'You look exhausted. Did you just get home?'

He nodded. 'I've got about thirty minutes before I have to head back. Sorry I missed your messages.'

'No worries. I was with Bridget when she got summoned. Should have realised you'd be there too.'

'Yeah, I probably should have said. But, you know, we were working flat out trying to get the lab in a fit state.'

He didn't add, and hoped she didn't need to hear, the unspoken subtext: *working, no time to notice Bridget, to feel happy to be spending an extra ten hours with her, or think how a few months ago spending the night with Bridget would have been a dream come true. Although, of course, even if there was time, I wouldn't have, because now all my spare happy thoughts are about you...*

'Did you manage it?'

She didn't seem mad. But then, she had no reason to. She knew Bridget and Cooper were workmates, friends.

'I think we've pulled it off. Cole might feel differently when he finally rocks in. Anyway, coffee's ready when you are.' He left her to get up, still nervous about where the privacy boundaries lay. They hadn't kissed properly since Derbyshire. Hadn't talked properly, really. It was beyond selfish and heartless to even consider it, but from an objective point of view Sam's accident couldn't have been worse timing. He was prepared to be patient while Emma did what she needed to do for her family – after all, they were his family now.

But it wasn't easy, living in relationship limbo.

Especially working with Bridget every day.

Right now, Bridget was still the person he automatically thought of when he saw an advert for a new tapas bar, or heard a crazy story he wanted to share, or simply wanted someone to sit and veg on the sofa with after a long day. If he could spend more time with Emma, so they could get to know each other properly and create some more memories, then he was sure she'd become his go-to person.

He could at least start by having breakfast with his wife.

Emma came out of the bedroom in her running gear, and sat at the kitchen table with her coffee while he ate.

'So, was breakfast in the B & B a one-off?'

'At work I'm constantly sampling whatever I'm making. That's more than enough.'

He nodded at her outfit. 'How often do you run to work?'

'Maybe four days a week. I usually keep the van at the Cakery.'

'I run with Ben most weekends. But we could run together. If you wanted.'

She eyed him over the rim of her coffee mug. 'I'm not sure I could keep up.'

He eyed her back, porridge spoon halfway to his mouth. 'I think I might end up eating your dust.'

Emma smiled, dropping her eyes, and Cooper breathed a sigh of relief. He liked Emma. It wasn't hard to find her attractive. They just needed more chances to create moments like this.

'What time will you be home this evening?'

Emma pulled out her phone to check her calendar. 'I'm not needed at Orla's tonight, but I've got tons of catching up to do. Ideally, I should be copying you and pulling an all-nighter.' She looked up then, and the realisation dropped that the question was more than idle chit-chat. 'What time will you be home?'

'Six.'

'Then I'll be here at six.'

'Or...' Cooper put his spoon down, '... I could come to the Cakery. See the magic happen.'

Emma smiled. 'That would work. Are you any good at washing-up?'

'I am excellent at weighing and measuring accurate quantities. Usually to the nearest microgram. Don't they say baking is a science?'

'Okay, but what about washing-up?'

Cooper smiled back. This was still unbelievable. Sitting across the breakfast table from a woman like this. 'Whatever you need.'

'I'll message you the address.'

'Great. I'll bring dinner.'

Emma's eyebrows jumped in surprise. 'It's a date.'

19

EMMA

This was one of those evenings straight out of a romcom. I'd been working flat out all day making base layers for some of the wedding orders that were stacking up, followed by one hundred heart-shaped cookies that Nita needed to ice by Thursday. Covered in smears of cake batter, my hair full-on straggles, I had burnt my thumb and was rinsing it under the cold tap when Cooper came through the kitchen door carrying a large brown paper bag that smelt so delicious I could have kissed him.

Only he kissed me first. A peck, but it was on the lips, and it felt only a little weird.

'What have you done?' He took hold of my hand, gently inspecting it.

'Just caught it on the oven. Occupational hazard. Especially when I'm about two weeks behind at the start of wedding season.' I showed him some of the faint scars on my hands and wrists before drying my hand on a clean cloth.

'Good day apart from the burn?'

'I got loads done. So, yes, a good day.' I leant back against the counter. 'How about you?'

'I got nothing much done apart from repeating the same fifteen-minute demonstration to twelve different groups of people who understood virtually none of it.'

'Oh, dear. Should you have gone with an easier demonstration?'

Cooper shook his head. 'No. Prof Cole wants them to be baffled by something seemingly so complicated that only scientific geniuses can hope to understand it. He thinks that will impress them, so they keep giving us money for this highly technical, deeply complex, cutting-edge research.'

'So, you didn't tell them about the compatibility project, then?' I couldn't help grinning.

'I'm no longer responsible for that project, remember? I left it to your sister to decide whether to do a presentation explaining how one of their funded postdoc positions had spent their time trying to matchmake random strangers, or instead to discuss how her highly acclaimed collaboration with a Chinese university was leading to incredible new breakthroughs in our understanding of ME, as detailed in her recent paper in *The Lancet*. Anyway, I've really done enough talking about work for one day. Are you ready to eat, or do you want to show me around first?'

'My lunch consisted of licking leftover batter off a spoon, plus a handful of raisins meant to go in a carrot cake. I'm beyond ready for a proper meal.'

He started unpacking the food while I got plates, forks and glasses.

'I presume Nita let you in?'

'She said she was signing out for the night, and if you're heading to the wholesalers in the morning could you look for black and gold edible glitter?'

I made a note on the whiteboard. 'She's designing a Nottingham Panthers fan's fiftieth birthday cake. I've so far vetoed life-size chocolate hockey sticks and anything involving a stuffed panther.'

'Ambitious.'

'That's one word to describe her designs.'

Cooper had brought wine, along with a Moroccan tagine and crispy falafels with tabbouleh salad. We ate sitting at the tasting table in the consultation room, relaxing in the comfy chairs away from the kitchen clutter. Conversation was largely about how Sam was doing, and whether Orla was totally out of her mind to take him home, along with whether Annie was even crazier to have abandoned her business to help.

'There's clearly something going on with her and Greg. We've not heard them talking on the phone once. And she told us he was in Singapore, but according to Insta he ate at Vinnie's Pasta House in New York last night.'

'Surely he wouldn't be stupid enough to lie about what country he's in and then post pictures proving otherwise?'

I shrugged. 'I think it's more likely she's lying to us. I'm wondering if she's left him, and has no intention of going back to New York. Her business website says that she's on vacation, and is taking no bookings for the foreseeable future.'

I took another bite of falafel. 'Anyway. Enough of my family. Let's talk about us.'

'Is this a "Where is this relationship going?" conversation, because I think that's sorted for now.'

I laughed. 'No, it's a "tell me about yourself" conversation. In Derbyshire we did the heavy stuff. How about the everyday, normal stuff that most couples already know by the time they've reached "I do"?'

'Okay. I like that idea. How should we do it?'

'We each take turns asking questions on a topic. Both have to answer.'

'Agreed.' Cooper poured us both another glass of wine. 'How about first topic – things that really get on our nerves?'

'Ooh. Good choice.' I thought about it for a couple of seconds. 'Lateness.'

'Yes! Me too.' Cooper narrowed his eyes. 'How about answering a question with another question?'

'Oh no, I hate it much more when people reply with something vague like, "Soon".'

'Maybe that's as precise as they can get, given the available information.'

'Which is why they need to ask another question before they give an answer!'

'Fair enough. What else?'

I took another sip of wine, stalling for time. 'People who ask us for free cakes, in exchange for featuring it on their social media. They pretend they're doing us a favour, as if we're desperate for publicity and their two-hundred followers will make all the difference.'

'Okay, I see where you're coming from. How about adding a running commentary to films?'

'I love talking about a film I'm watching! Even if I'm by myself. And as long as I'm not in the cinema.'

'Duly noted.'

'So, what about films as the next topic?'

And so we went on...

It was turning into the perfect date. Great food, easy conversation, a crackle of potential in the air. Once we'd finished eating, I fetched throws from the design room and we watched the twilight settle through the shop window. Beyond the faint hum of cars from the main road two streets away, the night was quiet and still. Cooper angled his chair so that I could rest my feet on his lap, and we held hands under the blankets.

We spent a while playing each other our favourite songs. I introduced Cooper to *Hamilton*, and to my surprise and amusement he revealed a love of the sappiest, cheesiest, verging-on-the-slightly-sexist country music.

'I didn't know you could get country music like this. I thought it was all Dolly and Johnny Cash.'

'Come on now, lady,' Cooper said in a terrible country drawl. 'Get with the times.'

By the end of the first song, I was mesmerised. 'That was ridiculously sad. But somehow at the same time, it wasn't bleak or depressing. Like sad but happy sad. I don't know how to describe it.'

'It's straight down the line,' Cooper said. 'That's why I love it. Too much of my life has been bleak. However sad country music gets, it's never bitter.'

He put his glass down. Uh-oh. I knew what was coming next.

'Come on, wife of mine, this country boy wants to dance with his woman.'

'I don't know if someone once told you that voice was sexy, but it really isn't.'

'You sure 'bout that?'

No. I wasn't sure. It might have been the wine. Could have been the beautiful night. Either way, I was feeling a definite something sexy for Patrick Charles Cooper as we swayed to the next hopelessly romantic ballad, my face pressed against his shoulder.

'Does Bridget know about this secret music obsession?'

Did I imagine it, or for a brief second did Cooper's whole body stiffen?

I must have imagined it, because the next moment, he pulled back, took my face in both his hands and kissed me.

* * *

Cooper

By the end of the week, Cooper still didn't know what to make of married life. After filming more predictably restrained interviews, Ben had headed off to Dublin to shoot a wedding, so it had just been the two of them. Which should have been easier. Only, he'd realised as he'd pounded out a ten-K run that Sunday morning, Ben had been a good excuse for the distance that still hovered between them; his easy-going manner created a flatmate atmosphere, removed the pressure to act like a newly married couple.

The date had been good.

The kiss had been lovely.

But when Emma had gone to fetch them coffee, he'd fallen asleep in the chair.

He'd done the same in the taxi home.

And on the sofa.

And then in bed, while she was in the bathroom brushing her teeth.

He'd apologised several times. Too many times, judging by the flash of irritation when he tried to explain once again about how he'd been up the entire night before...

And, of course, he couldn't help thinking what could have happened if he'd stayed awake.

Wondering if Emma had *wanted* him to stay awake.

Wondering if a tiny part of him was glad that he hadn't. Somehow, once the marriage had been consummated, it would feel a whole lot more real. And if it didn't go well, what then? He liked Emma, a lot. But he knew he wasn't in love with her yet. Would having sex breach the gap, or only highlight it? It was probably pointless to even think about it, seeing as Emma had given no indication of wanting to take things further since their date. They'd exchanged morning and hello kisses. He'd rubbed her feet after a

long Saturday at work. Held her hand as they sat through Moses'
sermon in church on Sunday morning. As they'd joined the convoy
to the farmhouse for Sunday lunch, got stuck into setting plates out
and carrying serving dishes, pouring drinks and eating more food
than he'd thought humanly possible, he'd felt one of the family.
Then when Gabriella announced that Helen Richards had given
birth to a ten-pound baby boy, Emma had rolled her eyes and
smiled at him over the top of her water glass in a way that made his
heart squeeze.

'To Jake and Helen.' Bridget held up her glass in a toast. 'What a
good job he found the contents of her jumper so irresistible.
Wouldn't you agree, Cooper?'

In the warmth of the Donovan family, surrounded by everything he'd hoped for and more than he'd ever dreamed of, he
would agree, yes.

* * *

By Tuesday evening, he wasn't so sure. Bridget had burst into his
office at lunchtime.

'I need your help.'

He saved the table he was working on and swivelled around to
see her pacing up and down the tiny square of empty floor space,
her lab coat flapping over faded jeans and a multicoloured T-shirt.
'What's Prof done now?'

'Prof? Oh, no, nothing. It's not work. I got an email from the
freaky shop lady saying my dress is ready, but I feel weird and I
think I might hate it now. I think I want a normal dress. Something
stylish and classic like Emma's. Beautiful and wifely and like something someone would wear who's ready to commit and has no
reason whatsoever to change her mind now. None of them good
ones, anyway.'

Cooper looked at her. 'Given that I'm assuming in the middle of all that you were referencing a wedding dress, why would you want my help?'

'I need you to come with me for my final dress fitting. Emma's too busy making one million wedding cakes.'

'Bridget, you have three other sisters.'

She looked at him, eyes wide with pleading. 'I'm not asking Annie or Orla, even if they weren't flat out already. And Sofia would talk me into wearing something that costs ten pounds from Oxfam. Or her old dress. Which was fine. For her.'

'And you think I'll do a better job of making sure you get what you want?' He shook his head, incredulous. 'You'd be better off asking your mum.'

'Look, it's not really about the dress though, is it?' she replied, veering dangerously close to a shriek.

He waited until she'd taken a few deep breaths, hand pressed against her chest, and opened her eyes again.

'I'm having a bit of a freak out. And it might not really be about the dress. I don't want one of my sisters' probing interrogations, prodding me about why I'm not skipping about with bridal glee. I can't hack their judgements while I'm trying to figure out if I'm ready to be steamrollered into this wedding yet.'

What?

Cooper swung back to his desk and pretended to be checking his phone while concentrating on holding his mouth closed to prevent his jaw from hitting the floor.

'I was doing fine at ignoring my niggles, and then seeing Sam and Orla, and how they've always been so in love but ended up drifting and nearly shipwrecking their whole family anyway. And now she's given up her job to take care of him. To repair the damage.' She threw herself into a chair. 'I just suddenly thought what if I'm only marrying Paolo because he's always been there, and we love each other and it's a good fit with the shop and everything?'

Cooper kept his gaze on the stapler on his desk. 'Aren't those all very good reasons for marrying him?'

'Then why am I freaking out about a dress?'

He spoke slowly in the hope it would hide the tremble in his voice. 'Because you aren't sure if you like the dress?'

'Will you please come with me so I can see? I trust you to be honest and tell me if it's the right one for me or not. However much hassle that might cause.'

He didn't ask if she meant the dress or Paolo.

* * *

The dress was perfect.

When Bridget stepped out of the changing room his heart slammed so hard against his ribs Cooper had to stifle a gasp.

Even with hair in a mussed-up ponytail, face free of make-up, Converse trainers clearly showing beneath the skirt, she was perfect.

He blinked a few times. Cleared his throat. Stuck his hands in his pockets.

'So?' she asked, chewing on her bottom lip. His heart gave up thumping and simply dissolved.

He managed a nod. 'It's great.'

'*Great?*' The shop assistant tutted. 'Is that the best word you can come up with?'

It's the safest I can come up with, for now.

This was wrong, him being here. He'd thought he was ready. Had even sent Emma a text while Bridget was getting changed, saying that he was thinking of her, compelling himself to think about her, and what she meant to him, the promises he'd made, just in case seeing Bridget in the dress resuscitated impossible dreams that should have died years ago.

He'd been wrong. He wasn't close to being ready to stand in front of Bridget in her wedding dress.

What scared him witless was the possibility that he might never be.

And she expected his honest opinion?

Damn.

He needed to go, now.

Only that would require an explanation he couldn't tell her. So, he did what he'd always done in order to survive being hopelessly in love with Bridget Donovan. Shut the feelings down, got a grip and shunted back into Friend Mode. He could handle this. He'd had enough practice.

Bridget took a few steps closer to the wall of mirrors. Swung her dress from side to side so that the millions of tiny coloured flowers sparkled in the shop lights. 'You're right. It's awesome.'

She promptly burst into tears.

Not happy tears, although thankfully the shop assistant didn't figure that out, promising to package the dress and have it waiting for her, even as Bridget sniffled and sobbed and used up nearly a whole box of tissues.

'We'd better get back to work,' she croaked as they left the shop.

'Let's grab some lunch first.' Comfortably back inside the Friend Zone, Cooper didn't need to add what Professor Cole would say if she returned to the lab still crying her eyes out.

'No. I'm fine. And I don't want to think about it, let alone talk about it. I'm clearly deranged. I have a great man, we love each other, no issues, no drama, it's cool.'

She accepted Cooper's offer of another tissue, giving her nose a long, honky blow.

'It's been an exhausting few weeks. All the work stress. Sorting out everything for you and Emma. Sam and Orla. Worrying about Annie. Living by myself for the first time ever. I think my brain's had enough change. I just need a moment to catch my breath. Probably nothing a pyjama day and a giant box of Maltesers wouldn't sort.' She grimaced. 'Only this Saturday I'm at Hatherstone Hall with Paolo's parents doing menu tasting. Then Annie's on at me to get bridesmaid dresses sorted. According to Emma's list I need to choose shoes, flowers, décor, transport, favours, a gift list. Sofia wants us to arrange marriage preparation classes and finalise the ceremony. I'm tired already and there's still over a month to go.'

They began walking back towards the tram stop. 'I wish I was marrying you.'

Cooper tripped over the pavement, crashing into an elderly man and nearly sending him flying. Bridget waited until the man was safely on his way before continuing.

'Well, not you, obviously! I mean, I wish Paolo would agree to a wedding like yours. You very sensibly avoided all this palaver. Three-week engagement, a few fairy lights in the barn and Nita's buffet. Family and might-as-well-be-family only. Do you think Paolo would mind if we moved the date to this weekend, just rocked up and said "I do"?'

If he did mind, he'd be a bigger fool than Cooper had previously pegged him for waiting even this long. And while on the one hand, Cooper's insides crumpled at the thought of them finally being married, on the other one, maybe that was the missing piece that would ensure he'd finally moved on.

The closer they got to the lab, as Bridget returned to her normal, relentlessly cheerful self, the more Cooper convinced himself that today was an entirely plausible blip.

'Let me know if I need to keep this weekend free, Widget.' He gave her a quick nudge as they reached her lab door.

'Do you think that's the answer? That moving the wedding

forward will sort all this anxiety?' She stopped, clutching the lab door handle, face scrunched with stress.

'How do you feel at the thought of getting married this weekend?'

'Like I want to vomit.'

'Then, from a neuroscientific point of view, I'd say that's probably not the answer. But I'm hardly the expert on marriage matters.'

'You're an expert on Widget matters.'

Man, she really did have no idea.

'Talk to your sisters.' He began to move away before pausing to add, 'Even better. Talk to your dad.'

Things were still a bit strange.

'Of course they are!' Nita shook her head, comparing two shades of pink ribbon against a cream background. 'What did you expect? Things take time to settle down when any two people start sharing a house together. Let alone with the added pressure of being married.'

'Was it strange when you and Vik first got married?'

She burst out laughing. 'Strange? The only man I'd ever been alone with up till then was my father. I was terrified, baffled, lonely, miserable. I called my mother and told her it was a terrible mistake, begged her to let me come home. She told me to give it time, we'd get past it. And she was right.'

'So how did you get past it?'

Nita pulled out another ream of ribbon, darker pink this time, and carefully snipped it with a pair of gold-handled dressmaking scissors. 'We boinked four times a day. Soon broke the ice.'

I closed my eyes, shaking my head even as I smiled.

'You should try it.'

'I don't know if he's ready.'

'Hah! Over thirty years old and you know even less about men than I did at twenty. He's your husband, isn't he? You're a stunning woman, inside and out. He's ready.' She laid the ribbon to one side, flicked through her basket to find another colour.

'So why hasn't he... tried to take things further?'

'Because he doesn't know you're ready.'

'*I* don't know if I'm ready!'

Nita looked at me out of the corner of her eye, smirking. 'Trust me, you're beyond ready.'

'So, what do I do? You know I'm hardly the type of woman to jump him when he gets home.'

'It's not rocket science! Even for Lady Uptight-and-Organised. A lovely meal, candles, soft music. Hunt through your wardrobe until you manage to find that one, long-forgotten item stuffed right at the back that's a little bit sexy. Or else borrow a dress off that sister of yours – Orla. Look at him like you've been thinking about jumping him, even though he knows that you wouldn't. He'll get the message.'

* * *

I followed Nita's advice to the letter. I knew my sisters would tell me the same thing. Cooper arrived home to find the lights dimmed, Spotify romantic country-music playlist warbling and his wife wearing a silky, silver halter-neck dress that skimmed my thighs and hung low enough on my modest cleavage to hopefully get his imagination stirring.

'This looks nice.' He glanced in appreciation at the table set for two, the steak waiting to go on the griddle. 'Have I got time to get changed?'

'That depends how you like your steak.' I tried to give him a sexy smile. It might have worked, because he raised his eyebrows and smiled in return.

'Medium rare.'

'Four minutes.' Or so Google had told me. The only steak I'd ever cooked was made of cauliflower.

He strolled to the door, then stopped and looked back at me. 'Or you could wait a few minutes before starting to cook it? I feel like this isn't a night to be throwing on a T-shirt and joggers.'

'Okay. Great.'

It wasn't great. I felt as though I was on the brink of a cardiac arrest. I only remembered to breathe once I heard Cooper turn the shower on.

Surely it wasn't supposed to feel this hard? I mean, I knew real-life relationships were nothing like the films, that they were mostly made up of a whole lot of normal, everyday, potentially awkward and really not very romantic or sexy moments, not whirlwinds of all-consuming passion.

Still, though.

Once the thought had popped into my head it was difficult to wrangle it out again: if I had been dating Cooper, I might be thinking about cooling things off about now. It wasn't that I didn't like him. More that we'd gone so far, and then seemed to get stuck there.

I was shaping up to be a terrible wife.

Needless to say, I was not in the mood for boinking.

I ate and drank and managed to listen to Cooper's stories and laugh a few times anyway. He also seemed a little tense, but that was hardly surprising given that, as Nita had predicted, he knew full well that this was my shaky attempt at foreplay.

We had made it all the way to the sofa, the coffee had been drunk and the candles nearly burnt down when I reached the point where I knew it was now or never. Or at least, now or have to endure this whole thing all over again on another night, only even more forced than this time.

I put my empty mug down, smoothed my hair behind my ears, and brazenly leant over and kissed him.

Again: nice enough.

As if by some sort of country miracle, the playlist moved onto the song we'd danced to the other night, and we smiled against each other's lips. Cooper placed one hand on the back of my head, his fingers gently burrowing into my hair. The other one slid against my waist, and to my enormous relief my skin tingled in response. After a good few long, slow, sighing kisses, I braved placing one hand on his chest, my fingers brushing against his shirt button.

And then it happened again.

It was only for a couple of seconds, but Cooper went rigid. His breath froze in his throat.

As he unpaused, and carried on kissing me, I tried to decide whether or not to pull away. Was his reaction anticipation or panic? Or worse – horror. Was he nervous in a good way, or was my husband bracing himself at the thought of me touching him?

Continuing to kiss him while my mind spiralled into a whirlpool of agitation, I had a flash of revelation that I was far too old and had far too much self-respect to leave this hanging. No way on earth was I about to plough on into having sex with someone for the first time while wondering in the back of my mind if he was secretly hating every second of it. I sat back, anxious to see some desire, if not quite love, in his eyes. But if there wasn't any there, at least I would know before things got any further.

Cooper ducked his head under my scrutiny. My heart plummeted into the depths of the sofa.

'I'm sorry,' he mumbled, voice riddled with anguish. 'It's been a weird day.'

I took a deep breath, not even sure what I was going to say, but knowing it had to be honest, no matter what that cost both of us.

But before I could speak, the front door rattled open and three seconds later Ben burst in, lugging his rucksack and an armload of photographic equipment.

'Hey!' He threw himself into the spare armchair. 'How's it going? I hope your day contained less drunk and disorderly idiots than mine.' Having kicked off his shoes, he glanced over at us. Dishevelled hair, flushed cheeks, my tiny dress riding precariously high on my thighs.

'Oh! Crap. Sorry.' Ben's eyes caught mine, before flickering away again. 'I'll get to bed, then.'

'No!' Cooper said, sharp enough to make Ben stop as he moved to pick up his bags. 'We were just chatting. It's your flat. Feel free to join us. I think there's some no-cheese cheesecake left.'

Ben furrowed his brow, gaze switching between the two of us.

'Tell us about the wedding,' Cooper added, his voice ending in a croak of desperation.

'Um, actually I'm whacked. It's been a long and uninteresting day and I'm heading to bed.' Ben grabbed his stuff and scarpered, leaving a mushroom cloud of mortification in his wake.

Cooper stared at the floor. His Adam's apple bobbed as he swallowed.

'I'm pretty tired too, come to think of it,' I said. 'Red wine always makes me sleepy. Shall we call it a night?' I wasn't lying about being tired. Not knowing where you stood was exhausting in a marriage.

'I'll clear up first.' Cooper stood up, still unable to meet my eye.

'Yes, good point. I'll help you.'

'No, really. You cooked. I can clear up.'

I left him sorting out the evening's mess, while I lay most of the night staring at the ceiling and wondering if there was any way to clear up the far bigger, seemingly impossible mess we appeared to have landed ourselves in.

We had to talk about it at some point.

Only maybe I would talk to my sisters first.

* * *

Wednesday Wine convened at Orla's house. The kids were eventually herded upstairs after overly prolonged hugs and kisses with their favourite aunties. Sam was resting in bed.

Collapsing into the old, squishy sofa, Orla closed her eyes. 'I don't know how I ever had the energy to work.'

Annie, who'd been taking care to divide the bottle of white wine equally between four different glasses until Sofia nudged her glass over to make it five, paused to pat her on the knee. 'You didn't have a recuperating man to take care of when you worked.'

'Maybe not, but I didn't have you, either.' She opened her eyes and gratefully accepted a drink. 'I don't know what I'm going to do without you.'

'Well, I'm not going until Sam's much better and the kids are settled back down, so there's no point worrying about it, is there?'

'How long is that going to be?' Sofia said, taking her first sip of wine in years as she curled up in a faded leather armchair. 'You must be dying to get back home.'

Annie shrugged. 'This is home too.'

'Okay, so how about back to your business, and your *husband*?'

Annie made a big show of checking the clock hanging on the wall behind the giant TV. 'Ooh, that's a new record. Less than four minutes before you started prying into my life.'

'Yeah, come on, Sofia,' Orla grumbled. 'Are you trying to get rid of my help?'

'Well, maybe if you didn't lie to us about Greg being in Singapore then we wouldn't have to pry!' Bridget said, her voice wobbling as she reached for a drink.

Annie jerked back the glass, leaving Bridget hanging. 'Have you been talking to Greg? I can't believe my own twin would go behind my back like that!'

Bridget's mouth fell open. 'Of course I haven't spoken to Greg! But we all follow him on Instagram, and, while my knowledge of Asia isn't great, even I can figure out that "hashtag best spaghetti in Manhattan" is probably not referring to the little-known-because-it-doesn't-exist suburb of Manhattan, Singapore.'

'Why don't you tell us what's really going on, Young One?' I asked, moving a cushion so that Annie could plop down next to me. 'Whatever it is, we love you and we're here for you and none of us are going to judge you, given some of the questionable choices we've all made lately.'

'Ahem.' Sofia looked at me, affronted. 'What questionable choice have I made?'

'You've just downed a glass of wine after nearly a decade sober. I can promise your head will be questioning you about it in the morning.'

'It tasted nice.'

'We could tell. Now, back to Annie...'

Annie took a handful of nachos and stuffed them in all at once, chewing aggressively, perfectly groomed eyebrows beetling.

'Of course,' Orla interjected, 'if we were really worried, we might have to phone Greg after all.'

'Or maybe we should ask Mamma if she's got any idea why you'd be lying about Greg?' Bridget mused.

'Fine!' Annie spluttered, spraying crumbs of tortilla chip across the table. 'Things haven't been... easy between us. And before you all start with how marriage isn't easy and how does running away help and you're hardly going to solve things by living on different continents, I know that.' She paused, taking in a deep breath. 'I know, okay? I didn't come here to run away. And I had no intention of staying. The reasons I gave for staying were true. They just weren't all the reasons.'

'So, what are the other reasons, apart from being a selfless sister?' Sofia asked, brushing up the sprayed chips with a napkin.

Annie, to our collective shock and amazement, burst into tears. 'If I tell you you'll hate me.'

'We won't hate you!' I looped my arm around hers, pulling her up against my shoulder. We hadn't seen Annie this upset since Mum told her she couldn't get her belly button pierced (she was eleven at the time).

'You won't hate me,' she choked through a face full of gloop. 'Sofia will.' And then she started crying so hard that only a twin could decode it.

'He wants kids,' Bridget said, her face screwed up in sympathy.

Annie nodded, grabbing another mouthful of nachos before wiping her eyes and nose. 'Preferably as many as possible as soon as possible. He's forty-four, after all, and isn't "getting any younger"!'

'Didn't you discuss this before you got married?' Sofia asked, gently.

'We had ninety days to plan a wedding! We discussed it in the same way we discussed having a house with a porch swing to swing on when we were old and wrinkly. Or when he was, which of course will be two decades before me. More like three, given my skin-care routine and his work addiction. We discussed kids like we talked about how we'd celebrate Christmas and rent a beach cottage in the summer. None of it was real!'

'It was clearly real to him.' Bridget frowned.

'So, what are you going to do?' I asked. 'Is the problem having kids, or having them now?'

Annie gave a miserable shrug.

'Are you leaving him? Is that why you're here?'

'I don't want to!' she cried. 'But I don't know how we can solve this and I'm so, so scared he's going to leave me.'

'And how is you hiding here supposed to help that?'

'Because then we can't talk about it and I can't tell him the real reason I don't want kids, and he can't leave me.'

'So, what is the real reason?' Bridget asked.

'I'm definitely not going to talk to you about that when I haven't spoken to him yet.'

'Then you'd better book a plane ticket,' Orla retorted.

'I thought you liked me being here!' Annie bit back. 'I could always move into the farm if you'd prefer.'

'Don't be a numpty. I love having you here. For someone who supposedly hates kids and anything remotely housewifely, you are an awesome stand-in mum and housewife.'

'I don't hate kids!' Annie started crying again. 'Now can we please move on the interrogation to why Sofia is on her second glass of wine?'

Sofia hastily banged her glass on the table, her expression frozen.

We waited.

She hiccupped.

We waited some more.

'I, also, am not trying to have kids any more.'

'Oh, Sofia.' Before we could get up and cluster around her, she held up quaking palms. 'Don't! I'm a kind word and a cuddle away from falling to pieces. Which is stupid. It was my idea, for goodness' sake. It's the right decision. I'm relieved. And finally at peace after years of relentless, harrowing hope. We can start making love again, instead of desperately trying to make a baby. I can stop wondering whether it's okay to book a flight or bother spending money on a fitted dress. Stop feeling bitter about not having the income to keep trying. Stop dreading having to go through it all again.' She paused to catch her breath, one hand pressed against the pain in her heart. 'What a complete waste of four years.'

'Oh, Sofia!' We ignored her flapping hands, gathering round and offering tissues, murmured sympathies and hands to hold.

'You needed to try,' I assured her, once her sobs had stilled and she sat propped up against my shoulder. 'You and Moses had to decide together when it was time to lay it down.'

'How does Moses feel?' Bridget asked, sitting on the floor by Sofia's feet.

'He was sad. But then once we talked about fostering, maybe even adoption... Well. You know Moses, always so blummin' enthusiastic and positive about things.'

'It's his one major flaw,' Orla agreed.

'Especially if the thing involves helping someone else out. And helping out a child in need? It's like he can't believe we waited this long to consider it. Now he wants to call social services and make an appointment. All his spare time is reading up and making plans. Talking about how old and how many and whether we should move to somewhere with a garden and a decent catchment area.' She paused, burrowing her head back into my shoulder. 'But I'm still mourning. Mourning the babies I longed and prayed for all this time. The blue line on the pregnancy test. Messaging you all with the baby scan photo. Moses stroking my bump and crying the first time he feels our baby kick. Discovering that they have my eyes, his voice.

'I mean, I want to do this. It's not like we haven't opened our doors to kids in need of a home before. I'm up for the challenge, I know it's right. I just need some time to be a selfish, irresponsible, puts-herself-first twenty-eight-year-old childless woman first. So. I'm drinking if I feel like it. I ate a whole box of cheap, nasty doughnuts for breakfast yesterday. I texted Carmen Wallis on the day of her fundraiser and said I was feeling unwell and then I went shopping in town and bought underwear that cost more than my wedding dress.'

'You took it back first thing on Monday though, didn't you?' Annie asked, smirking.

'Well, yes, but I bought it!' She screwed up her face in exasperation. 'I want to explore this as an option, but I don't know if I can do it without a break from trying to give a crap about all the people whining on at me about their piffling problems. I'm tired.'

'My darling sister, would you like a top-up of wine?' Orla asked.

Sofia looked at her, and hiccupped. 'Yes.'

'So,' Orla said, once all that was left of our nachos was a smattering of crumbs, and we'd moved on from wine to decaffeinated tea and my millionaire's shortbread. 'We know Annie's problem. Or at least as much as she's going to tell us right now. We're fully behind Sofia's selfish sabbatical. You all know what's going on with me. What about you, Young One? Still raring to become Mrs Russo?'

'What?' Bridget squeaked. 'Why would you ask that?'

'Bridget, you're second only to Moses when it comes to enthusiasm.' Annie shook her head. 'This is the one time when we have to tolerate your relentless messages about centrepieces and shoes, but we've not heard a peep from you in days.'

'Well, it's hardly been the time, given what's been happening, to be parading my wedding all about the family.'

'Bridget,' Orla replied, 'when something horrendous happens to one of us, that's exactly the time we should be bigging up the good stuff. We could all do with something beautiful and joyful to take our minds off Sam scaring the life out of us.'

'Oh. Well. I didn't know that. And anyway, Emma's organising it. I've virtually lost track of what needs doing and when.'

'Well.' I wriggled a bit straighter in my seat. 'Most things are ticking away nicely, although Nita will need catering numbers soon and Moses needs to let me know how long his band are playing for. The only thing on the list for this week is the dress fitting.'

'Ooh, yes!' Sofia said. 'Why don't we all come? We can try on our bridesmaids' dresses at the same time.'

'Urr...' Bridget started inspecting her usual loose strand of hair intently.

'Urr what?' I asked, feeling a little alarmed. 'Have you changed your mind about the dress?'

'No. The dress is perfect. But I already did the fitting.'

'What?' I scanned my sisters to see which one of them had traitorously accompanied Bridget to this momentous occasion. They all appeared as mystified as me. Even Annie.

'You didn't take *Mamma*?' Annie's nose scrunched up at the thought.

'No!'

'Then who?' Orla asked, brow furrowed.

'It was the middle of a workday, I only had my lunch break and I suddenly felt like doing the fitting so I didn't have time to ask any of you. You should be pleased I proactively did some wedding arranging.'

'Did you go by yourself?' I was astounded. 'To try on your wedding dress?'

Annie paused, a slice of shortbread halfway to her mouth. 'Bridget, did you go wedding-dress shopping with Cooper?'

A prolonged silence in a room full of Donovan sisters said it all.

I took the opportunity to try to decide if I felt more flummoxed by Bridget having gone to try on her wedding dress with my husband, or that neither of them had mentioned it.

'Bad call,' Orla said, eventually.

'Does Paolo know?' Annie asked, knowing full well that he wouldn't.

'Bridget, that was not a good idea on so many levels.' Sofia took hold of my hand. 'You know Paolo's jealous of Cooper. You can't meet up with another man in secret once you're married.'

'She's right,' Orla added. 'Don't repeat my mistake.'

Bridget jolted her head up, dropping the twisted strand of hair. 'How dare you compare my friendship with Cooper to your sordid shenanigans with Gym Jim?' she cried, eyes blazing.

'*Shenanigans!*' Orla yelled back, dumping her mug on the table as her eyes nearly bugged out of her head.

'But that's only part of it,' Sofia carried on. 'Cooper married Emma. You have to back off and give them some space.'

'How weird would you have thought it if I'd taken Sam or Moses when I tried on my wedding dress?' Annie interjected. 'And there's no point pretending to yourself or us that you don't get it. If you thought it was all fine and innocent, then you'd have told Emma.'

'So I have to give up my best friend? I'm not allowed to see him now without asking permission first?' Bridget glared at her sisters, her expression defiant, her wobbling voice less so.

'I thought *I* was your best friend,' I said, barely above a whisper.

Bridget closed her eyes. 'It wasn't meant to be that big a deal. Like I said, I was at work when the shop called, and it was a spur-of-the-moment thing. It wasn't like he was there when I chose it.'

'What's even weirder is that he went with you,' Annie barked. 'Someone needs to have a chat with him about how relationships work. I vote Moses does it.'

'Look, I'm sorry, Emma. Genuinely. I guess I was wrapped up in my own situation and didn't take time to think how it might appear to you. And Cooper knew that it wasn't a big deal, that's the only reason he came.'

I took a long, hard look at my youngest sister. I thought long and hard for most of that night as I lay beside a man I barely knew. I thought about how in order to make a marriage work, it took sacrifices. And the whole point of a sacrifice was that it cost, it meant something.

As soon as the first rays of dawn probed their fingers through the curtain, I dragged myself out of bed and texted Sofia.

Yep. He'd totally blown it. Cooper glanced at the clock on his phone and then back at the empty bed beside him. Six a.m. and Emma couldn't wait to get out of there. He'd flaked the other night. There was no hiding behind excuses. *'It's been a weird day.'* Every time he thought about it – which was about as often as he thought at all – he pictured Emma's face when he basically, in a roundabout way, rejected her.

Everything he'd vowed he wouldn't do – messing this up, acting like a fool, hurting her, not being the man she deserved...

Ugh.

He needed to make it up to her.

And fast.

If only he had the first clue how.

He could make a move, *un*reject her. Come up with a date so spectacularly romantic it'd make it clear beyond a shadow of a doubt how he felt.

And how's that?

He made a mental note to talk to Ben, see if he had any ideas about how to redeem himself, then he got up, had a shower, shovelled in a piece of toast and went to work, pretending to himself and everyone else that he wasn't trying to avoid his sister-in-law.

* * *

Emma

I had arranged to meet Sofia for an early dinner. Given that she was squeezing me in between after-school club and visiting someone to talk about his wife's funeral, we were settling for a hearty salad in her office.

Propelled by my anxiety, I power-walked the journey to the church building, arriving as Sofia and the other helpers were finishing off the club.

'Right,' Sofia called over the general hubbub of twenty-odd primary school children, as I found a discreet chair to perch on near the entrance. 'Last few bits to tidy up, and we should have time for Ask Anything.'

The mulling grew decidedly more focussed at this point, fuelled by a buzz of anticipation at whatever Ask Anything might be. I was interested, too. Surely Sofia wasn't going to allow a bunch of kids to ask her whatever they liked?

A few minutes later they were sitting in a semicircle of chairs, eagerly waiting for Sofia to start.

'Right. Ten minutes on the timer. Ask Anything. Go.'

It took about ten wasted seconds for a group of boys all clustered at one end of the chairs to start elbowing and jostling each other, until one boy put up his hand, his face a mask of serious intent.

'Leon?'

'Why does poo stink?'

The boys collapsed in a pile of guffaws.

Sofia didn't miss a beat. 'Well, I guess that would be because it's dirty, and has a lot of germs in so can make you ill. Being really smelly means we don't want to touch it, which protects us from catching the germs. That's my idea. Anyone else?'

'It's because of the intestinal bacteria and the different things that your food gets broken down into,' another boy added, sitting between two girls towards the other side. 'What you eat will affect the smell. For example, the crisps Leon ate at snack time could make his poo smell worse than if he'd had an apple, because of the higher fat content.'

'Uuurgggh! Leon's poo stinks!' A load of the other kids called out, holding their noses and trying to move their chairs away. Leon, his face scrunched with rage, stood up, causing his chair to topple over. 'No, it doesn't! Anyway, Conor and Rhys had crisps too!'

'UUUUGGGH! Conor and Rhys toooooo!' Other kids cried, jumping up and sending more chairs flying.

'PEEEEEP!' Sofia blew hard on a whistle, pointing at various children in the three seconds it took them to grab their chairs and sit back down. 'Matthias, thank you for that interesting scientific input, but please remember not to make it personal. Right, that's your one permitted poo question out of the way. We have under six minutes left so who's next?'

'Why is Matthias such a geek?' the boy next to Leon asked.

Sofia looked at him. He put his hand up and then repeated the question.

'Explain geek, please, Conor.'

'Um.' Conor shifted about on his chair, a grin tickling the edge of his mouth. 'I dunno. Like, he's always going on about science and facts and using long words and talking about everything that normal people don't know.'

'Hmm. Why does Matthias know lots of interesting information that he enjoys sharing with people? My guess is that he likes to read books and go online and watch interesting TV programmes and ask lots of questions so that he gets to find out all about the world and how things work. And then because he likes knowing all those things, and he's kind, he likes to share what he's found out in case other people would like to know it, too. What do you think, Matthias? Is that about right?'

Matthias nodded, gravely. The girl next to him said, 'Yes, he's really kind so I think that's definitely true.'

'Now, four minutes left, who's next?'

'Is my dog in heaven?' one of the younger girls asked, having raised a shaky hand.

'Well, last time you asked me that question Scampi was playing in the garden at home.'

'But now he's died.'

'Oh, I'm very sorry to hear that, Kiesha. There are lots of different thoughts about whether our pets go to heaven or not, but, given that Scampi is an imaginary dog, I think he's wherever you imagine him to be.' Sofia smiled and nodded reassuringly, checking that Kiesha was okay before moving on. 'Next?'

'Is everybody going to get washed away in the floods and then run out of food and die because of the environment?'

And so it went on…

There were only a few seconds left when Milly asked her question:

'My question is in three parts so it's really only one question, and it's where are your children and how old are they and what are their names? Ooh! And can they come to kids club one time and that's still part of the question only I forgot to say it before so it's still one question.'

Sofia stared at Milly. Some of the kids started to fidget and mutter, while others fixed expectant faces on Sofia, probably feeling confused at why, instead of replying, she didn't even blink.

'Well?' Milly asked, her little forehead creasing.

'Um.' Sofia opened her mouth, closed it again, and then, to save me having to jump up and create an intervention, the timer went off.

'Oh!' Sofia snapped back into life. 'Right, well, time's up! Thanks, everyone, for your fabulously fascinating questions. I hope you all learnt something new. It looks like your parents and carers are waiting, so once you've stacked your chairs you can sign out with Gemma.'

I helped one of the playworkers stack the empty chairs, then stood and watched my sister smile and wave while gathering stray bags and coats and making sure she spoke to each of the children's collectors. My heart splintered. Ten minutes in a room with those kids and I was wondering if filling in 'yes' to the children question on the compatibility test had been a foolish mistake. Sofia was born for this.

Where are her children? That was my question, too. *Well, God?*

Once all the kids had gone, Sofia left the team to clear up and we relocated to her office.

'Well, that was... enlightening.' I tugged two plastic boxes out of my bag.

'I love Ask Anything.' Sofia grinned.

'Those boys.' I shuddered. 'Are they always so... yuck?'

'Oh, come off it, Emma. We could be just as bad. The trick with the Young Ones' potty?'

'I had nothing to do with that!' I cringed in remembrance.

Sofia squinted as she thought about it. 'No. You're right. You were very rarely yuck.'

'Well, I think you were a phenomenal fount of knowledge. I'm impressed, as always. And I'm sorry about that question from Milly.'

Sofia placed two glasses on the table in between us, pausing before she sat down again. 'Yeah.' She pressed her lips together, which I knew from experience was an attempt to stop her chin from wobbling. 'That one caught me off-guard. I don't know why. It's not like some of the adults in church haven't been making comments about me starting a family.'

'Do you tell them to bog off and mind their own business?' I handed her a plate.

'Wouldn't make it any less painful that they'd asked.' She shook her head briefly then, looking back up at me with a bright smile. 'Anyway, we aren't here to talk about my same old problems. What's up with you, Old One? Sounded a bit urgent when you messaged.'

How Sofia could deduce that from my ten-word message, I would never know.

'Yeah. No. Not urgent as in an emergency.'

'Urgent as in, "I can't stop thinking about this and it's driving me bananas so I need to talk to someone sensible about it soon to avoid imminent emotional implosion."'

I shrugged, popping open a pot of salad, and started dividing it between the plates.

Sofia smiled. 'Yeah, most of my urgent appointments tend to be in that category.'

'I'm sorry to bother you, especially when you've so much stuff going on...'

Sofia sat back. 'Don't be stupid. You're my sister. I always have time for you. And we never got around to catching up properly last night.'

I took a forkful of lentils and sweet potato.

'Are you worried about Cooper and Bridget being friends?'

I swallowed carefully. 'Do you think I should be?'

Sofia considered her answer. 'I think Bridget is struggling to adapt to all these changes, feeling off-balance and unsure of herself, and clinging onto an old friendship is her reaction to that. I'd be more worried if you couldn't talk honestly with her, and, more importantly, Cooper, about what boundaries you feel comfortable with and why.'

'What, like please stop being friends with my sister, because I'm jealous that she knows everything about you and I don't even know your favourite colour?'

'Well, yeah. If that's true. Or at least you can ask him to tell you if he's been hanging out with her.'

We ate a few more mouthfuls.

'Are you more jealous for Bridget or Cooper?' Sofia asked.

I thought about that and decided, in the inner sanctum of Pastor Sofia's office, I had better be honest, or I truly would find myself turning bananas. 'I've thought and thought about it, and I don't think I am jealous. That's what bothers me the most.'

Sofia put down her plate. 'Go on.'

I took a deep breath, ready to rush my words out in one go before I changed my mind. 'I think I might be hoping that Cooper has a thing for Bridget so that we have an excuse to split up and it's not my fault for not being able to fall in love with him.'

There. I sagged in the chair like a deflated balloon.

Sofia took a sip of water.

'I hate myself for even thinking it. It's been, what, two and a half weeks? We haven't made it past kissing yet. And I have no reason not to fall in love with him. I probably do love him, in one kind of way. He's so lovely and kind and sweet and I really respect his integrity and his decency and his sense of humour. He's perfect in so many ways. And I think he's very good-looking. I really do. There's just...'

'No boom.'

I pressed at a tear threatening to leak out of the corner of my eye. 'Exactly.'

'So, what are you going to do?'

'I was hoping you'd tell me that.'

'That's not how this works.'

I breathed out a long sigh. 'I don't want to take the easy option for the sake of it. I don't want to run away at the first obstacle. I got myself into this situation after weeks of thought and consideration, because I believed it was the right thing to do. I have to know I gave it everything. Nita said we needed chemistry, kindness and commitment. Kindness is a given. I think that there's at least some chemistry. Maybe the problem is I'm wavering on the commitment.'

'Sounds like you want to keep going.'

'I do.' I dragged my eyes up off the faded linoleum to look at her. 'I wish it felt a bit easier, though. It doesn't help that I find being with his flatmate so comfortable, either.'

'Ben? The best-man photographer?'

'Yeah, he's got that knack of putting people at ease, like Dad always does. Whenever he walks into the flat the tension dissipates.'

'Emma, do you like Ben?'

Oh, dear. I really hoped not.

I fiddled with my water bottle. 'I... don't find him *un*attractive?'

'Oh, boy.'

'He's that photographer from Mervyn's wedding. Remember? Who I climbed into the bin with? I seem to remember you being the one pointing him out. I thought he was nice. But we are totally incompatible. In the Cole Compatibility Test we'd score 0 per cent. And he's also a zero on the commitment factor. He doesn't believe in monogamous, long-term relationships. He doesn't even believe in love.'

Sofia looked right in my eyes. 'Emma, if you want things to work with Cooper you need to move out of Ben's.'

'We are going to move out! As soon as Bridget moves in with Paolo we're moving back into my flat.'

'Right.'

'Anyway, thanks for listening. I feel better now I have a plan.' I started quickly gathering up the salad containers.

'Remind me of the plan again?'

'Stay married?'

'Sounds like a great plan.'

* * *

My fledgling marriage crawled through the next few days. Nita and I were flat out with wedding-cake orders, and by Saturday evening I was longing to collapse on the sofa in my comfiest (and therefore probably least attractive) pyjamas with a reheated curry. To my relief, Ben and Cooper had gone out. I'd told Cooper not to expect me home until late, given that we had a christening cake with accompanying cupcakes to finish off ready for Sunday morning, and I blissfully sagged across the sofa, giving no concern to how undaintily I was eating, how much of a wreck my hair was or what anyone would think about me bingeing on *90 Day Fiancé*.

I made sure I was firmly tucked under the duvet and sound asleep at whatever time Cooper and Ben arrived home.

* * *

Sunday was family dinner as normal. At least, as normal as things got when it came to my family.

Firstly, it was always going to be impossible for certain family members to behave normally given that there was a camera rolling, even if there hadn't been a charming man coaxing them into action from behind it. Secondly... well. That came later.

'Benjamin, sit here!' Mum instructed, pulling up one of the Best Chairs that Dad had hand-carved her as a tenth anniversary gift. 'Please, make yourself at home. Here, next to me.'

'Thanks, Mrs Donovan, but—'

'Gabriella, please! You make me sound old enough to be your mother!'

'Mamma, please! That's because you *are* old enough!' Bridget cringed.

'I can get better shots if I stay in the corner.' Ben winked, at everyone in general so there was no reason for my cheeks to flush in response. 'Pretend I'm not here.'

I glanced at Sofia, busy scooping potatoes onto Oscar's plate, Orla having stayed at home with Sam, who for some reason didn't feel up to joining a Donovan Sunday lunch. I'd been handling things fine until Sofia had prodded and poked about in my feelings. I did my best to ignore the rumble of annoyance mixed with embarrassment as places were taken and plates piled high. Then Cooper took hold of my hand under the table, and when I glanced at him he gave a wink and a smile that was definitely only for me.

'So, how are you two settling in together?' Mum asked, smiling sweetly as she flicked a bushy clump of hair over the shoulder of her shocking pink dress, eyes remaining firmly on Ben's camera.

Annie groaned on my behalf, earning a 'Shush!' from Mum far louder than the groan had been. 'We are supposed to be talking about the marriage project, aren't we? To prove to all the big boffin scientists how love is blossoming between Cooper and Emma and finally, after all this time and all the many years of fruitless searching, because of Bridget's amazing work, Emma now has someone who can love her.'

'Um, well, that's not really...' Cooper said.

'We aren't meant to be proving anything,' Bridget replied, her voice terse. 'The whole point of scientific research is that you gather the data and then analyse it and draw a conclusion. You don't try to only gather data that proves your point. If Cooper and Emma put on a show to pretend things are great when they aren't, that's completely unscientific and the whole project is null and void.'

'But things *are* great!' Mum exclaimed, affronted. 'So, what's the problem?'

No one was going to argue with that point.

'Time to call New York,' Mum announced, once the panna cotta had been served.

'Um, hello?' Annie waved from the other end of the table. 'I'm here.'

'As if we hadn't noticed!' Mum harrumphed. Annie had taken her documentary debut seriously, with stand-out make-up and perfect waves crafted through her chin-length bob. She wore a cream blazer over a bottle-green crop-top with matching cream culottes that were way too expensive to risk wearing at a family dinner. It had taken her twice as long as anyone else to finish her minuscule lunch, due to trying to eat it in tiny enough chunks to avoid any potentially unattractive chewing faces caught on camera.

'Greg is not here though, is he? It is high time I saw my beautiful eldest son-in-law's face. I need to check he is coping without you.'

'Mamma, he's forty-four, with his own parents living two streets away. You don't need to check that,' Annie added, before suddenly remembering she was on camera, and smiling brightly like a toothpaste advert.

'Well, maybe you don't care whether he is eating okay and not working too hard, but I do! Harry, please dial in to Greg's number.'

Harry, with a nervous glance at his Auntie Annie, clicked on the laptop so that it called through to Greg.

'How did you even get his number?' Annie hissed, behind her fixed grin.

'Why would l not have his number?' Mum said, shaking her head as if baffled. 'You think I'm letting my youngest child move to New York to live with a man without getting his number? What if I want to check whether you already own the cardigan I picked out for your birthday?'

'Not a problem you need to worry about,' Annie muttered, glaring at the screen.

'I don't think he's answering.' Harry shrugged.

'Well, why ever not? Annie, where is your husband on a Sunday morning?' Mum waved one hand around as if that would conjure him up in the dining room.

'Maybe he's at church?' Lottie suggested, in between licks of her panna cotta spoon.

'Annie? What are your husband's plans for today?'

'This may come as a shock to you, Mamma, but I don't know his every move even when on the same continent.'

'You didn't message him to say good morning?' Mum's eyes narrowed.

'Nope.'

'Well, what about when you had a goodnight call yesterday?'

Annie scraped at the non-existent remains of her dessert.

'Annie, when was the last time you spoke to your husband? Have you any idea at all where he is?'

'Now's not the time, Gabriella,' Dad interjected, his voice soft but firm.

'I stopped recording as soon as pudding arrived,' Ben said, holding up his bowl as proof.

'Who's up for a game of frisbee?' Moses asked, 'Harry, Lottie and Oscar, excellent. Last one out there has to stand nearest to the compost bin.'

By the time they'd got their shoes on and clattered outside, declaring Paolo to be the last one out as they barged past, Annie was hiding in the kitchen. Mum, rather than retreating upstairs for her afternoon snooze, settled Dad into his armchair to watch the games outside, and went in for the kill.

'Antonia, what's going on? It's not normal to not know where your husband is. I don't care if he's living in the North Pole or on the moon. You haven't talked about him once the whole time you've been home. It's even worse than Bridget and her wedding.'

Bridget froze in the doorway, almost dropping her armful of pots. Mamma raised five daughters. She saw everything.

'Nothing's going on.' Annie wiped at the saucepan she was washing up, but it was half-hearted, and we knew she knew that she was cornered.

'Maybe that's the problem!' Mum replied. 'Maybe you need to get a something going on again! Stop pretending you don't have a husband and start showing him that you care where he is and what he's doing.'

In the background, the doorbell rang. 'I'll get it!' Cooper said, ducking out of the room before anyone else beat him to it.

Annie blew out a sigh, dislodging a clump of bubbles from the dishwater. 'I'm trying, actually. I've messaged and called him multiple times in the past twenty-four hours and he hasn't replied. I even emailed him, and got an automatic reply saying he's out of the office. So, in answer to your earlier question, I don't know where the hell he is. My money is on him having finally run out of patience with me hiding out on the other side of the ocean and avoiding his calls. So, if you must know what's going on, I think the answer to that is that, most likely, my marriage is in ruins, because I won't give my husband the only thing he really wants, and, even worse, would rather run away than dare tell him that, leaving him wasting time when he could be moving on and finding someone else to have a baby with.

'So, it turns out all the haters were right all along!' Annie continued, laughing bitterly as she dumped the still-dirty pan onto the draining board. 'I'm a selfish cow. Because I'd rather live like this, stringing him along with my excuses, than face up to it and be honest. Because then I'd have to let him go, and the one thing I've realised since coming here is that I don't think I can bear to live without him.'

'Well, thank goodness!' Mum cried, pressing a tea towel to her chest. 'I thought you had gone off him like with that hamster you were so obsessed with and then decided, poof, you didn't want it any more.'

'Amen to that!' A gravelly East Coast drawl had all of us spinning around to face the kitchen doorway.

'Greg!' Annie gasped, as dollops of suds dripped off her fingers onto the kitchen tiles. 'What are you doing here?'

Greg, hands tucked in his pockets, raised one eyebrow, his eyes fixed on Annie. 'I'm here to find out what the heck is going on with my wife. And, once that's straight, to take her home. To be honest, I wasn't expecting to get an answer before I'd taken off my jacket.'

'Cooper!' Mum exclaimed. 'Why didn't you take Greg's lovely jacket and hang it up?'

'Why don't you take it, Mamma?' I suggested, trying to shoo everyone else out of the room. 'Let's give Greg and Annie a few minutes to themselves.'

'But then how will we know what's happening?' Mum frowned as we herded her towards the living room. Then she spotted Ben. 'Benjamin!' She attempted to whisper. 'Where's your camera? You can zoom in, use the fancy microphone and tell us what's happening.'

Sofia shoved Mum into the room and firmly shut the door behind us. 'Or, how about we let Annie and Greg tell us what's happening when they're ready?'

Mum stuck her hands on her hips, huffing as we settled ourselves down onto the sofas. 'It's my house, my kitchen. Maybe I want to go and ask my newly arrived guest if he wants a cup of coffee after his long journey. Or a slice of panna cotta. You daughters are forcing me to be a bad hostess, and a terrible mother-in-law, making Greg feel unwelcome in the family home!'

'Well, if it's any consolation, at least you got to see if he's looking malnourished. And he's clearly taken some time off work, so you can lay those fears to rest too.'

We sat in silence for a while, listening to the kids squealing and laughing through the window as they piled on top of Moses, Dad snoring faintly in the background.

'So she did run away,' Mum said eventually, staring at a spot on the carpet. 'Because of this baby thing. I tried to teach all you girls that we talk about our problems, no secrets, we work them out together. Antonia would always prefer to hide rather than admit she was wrong. But that Greg. I knew he was the right man for her, wouldn't put up with her nonsense. Now he's here, they'll work it out.' She looked up, her jaw set. 'They will. They'll work it out.'

When, a couple of minutes later, the front door slammed, we all jumped to our feet, expecting to find Annie crying or stomping about in the kitchen. Instead, a moment later the door to the living room opened and Greg shuffled in, his face a picture of hurt and confusion.

'She ran away.' He shrugged. 'Like, literally *ran* out the door. That was not how I thought this would go down. I had a gift for her and everything.' He pulled an envelope out of his jacket pocket. 'Tickets. I finally booked us both a proper holiday. I thought she'd be pleased.'

He looked up at us, shaking his head in bewilderment. 'Well. This is kind of embarrassing. I guess I'd better book myself a hotel.'

'Don't you dare!' Mum exclaimed, eyes blazing.

'What? But... my flight home's not until after the wedding. And I don't want to leave until I've spoken properly to Annie.'

'A son-in-law of mine, sleeping in a hotel? Emma! Go and put fresh sheets on Orla's bed. Orla and Sofia always had the best room.

It's got a view right across the meadow, full of spring flowers this time of year,' she faux-whispered at Greg. 'And Sofia, Bridget, did I raise you to let your own family stand there without a drink or some dinner after travelling halfway across the world?' She flapped her hands in disgust. 'And Gregory, don't worry about Antonia. She's going to be on that plane.'

Cooper spent the following week focussing on being a supportive husband. The pop-up tea shop had metamorphosed into a full-on event, and while on the one hand Emma was pleased that Gabriella had railroaded so many people into buying tickets, the increase in prep required smack in the middle of wedding season was clearly not the easiest timing. Add to that Bridget's wedding a couple of weeks later, and even Emma's organisational skills were buckling under the strain.

'It's not that I can't handle the logistics,' she explained, after arriving home from work past nine o'clock one evening. 'It's relying on everyone else to carry them out. In the right order. At the correct speed. And to the required standard.' She leant back on the sofa, gratefully accepting the mug of lavender tea he'd made her. 'I mean, how hard can it be to pick up the dresses on Tuesday afternoon? It's no good replying with, oh, sorry, got held up, I'll do it tomorrow instead. The shop is closed on Wednesday. And Wednesday we need to go to the wholesaler's to get the dry ingredients for the afternoon teas and bake a hundred macaroons. There's a clear system and this whole thing is going to topple like dominoes unless everyone follows it. *I'm* going to topple unless everyone follows it.'

Cooper went and fetched the reheated tacos from the kitchen. He didn't know what sides Emma liked, so he added a dollop of salsa, guacamole and slaw alongside the black bean filling.

'Oh, my goodness, I love you,' she sighed, taking the plate. He didn't ask whether she was talking about him or the meal.

'I booked next week off work.' He took a seat on the other side of the sofa, making sure he wasn't crowding her as she ate.

'Oh.' She looked across, holding her loaded taco in both hands. 'Was there a particular reason? I mean, did you have plans? Because I'm going to be even busier then.' She scrunched up her nose. 'I know we could really do with spending some proper time together, after Sam and everything. But with the wedding so soon, this month is going to be ridiculous. I promise things will settle down afterwards. I mean, we'll be busy the rest of the summer, but, well, I could probably take off a few days in July... I'm sorry. Am I a terrible wife?'

'I meant so I could come and help.'

'Oh!' Emma put the taco back on her plate and swivelled round to face him. 'You mean, help in the Cakery?'

'Or picking up the dresses.' Cooper nodded at Emma's wedding planning folder. 'Folding order-of-service cards. Hanging bunting for the pop-up. Whatever you need. Treat me as an all-round dogsbody.'

'Cooper. That's amazing. You really didn't need to do that.'

'Well, I have a meeting Monday morning, and should probably check in with a couple of students at some point during the week. Other than that, I'm all yours.'

'Thank you. That's... it's... I...'

Then, to his surprise and consternation, Emma burst into tears.

Cooper tried to ignore the instant rush of panic and think how a supportive husband would respond. He tried to imagine what Moses or Bear would do, but he was too disconcerted to think clearly, so decided to go on instinct and take hold of her hand. When that seemed to go down okay, he shuffled up closer and put his arm around her, grabbing a tissue from the box she'd left on the coffee table and handing it to her. He couldn't come up with anything to say apart from, 'It's okay,' and her gasping sobs indicated it wasn't at all okay, so he kept quiet.

'I'm sorry,' she said, eventually, words thick with tears. 'I'm so overwhelmed with everything right now, and so tired and there's still so much to do, and Mamma keeps texting me to say actually can we have quiches with the afternoon tea and remember that Uncle Kenny can't sit near cousin Keith at the reception because of a thirty-four-year-old feud about a missing bottle of Tizer and, I mean, why not? It's not like I've got anything else to do, being wedding organiser and chief bridesmaid! And then Paolo's grilling me about what Bridget would want in his vows, as if I should know better than him. Orla's asking if I can pick the kids up and Annie's wondering what I had in mind for the hen-do, as if I have any brain cells spare for something like that. Then you take a week off work. To be my dogsbody. And I think that's the nicest thing that anyone's done for me in ages.'

'You're welcome.'

Emma tucked her head into his neck, resting her hand on his chest, and Cooper breathed a sigh of relief that he'd got this right. Then, after a minute or so she moved her hand to his cheek, tilted her head up and kissed him gently on the lips. 'Thank you.'

He swallowed. She must have felt it, because she pulled back, dropping her hand to take his again.

'Look, while we're talking about stuff – although I know we weren't talking about *that* stuff – I wonder if, what with it being so busy, and my head being a frazzled mess, if we should agree to maybe put some... *things* to one side for now. I'm not sure now would be a good time to try taking our relationship to the next level. If you know what I mean.'

Cooper coughed sharply, instinctively straightening upright and away from her. 'Yes, I know what you mean,' he blurted. 'And that's fine. Of course. I wasn't even thinking that...'

'I mean, if it ends up, well, happening, at some point, that's great. I mean, I hope it'll be great, obviously. Oh! No. That came out wrong.' Emma's eyes widened with horror.

'Emma.' Maybe it was because booking the time off work had gone down so well, maybe they'd simply got beyond the point of faffing around the subject, but Cooper decided to step up. 'We've known each other less than a month. And for a lot of that time things have been, well, stressful for you. We've had a handful of dates. I'm not expecting anything, until we both know it's absolutely right. No pressure. No clock ticking. We've got a long time to get to that. The last thing we want to do is push things and then regret it later.' He cleared his throat again. 'I'm sure it'll be worth waiting for. But there are other priorities, like getting to know and trust and... love each other. That and making one hundred top-rate macaroons. So, no worrying about when or where or how it's going to happen, okay? Deal?'

Emma nodded. 'Deal.'

'You don't sound very sure.' He picked up their mugs, handing Emma hers.

She looked down for a moment before lifting her eyes to look straight at his, a smile beginning to curl at the edges of her mouth. 'Deal.'

They clinked mugs. 'Although keep on making speeches like that and it'll be happening sooner rather than later.'

Cooper choked on his coffee.

* * *

After spending the Monday afternoon before the pop-up picking up tablecloths and homemade bunting from a Mrs Milano and dropping them off at the farmhouse, Gabriella insisted he stay and have a coffee on the patio with Greg, who was apparently 'rattling around with nothing to do but stare at his phone and hope it starts ringing.'

'You should come and help Emma,' Cooper found himself saying. 'Come tomorrow.'

'Oh, now, Emma is perfectly capable of managing a few scones and cakes.' Gabriella tutted, unloading a tray of drinks and loaded bruschetta on the patio table. 'She runs a very successful business! Greg is a Senior Accounts Manager. He doesn't want to be stuck in Emma's kitchen being bossed about. I love my eldest daughter, but she is a baking bossy boots.'

Cooper raised his eyebrows at Greg, hoping that conveyed the other reason why he might want to be there.

'Actually, I like a bit of baking, Mrs D. Tell Emma I'll be there.'

Cooper shook his head, gently enough that Gabriella didn't spot it.

'Or not. I'm still a bit jet-lagged. Might need to check in with the office. I'll think about it, see how it goes. Best not tell anyone about it, so I don't end up letting them down.'

Cooper messaged Emma as soon as he got back in his car to tell her Greg would be at the Cakery the next day.

She replied a split second later.

Perfect!!

He couldn't help grinning as he drove away. Afternoons like this felt pretty damn close to it.

* * *

Emma

My Cakery kitchen had never been so crowded. I was loving it and hating it at the same time. Nita was in one corner icing lemon drizzle cakes with Eli, the fifteen-year-old who was staying with Sofia and Moses again. We didn't ask why. Neither did we ask why he was here, zesting lemons, rather than in school. He dropped his haunted expression and very nearly smiled when Annie asked Sofia if she was going to 'start beating those eggs, or just pray the power of love can whip them into shape.' So we figured being here was doing some good.

Sofia had raised her eyebrows at me when she walked in and saw Cooper grating cheese in one corner. Sister-speak for, 'So, things are going okay, then?'

I nodded, glad that Cooper had his back to us and couldn't see the heat flushing my cheeks. Ben was in Tuscany, Cooper was here rather than squirrelled away in a laboratory saving the world with Bridget and, for now at least, things were going okay.

I set Annie and Sofia mixing the quiche fillings. I didn't trust anyone but me to make the pastry, but Cooper was happy cutting miniature cases out of my pastry sheets, using scientific precision to create minimum wastage.

A few minutes before lunch, the door to the kitchen swung open and Greg walked in.

Annie froze, eggy batter dripping off her spoon onto my stainless-steel worktop. Her eyes swivelled to me, then back to Greg again.

'Anyone use a hand?' Greg asked, already rolling up his shirt sleeves as if senior account managers at top New York advertising firms made a habit of turning up in tiny kitchens in Nottingham to bake scones.

'Why are you here?' Annie asked, somehow managing to get the words out without moving her lips.

'Heard you were pretty busy.' He shrugged, nodding hello to the rest of us. 'All Donovan hands on deck.'

'I told you I'm not ready to talk yet.' Annie had subtly shifted her posture to that of a cornered animal.

Greg put his hands in his pockets, waiting in the doorway until Annie met his gaze. 'Are you ready for me to stand here quietly and do the dishes?' he asked, his voice soft, face grave.

'You hate doing dishes.'

'Honey, I'm staying at your mother's house. You know I love your parents, but there's only so many times a man can hear about Mrs Cumberland's wayward grandchildren and Gwendoline Jones's rip-off builder before any form of manual labour becomes an appealing alternative.'

Annie pursed her lips.

'She keeps telling me stories about what an amazing, perfect daughter you were growing up, and, no offence, but she's having to dig real deep to keep finding more of those, you know what I'm saying?'

'Fine.' Annie huffed and puffed, and if looks could kill she'd have slaughtered me right there on the vinyl floor, but it didn't take long before she picked up a tea towel and started drying the mountain of clean pots piling up on the draining rack.

The rest of us carried on drizzling and whipping and cutting out pastry circles, joking and chatting about nothing as if this were a perfectly normal way to spend a Tuesday and there weren't a marriage dangling by a thread right in front of us.

At three, when Annie had to pick Lottie and Oscar up from school, and Greg immediately offered to go with her, she shook her head tightly, marching out of the door and all the way to Orla's car before striding back in again a minute later. 'I'm busy tomorrow morning but will be here from two. Emma could probably do with the help again. If you're looking for something to do.'

'Okay. Great.' Greg was a man used to playing it cool. He nodded, smiled gently and waited for Annie to get in the car before he collapsed his head into his hands, his body leaning on the side of the sink for balance. 'My apologies,' he huffed in a breathless wheeze. 'That must have been really awkward, witnessing my critically ill marriage flailing about in front of you.'

'Urr, hello?' Nita rolled her eyes. 'Given that you're married to a Donovan, I would have thought you'd learnt by now that they aren't bothered about awkward. Or polite. They give the phrase "life out loud" a whole new meaning, if you get *my* meaning. I think you've probably earnt yourself a test-slice of raspberry-ripple cake.'

'I think we all have,' I added, fetching a knife off the rack.

Nearly everyone left soon after that, leaving Cooper and me to continue working until everything was ticked off the day's to-do list and tidied up, by which time it was gone seven.

'Your calendar is blanked out for nearly the whole of June,' Cooper said as I was locking up.

'Well, we have a wedding on the twenty-second and a fiftieth birthday cake for a few days later, but they were already booked in before Bridget's date was set. The cakes are in the freezer. Nita'll be able to ice them and drop them off.'

'You must have turned away a lot of business.' We began walking towards the bus stop.

'Well, I'm not going to have my sister pay someone else to make her wedding cake.'

'No. But I'm guessing the wholesaler sells mini quiches. And macaroons. And given that people are coming to donate to a good cause, they're not going to kick up a fuss or ask for a refund if it's not all Emma's Cakery standard.'

'Maybe not.' I did a brave thing, brushing my hand against his so that he quickly wrapped his fingers around mine as we strolled through the evening sunshine, the faint scent of cut grass mingling with the birdsong. 'But I'm not doing this for them. I can't help my dad get better or make his life any easier. I can't stop his muscle tremors or give him a decent night's sleep. I can't beaver away in a lab like you and Bridget, using my brilliant brain to find a cure, or even some sort of treatment. But I can pour some energy, along with my love, and my care, my heartbreak and my hope into magically combining flour and fat and sugar into something that looks and tastes beautiful. That makes people happy, and forget their troubles and their aches and their worries about the future as they sit and eat something so delicious they get lost in a moment of pure joy. That's what I can give him. When he sees everyone laughing and eating and filling up his farmyard with fun, he'll have a moment of joy, too. And that means more to me than earning money.' I swallowed back the tears now clogging up my throat. 'That's priceless.'

We reached the bus stop. Cooper let go of my hand and pulled me close, wrapping his arms around me as he pressed a kiss into my hair.

'Thank you for letting me help you with that.'

'You're welcome,' I sniffed back, aware that I'd probably ended up smearing snot on his T-shirt as I buried my head into his chest.

As we stood there, waiting for the bus, I took another step closer towards falling in love with my husband.

Friday was the kind of day Cooper had dreamed of when he wondered about marrying Emma. A dozen outdoor tables and ten times as many chairs had been delivered from a local event-hire company along with a giant bouncy-castle assault course. Emma and her sisters would be spending the day picking up drinks and other extras like jam and cream for the afternoon teas from the wholesaler. They'd then load up Emma's van with crockery, glasses and cutlery along with varying mismatched teapots and the giant coffee urn from Sofia's church, before finally fetching cake stands, more decorations and anything else they'd need from the Cakery.

In the meantime, that left Cooper, Greg and Moses to pop up the pop-up, using yet another one of Emma's lists to provide instructions.

Gabriella was busy in the farmhouse cleaning, because, 'you never know which of those sticky-beak women are going to be peeking and poking through my windows, making up excuses to mysteriously end up in my kitchen. "Oh, Gabriella, I was looking for a baby changing table and must have missed the clearly signed bathroom right inside the back door and somehow ended up in your bedroom instead!" That Mrs Windermere. I'm giving her not one single reason to be spreading gossip about my skirting boards this year.'

Even better, Paolo was manning Donovan's DIY, so that he could take the day off on Saturday. Not that Cooper had any reason to mind Paolo being there. It might have been a good thing, a chance to hang out together without Bridget complicating things. To show Paolo he had nothing to worry about, no reason to hold a grudge.

Instead, he had a whole day of scrubbing, sweeping, setting out chairs and standing on stepladders hanging bunting with men who had no issue with him, who seemed as if they might consider enjoying a couple of pints together to not be totally out of the question.

'How's it going?' Moses asked as they settled on a bench for a tea break while inspecting Emma's diagram to ensure the table layout matched it to the inch.

'Yeah. Not bad, thanks.'

'Not bad?' Moses winced. 'I'd be hoping for something a little more positive for someone, what, a month into their marriage.'

Cooper plucked a piece of grass off his jeans. 'No. Yeah, it's been... a big adjustment. Obviously. We're still early days. But this week's been good.'

'Sofia said you've been helping in the kitchen.'

Cooper nodded. 'Yeah, it was a change, weighing out flour instead of chemical compounds. Swapping a lab coat for an apron. I enjoyed it. Seeing a different side of Emma. I kind of get now why her sisters say she's bossy.' What was it about Moses that made him talk about this stuff? 'In a good way. Bossy as in like a boss. But watching how hard she's worked, bringing all this together – on top of spending most of her evenings sorting wedding prep at Bridget's – it's impressive.'

'Glad you've had a good week.'

Cooper thought about that. It had been better than good. Working all hours at the Cakery with whoever happened to be free to pitch in, starting to get to grips with the in-jokes and the ebb and flow between family members. Seeing Emma in her element had definitely been a good thing. He felt a wave of something – Guilt? Fear? Relief? – at the realisation that not seeing Bridget all week had been a good thing, too. Although, spending those evenings in alone, he couldn't help wondering if Emma had chosen to go to Bridget's on purpose, if she'd felt at all threatened by his friendship with her sister. Or whether she'd been missing her old life, and it was a relief to escape this new and uncertain life for a while.

Yes, lots of Emma and no Bridget, keeping busy and spending every day at the heart of the Donovan family, had made for a great week, when he thought about it.

What he tried not to dwell on was whether the decision not to take things more physical with Emma was one of the reasons things had been so much easier between them.

Should there be some sense of anticipation building?

He'd considered it, of course. Thought about what Emma would look like, how her skin would feel against his.

How it would be.

How it would be *afterwards*.

But he knew what it was like to long to touch a woman. Press his lips against her collarbone and breathe in the scent of her. To dream of a woman. To yearn for the freedom to unashamedly study every inch of her face and the shape of her neck and the flow of her curves and, yes, everywhere else. And not to have to conceal his love with a friendly smile or a throwaway comment. But to be able to pour all of it out, to show her with his gaze and his words that she was the reason for everything.

To be naked, and without shame.

But was that love, or obsession? A messed-up kid's infatuation?

Was he wrong to wish he could feel that longing for Emma? For his wife? Or should he be grateful for respect, admiration, the fondness that felt closer to love every day?

Was it a pointless, hopeless fantasy? The patina of lust that soon wore off with bill-paying and dishwasher-emptying and all the other million minute tasks that made up real life.

He was certain that he needed to find a way to be able to think about Emma without circling back to the time when he'd felt that for someone else.

Those feelings were nothing. A past illusion.

This, today, was real. This was what mattered. Belonging. Family. Being part of a bigger picture that wasn't all about him and what he wanted.

In the meantime, he had over a hundred chairs needing to fit a very precise diagram...

* * *

Emma

Friday night, I shuffled in well after midnight. I'd spent all evening with Nita, putting the finishing touches to the cakes for the next day, whipping cream and decanting jams into ramekins. The Cakery fridges were stacked with neatly labelled containers. When I'd left the farmhouse earlier in the evening it had looked fantastic, pretty bunting draped from every tree branch and rafter, pots with bushes in blossom and hanging baskets bursting with spring flowers filled the barn with colour. We'd borrowed every cushion from all of our respective houses, as well as the Cakery and church, and strewn them across the chairs and rugs at the far end of the barn. More cushions and picnic blankets waited to be set outside on the lawn in the morning. The signage was up ready. The menus were artfully scrawled across a chalk board. There were tables lining one side of the farmyard waiting to transform into a face-painting station, a craft stall and an information stand about ME.

Everything had been ticked off the list, which was the closest I got to perfect happiness.

That, and coming home to a bowl of chilli and a note from my husband tied to a bottle of gin with a tiny tick-list, the first few items ticked off, the last two still waiting:

Do an unbelievably amazing job getting everything ready
Complete every single item on all the other lists for today
Make everyone, especially your husband, proud of you
Have a drink, enjoy your dinner and relax
Stop worrying

Smiling despite the exhaustion seeping out from every bone, I took a generous G and T and the chilli into the living room, getting the fright of my life when a figure loomed in the shadows.

'What?' I stood there, hands full with the bowl and now half-empty glass, and looked down at the slop of gin now soaking my T-shirt. 'Why are you sitting here in the dark?'

Ben clicked on the only lamp in the room, which happened to be next to his chair. He squinted at me through the sudden glare. 'I was thinking. Hadn't noticed how dark it got.'

'You didn't *think* that lurking here might scare the life out of me?'

'I assumed you were in bed. I didn't hear you come in.' He stretched his arms above his head, his crumpled T-shirt rising up to reveal three inches of stomach. I ignored it. I'd seen a lot more of him once before, after all. 'Why didn't *you* put the light on? You're the one creeping about in the dark, when you think about it.'

'The kitchen light *is* on. And I'm the one who was going to put down her plate and glass before switching the light on in here, given that, as well as having only two hands, I'm tired and likely to be clumsy and didn't want to end up spilling gin on my top.'

Ben eyed my top in a way that sent heat prickling across my skin.

I briefly wondered how I'd have felt if Cooper had looked at my chest like that.

'Let's agree mutual culpability, then. Here.' He chucked over what looked like an old dust-rag, but turned out to be a T-shirt. It ended up draping over the glass.

'Is that for me to change into?'

Ben grinned that grin that somehow made every transgression instantly forgivable.

'To mop the wet patch.'

'I'll settle for getting changed. But thanks for being willing to donate a T-shirt to the cause.' I turned back towards the doorway.

'No worries, it's Cooper's.'

I turned back. 'What are you doing here anyway? Aren't you supposed to be in Mexico?'

'I was. Now I'm back. I'd been planning on hanging around a few more days, but the wedding depressed me so much I changed my mind, rebooked my flight.'

'Don't you find all weddings depressing?'

'I liked yours.'

I should have gone then. Instead I stood there in a sopping-wet top holding a bowl of congealing chilli and a half-empty glass. Waiting, I suppose, for Ben to say something that proved to me he wasn't worth standing around waiting for.

Eventually, he shrugged. 'I don't know. I'm finding them depressing for a whole lot of different reasons these days. This couple were early forties. They've already been living together for well over a decade. They were clued up, morally sound, intimidatingly intelligent. Had three kids with them and both sets of parents. And they were, I don't know.' He shook his head, as if baffled. 'Not just happy. I mean, they *were* happy, ridiculously so, but it was deeper than that. *Content*. Satisfied. Like they'd made this choice, eyes wide open. With their heads and hearts in full agreement, love and logic in perfect sync.' He pressed his hands together to illustrate the point. 'And they really *worked* together.'

'Don't you simply put that down to being a one-in-a-million fluke?'

He looked up at me, eyes black holes in the semi-darkness. 'I used to. But lately it seems as though those odds aren't working out any more.'

'Why on earth would that be depressing? It sounds like the wedding was wonderful.'

'Yeah. It was,' he replied, so softly I had to strain to hear. 'I guess I've been at too many wonderful weddings lately. If I'm honest, and I'm expecting this to remain in the same category of secret as me catching you spying on me in bed naked, I almost felt, sort of *envious*.' He sighed. 'Maybe not quite envious. But definitely veering towards the... wistful.'

'Wow.'

'Yeah. And that made me feel beyond depressed. So I came back to reality as fast as possible.'

'Where is my housemate Ben, what have you done with him and please can we have him back?'

He grinned again, but it twisted up in a way that didn't fool me for a second. 'Ah, I've got a couple more weddings booked in – the odds are that the old Bitter and Twisted Ben will be back soon enough.'

'Given that one of those weddings is my sister's, I should hope not!'

I hoped not. But if I was honest, I was starting to wonder about those odds.

What I really shouldn't have wondered about was what would have happened if Ben's revelation had been *before* asking me out at a wedding.

* * *

Cooper

'I'm so glad I married a scientist.' Emma jumped down from the van, walking to meet Cooper coming round the back from the passenger side. 'I couldn't have followed the plan more closely if I'd tried.'

She beamed at Cooper before opening the doors.

Cooper started unloading the boxes. 'These all going to the barn?'

'Yes. Ah, and here's our unwelcome shadow.' She squinted at Ben, strolling across from his car, camera in hand. 'Any chance you can help?'

'And miss documenting your fantastic teamwork?' He gazed at her steadily, a smile lingering at the corner of his mouth that made Cooper's jaw clench. 'In the interests of the project, that would have to be a "no". Right, Cooper?'

'Whatever.'

Emma shook her head, looking more amused than irritated as she picked up one of the larger boxes and marched off.

'Just making you look good, mate. You can thank me later with a pint.'

Cooper said nothing. Ben always brought out Emma's lighter side. He knew she relaxed with Ben in a way that she couldn't – yet – with him. He also knew Emma was committed to building something that went far deeper than surface interactions and he didn't have to worry about Ben. More importantly, he needed to act as though he weren't worried about Ben. Especially while he had a camera zooming in on every cantankerous expression.

In the end, however, the camera didn't bother him for long. By the time they'd unloaded the van, the rest of the family had arrived and for the next couple of hours they were so busy getting everything ready he barely saw Emma.

By five to eleven, the second Donovan Family Fundraiser was good to go. There was even a queue of a dozen or so people hovering on the other side of the makeshift ticket booth waiting to be let in.

'Righty-ho, then!' Gabriella called from the middle of the farm-yard, clapping her hands as though her bellow weren't enough to get everyone's attention. 'Everybody gather round, time to pray that God brings all the people here, and keeps all the rain away!' She put her hands on her hips, scanning the stalls and tables. 'Where's Emma, then? Cooper! Please fetch Emma, tell her the only thing left on her list is to open the doors so people can start giving us money.'

He held up a hand in acknowledgement, guessing that Emma had gone to take a few deep breaths somewhere. He passed Ben as he made his way towards the barn; his housemate nodded. 'She's in there.'

'Thanks.' He bit back yet another completely unreasonable stab of jealousy and carried on past him.

'Hey.' He entered the wide-open barn doors to find Emma standing at the far end, staring at the display table. He'd got used to seeing her in her work uniform over the past few days. She'd changed into a sundress at some point, navy blue with white spots and a wide red belt. It suited her. 'Your mum's summoned the prayer huddle.'

'Yeah, they messaged me. I don't appear the moment I'm called and they send out a search party. Sometimes it's exhausting being the responsible one.'

'Well, someone's got to hold it all together.'

She checked her watch. 'Two minutes to go.'

'Everything ticked off?' Cooper walked up to join her.

'It better be!' She let out a shaky sigh. 'Oh, stuff that. If it's not, what's the worst that can happen? We've got cake, and tea, and the sun's shining. What more do we need?'

'We've got a lot more than that.' Cooper smiled, coming to a stop a couple of paces away, knowing he wasn't the only one remembering the last time they had stood here together in the exact same spot.

Emma smiled back, ducking her head as a tinge of pink coloured her cheeks.

'You've done an incredible job, Mrs Donovan.' He stepped closer, taking her hand as he brought his face within a few inches of hers, near enough to make his intentions clear, while pausing long enough to allow her to respond either way.

'Please don't call me that. There's only one Mrs Donovan and I really don't want to be thinking about her right now.' She lifted her head, leaning in so he felt the breath of her words against his lips.

He couldn't help laughing. 'Me neither. Quick. Change the subject.'

'I'm all of a sudden finding it impossible to think about—'

Before she could finish the whispered sentence, he breached the now microscopic gap and gently pressed his lips to hers. Closing his eyes, he wrapped both arms around her, feeling her shoulders drop as she relaxed into the kiss. Seconds after it crossed over from gentle into something deeper, an exclamation burst out behind him, causing them both to spring apart.

'Oh!'

He spun around to see Bridget in the entrance, her face flushed.

'Everyone's waiting to start,' she said, before turning round and disappearing back out of the barn.

'We'd best go.' Emma wrinkled her nose. 'Goodness knows they can't possibly start without me.'

'I'm sure they'd manage without you for a couple more minutes.' Cooper didn't know why he said that. Bridget interrupting them had caused his stomach to concertina in on itself. It was probably best to let the moment pass.

'Yeah, but you and I both know your wife can't cope with not being there to make one final sweep to check everything and everyone's in place.' She released a mock shudder.

Cooper felt his stomach settle back down into a pool of warmth. Yes. He did know that. He was getting to know more about her every hour they spent together.

'To be continued, then?' he asked, in a moment of daring.

Emma smiled, taking his hand. 'To be continued.'

The next few hours passed in something of a blur. I spent most of the time in the barn, serving drinks and food, checking that Sofia and Orla were plating up the afternoon teas correctly, nudging them when tables needing clearing, sending them up to the farmhouse kitchen when we needed more milk or cream from the fridge there.

In the brief moments when there was a lull in the queue, I dashed outside to check whether everything else was running smoothly, winding my way past the stall where Annie was painting young faces and older nails. Paolo was supervising the giant inflatable, Eli and Harry assisting him in taking the money and making sure the children (and their parents) took turns. Moses had set up his kit beside the rugs on the lawn, and by the early afternoon some people had begun to dance, couples and toddlers bopping to his swing classics.

Ben had long since given up filming, and found a seat at what my father and the couple of his ME friends were calling the 'invalids' corner'. Every time he said this, Mum let out a tirade about ableism, and people's perceptions and how nobody asked them to go in the corner. Dad's friend Margo, who was well enough at the moment to have managed a brief dance, held her bottle aloft at that and shouted, 'Nobody puts Baby in the corner, isn't that right, Bear?' and they all burst into guffaws so loud that none of them could have heard Mum even if they'd been listening.

'They're having fun, no harm done.' I gently took her arm and began to lead her away. 'Dad's not had this good a spell in ages, let him enjoy his day.'

'It's plenty of harm, nearly two years of fighting to get this terrible illness taken seriously. The whole point of today is too many people trying to shovel those with chronic illness and other disabilities into the corner. Away where we can't see you, so it doesn't matter. Now they want to make their own corner, for real? And calling themselves *invalids*. Like a worthless ticket or out-of-date licence. They are not worthless! Bear is as valid as any man I know!' She swiped at a tear.

It was so rare to see my mamma cry, I resisted the urge to rush back to the barn and stopped to give her a hug. 'The main point of today is to raise money and awareness, while people have a brilliant afternoon. And look at all these people you managed to get here. Having fun, giving generously, because you've let them know how important this is. And because they all know that Bear Donovan only belongs in the corner when he chooses to sit there. Plus, the whole point of setting up the comfy chairs over in the shade was because some of his friends with ME can't cope with being in all the hustle and the noise. Let them enjoy their corner while they can.'

She sniffed. 'Okay, so I'm going to check that Sandra Bebbington is not trying to wangle a discount. She'd be expecting money off her own coffin.'

I watched her hurry off and then I headed back towards the barn. Bridget and Cooper were in the farmyard manning an information stall about ME alongside another member of the support group. I spotted Cooper talking to a couple I knew from the village. To my surprise, rather than joining in with the conversation, Bridget was standing behind the desk, fiddling about with the leaflets.

'Hey,' I said, smiling at Cooper as I wandered over. Bridget's fascination with the alignment of the different information sheets seemed extreme even for a postdoctoral scientist.

Once the couple had moved on, Cooper came over to give me a kiss. 'Hi.'

'Everything going okay?'

'Yeah, great. I can conclusively state that the awareness of ME has been raised to a statistically significant degree during the past two hours. By my calculations, by the end of the day we'll have raised awareness by ten point four to the power of awesome.'

'Excellent. I'm very impressed.' We smiled at each other.

'Do you want to get some lunch?' he asked, glancing back towards Bridget. 'You'll be all right on your own for a bit, won't you?'

Bridget didn't look too sure.

'Bridget, are you okay?' I asked her, stepping up to the stall so that she could reply without Cooper hearing.

'Yes!' She jerked her head back, as if startled by the utterly preposterous question. 'I'm fine! Having a lovely day. Talking to people about my research, and other science. It's, like, one of my favourite things to do!'

It would have been easier to believe her had she not directed her reply at a clump of grass about three feet to the right of me.

'Well, feel free to take a break whenever.'

'I will! Don't worry about me! I'm fine!' She shook her head at the clump, as if, honestly, there was any reason to think anything to the contrary.

I looked at Cooper. He shrugged.

'Right, well, I really need to get back. I promised not to leave Sofia and Orla for long. But we can grab a bite to eat together later?'

Cooper smiled. 'Later, then. It's a date.'

I left them to it, my concern about Bridget swiftly dispersing once I entered the barn and found a drama unfolding that no checklist, however long, detailed or perfectly colour-coded with stickers, could have foreseen.

Greg was standing in the middle of the barn, holding a bunch of flowers. Annie was behind the cake display, Orla and Sofia either side of her.

'Come on, now, honey. Please, you have to talk to me.'

'What, here?' Annie scanned the tables, packed with people who all seemed to have suddenly lost their appetite.

'I don't care where! But I can't stand this. I can't go another day fighting with you.' He stopped, wiping his face with his free hand as he spoke more slowly. 'I'm not interested in fighting you, Annie. Will you please tell me what's going on, what it is that you want?'

'Okay. Fine. How about I tell you what I don't want? I don't want to be another one of those mums at your little league games. The ones who throw themselves at you. Whipping up batches of homemade granola for the school bake sale. Spending their days hand-sewing Halloween costumes in between slagging each other off at committee meetings. I love my job, I'm proud of my business. I don't want to end up being the ex-beautician styling her boring, middle-aged friend's hair in the kitchen. Laughing about how I was once a cutting-edge therapist charging two-hundred dollars for the latest treatment and now I swap manicures for babysitting. I'm not ready for the rich housewife life. I don't think I ever will be.

'And I don't want my kids to be raised by a nanny, either. If I have a child, I want to be the one dropping them off at the school gate, turning up for the dance recital. To be around in the holidays, not packing them off to day care or band camp or whatever it is working parents do in New York.'

'So what about working part-time? Why not work half the week, close the shop the other half? It's not like we need the money.'

'The business will make a loss if I'm not open full-time. And that's not a business, it's a hobby. That's even worse than not working at all.'

Greg nodded. 'Okay, I understand.'

'Do you?' Annie snorted, tossing her hair, unshed tears glinting under the fairy lights. 'Do you understand that I might be ready at some point to become a mother? Living with Orla these past few weeks has shown me that I'm actually not that bad at it. I like snuggles and stories and I don't even hate wiping snotty noses.'

'I watched you face-painting those kids today. You were a natural.'

'Maybe so, but living with Orla's also shown me that it's unbelievably hard work. It takes everything you've got. Physically, emotionally, mentally. I'm not prepared to do that by myself. I won't be a single mum in practice, even if in theory we're parenting together.'

'Honey, if we have kids I'll do my bit. I'm not afraid to change a diaper or do the night feeds. I dream of doing all that.'

'How the hell are you supposed to do all that when you're in Baltimore, Singapore, Toronto, yet another late night at the office? Kids go to bed at, like, seven o'clock. They eat dinner at five. You'll be a weekend dad. That's not fair. On them, or me. And over the years I'll grow more and more resentful and angry and I'll learn to stop caring whether this time you'll make it to parents' evening or their birthday, because I can only take so many years of disappointment, and so can they. I'll learn to do it without you. To live without you. And I'm more terrified of that than anything else.'

'That's not going to happen! I won't do that to our kids!'

'Really? Then how come you keep doing it to me?'

Greg stepped back, his face ashen.

'My birthday? You cancelled last minute. I don't care if you made it up to me the weekend after. On the day I was sat in my new dress crying on the sofa alone.' She started counting it off on her fingers. 'Our anniversary, you were so late for our lunch we didn't have time for dessert. And the only reason we'd gone to Henry's was because we love the desserts. Christmas Eve, I'm left making awkward small talk with your brothers, trying to ignore the looks of pity. I can't do it any more, Greg. I'm so fricking lonely. I'm so blummin' homesick. I hate our life. How can you ask me to bring a child into our dysfunctional, practically non-existent family?'

'Why didn't you tell me how much this bothered you?'

'How couldn't you know?'

'You... you always seemed fine about it. You made other plans, saw your friends, enjoyed a night in to yourself...'

'I lied! I have no friends and when you spend every night by yourself, it starts to become less enjoyable.'

'Why would you lie?'

'Well, I'm not about to become one of those needy, demanding, overly dependent women, am I? Isn't that why you dumped Shania or Shauna or whatever her name was?'

'You are nothing like her!'

'Well, maybe I'm a lot more like her than you think!' Annie yelled, throwing her bunched-up napkin in Greg's direction, where it drifted to the ground about three feet short of him. She spun on her scarlet heels and started half running, half-skidding in and out of the tables towards the exit.

As she reached the barn doors, Greg called after her, 'Wait! Let's talk about this. I mean, go somewhere private and talk properly. We can work this out, Annie. Together.'

'How are we going to do that?' Annie replied, the words wrenching out of her, entangled in her sobs. 'You want kids. End of.'

'I'd rather have you.'

'Us not having kids won't make me any less lonely or miserable. And what if I do want kids? I just don't want them with you?'

'I'll give up my job.'

Annie spun slowly around. 'What?'

Greg had already pulled out his phone and begun typing frantically. 'There. I've written an email to resign. I'll take care of our kids while you build your business empire. No more lonely nights in waiting for me not to come home.'

'Are you crazy?'

'Crazy about you.' He took a few tentative steps forward, several people shifting their chairs out of the way to let him squeeze past. Until, encouraged by Annie's shocked expression, he increased his pace, walking right up to her. 'It's perfect.'

'How are we going to afford to live on my beauty-salon income?'

'Well, I happen to know an excellent business advisor. He can sweep floors and wash hair too, as it happens.'

Annie gaped at him. She reached forwards and grabbed his shirt. 'I can't believe you'd give up your job for me.'

'I'd do anything for you, honey. I'm sorry I failed to show you that.'

'Right. Well.' Annie took a good look around, still gripping onto Greg's jacket. No one even pretended not to be listening. 'Enjoy the rest of your day, everyone. My husband and I are off to practise getting me pregnant.'

And with that, she dragged him out of the entrance and off to I didn't want to know where.

* * *

A while later, Ginger, the woman who ran Hatherstone Hall where Bridget's wedding reception would take place, wandered into the barn.

'Today has been simply marvellous, Emma!' She handed me a wodge of cash in exchange for two cream teas. 'Keep the change. It's such a worthy cause, and we won't be buying tickets for the inflatable whatever-it-is, so we'll chip in here instead. Well done you, managing all this with Bridget's big day only a fortnight away. I would lure you away to come and work for me, if you weren't captain of your own tremendously successful business.'

'Thanks, Ginger. It was a team effort. I had loads of help from the rest of the family.'

'I'm sure you did! Oh, there's Sofia. Sofia!' Ginger waved brightly at Sofia weaving her way through the barn collecting dirty cups.

'Hi, Ginger.'

'Sofia, I spoke to that lovely registrar, Lisa Chan. She said she's booked in for Bridget and Paolo?'

Sofia paused, causing the cups to rattle precariously on the tray. 'Great! Brilliant! I'll catch you later, Ginger, just taking these up to the house to get washed.'

Sofia rushed out of the barn, Ginger carrying her own tray much more slowly behind her. I frowned, puzzled. I had a feeling there was something about that conversation that should have bothered me, and Sofia's quick exit only heightened my suspicions. But before my overloaded brain could process what that might be, Orla poked her head round the barn door.

'Em! Speech time. Get yourself out here.'

'Right.' I secured the takings, made sure the remaining food was all safely covered and got myself out there, through the crowd and over to the lawn where Mamma had commandeered Moses' microphone, her cerise sundress bright against the bushes behind her.

'Ladies, gentlemen, Annabel Finch and everybody else, I thank you with all my heart for coming along to this important event.'

'Like we had any choice!' someone snarked from the crowd. I couldn't see for sure, but it sounded like Annabel Finch.

'As most of you will now know, ME is a hidden disease. Stealing the purpose and the independence of a quarter of a million people in the UK alone. There is no cure and next to no treatment. Mainly because for too long too many of these fancy boffin doctors found it more convenient to believe it didn't even exist, apart from in the minds of all these weak, lazy, paranoid, hypochondriac people who pretend to be ill so they get to lie in the dark all day alone while the rest of the world carries on without them—'

'You had some more people to thank, Mamma?' Orla interjected from her spot at the front, no doubt positioned there precisely in order to keep things moving.

'Yes! Yes, I have so many people to thank.'

The crowd shifted with a collective mutter.

'I won't be long!' Mamma huffed. 'Please show your appreciation for Emma and Nita, from Emma's Cakery, for all the lovely food. Delicious celebration cakes, and they can even do food for if you want vegan or this or that free or whatever else people fuss about these days. It actually tastes not bad, too!

'Also, the rest of my wonderful family, who all helped. You know who they are, I don't need to go on about it.

'But, finally, I must say my biggest thank you to two most important and special people. Two people who give me hope and fill my heart. Their big, fat, brainy brains could do anything, but instead, they decided to work for a nasty little man who pays them peanuts so they can work, every day and lots of nights too, searching, searching to try to find something to beat this disease. Ladies and gentlemen, please extend a very big, Hatherstone appreciation for my daughter, Dr Bridget Donovan, and her wonderful assistant Dr

Cooper. Dr Donovan and Dr Cooper! Up you come! Quickly now, everybody is getting tired and ready to go home.'

No Bridget or Cooper.

'Oh, well now, where have they got to? Probably off somewhere discussing something very important and scientifical. Emma, Paolo, perhaps you can find them for us?'

The crowd grew increasingly restless.

'Moses, perhaps you could sing us another song while we are waiting?'

I scuttled off, wondering where they were most likely to be. Hurrying across the lawn and around the side of the farmhouse, I found them standing in front of the back door a few metres away. Before I had a chance to get any closer, my subconscious registered their body language and I drew to a sharp stop, before retreating swiftly to stand in the shadow of a pine tree.

'What's wrong?' I could barely hear Cooper's words over the roaring of my blood as it galloped frantically through my veins. 'You've barely looked at or spoken to me all day. Have I upset you?'

Bridget shook her head. 'It's nothing, honestly.'

'I know you. I know when something's wrong.'

'I'm probably just stressed and tired.'

Cooper cleared his throat. 'And that means you can't even look at me? Will you please tell me what I've done?'

Bridget pressed her hands to her face. 'Nothing. You've done nothing. Please stop asking.'

'Bridget.' Cooper tentatively reached forwards and tucked a strand of stray hair back behind her ear. A gesture I'd done myself a million times before over the past twenty-five years. He looked as though he'd been waiting at least twice that long to do it.

'If it's not me, then will you talk to someone else about why you're so upset?'

'I'm not upset!' She dropped her hands, the lock of hair falling straight back down again. Her shoulders shaking as she sobbed, in defiance of her words. 'You have to stop asking me. Stop talking to me. It's nothing. I'm fine. And you can't say anything to anyone else about it, either.'

Then my sister looked up at my husband, and behind the raw anguish, the fear and distress, I saw something that turned my blood cold.

Her face... melted.

Melted into an expression of complete and utter love.

I'd never seen her look that way at Paolo.

My heart just about stuttered to a stop then and there.

As I continued watching, frozen in some moment of hideous clarity, a thousand pieces from a seven-year-old jigsaw suddenly tumbled into place.

Not waiting to see any more, I stumbled back around the side of the house and started running.

I knew Bridget and Cooper loved each other. Of course they did. They'd always loved each other. Bridget loved practically everyone, and Cooper hadn't had anyone else to love back for so long.

But then, rewind back to the point about how my sister never looked at Paolo like that.

Because she loved Paolo differently? *Not* as a friend?

Because Paolo wasn't an orphan who got abused by his father and then neglected by his unfeeling aunt until ejected into the big wide world to fend for himself at eighteen?

Was it a pity look?

A friendly, caring hair tuck?

I paused to wrench open the farmhouse front door, replaying their faces in my mind once more.

Nope. That was not a friendly exchange.

I'd been to a lot of weddings in my time, and that was the look a bride gives her groom once she meets him at the top of the aisle.

Of course it was.

Of course Bridget loved Cooper.

Was *in love with* Cooper.

And of course he was in love with her back.

How could I not have seen it?

She didn't tell any of us that he was working at the lab until she had to.

She took Cooper with her to try on her wedding dress!

Did she think that by us getting married, she'd stop loving him, move on, live happily ever after with Paolo?

More to the point, *why the hell did Cooper say yes*?

I was so angry, so distraught, that I couldn't even think about it. Or care about the whys.

Dad, having lasted far longer in the invalids' corner than was probably wise, was now in bed.

He must have heard me thundering up the stairs, because he was already pulling himself to a sitting position by the time I burst through his bedroom door.

'Emma, what is it? What's happened?' He grappled to pull himself further upright.

'Nothing. Nothing, Daddy.' I held out my hand to stop him, knowing at this point that even a small action like getting out of bed could cost him dearly. 'I wanted to come and sit with you for a little bit, if that's all right?'

'Aye. Of course.' He manoeuvred himself on the pillows so that I could climb onto the bed beside him, resting my head on his chest. 'You sure you're all right?'

'Yes. I'm fine, honestly.'

My tears told another story as I lay, cradled in my father's arms, and wept.

After the crowd had dispersed, and most of the guests began making their way home, Cooper found Ben sitting in the cluster of chairs Emma had arranged off to one side for her dad and a couple of his friends. The otherwise empty chairs were now occupied by Sam, and Sam's foot, his leg still held straight by a heavy-duty brace, along with Moses and Paolo.

Paolo picked a bottle of beer out of a cool box and held it out. Cooper hesitated for only a second before accepting it, a wary glance suggesting that Paolo knew nothing about what had happened earlier.

Not that anything had happened.

Not really.

Only it had felt like something.

Cooper knew Bridget. He knew her happy, sad, stressed, excited. He could read her body language, interpret her moods and pick up on her hints. He hadn't known what to make of the woman he'd just spent the day with.

She'd been polite. Pleasant. Distant. Distracted. There was definitely something going on, and he knew it involved him.

But then the way that she'd looked at him when not long ago any kind of look at all had the power to send his head spinning, that look had been... too much. It had knocked him off-balance. Awoken old memories, old feelings, that really, really, needed to remain asleep. Or, preferably, to die once and for all.

Bridget had looked at him like, well, like he used to want to look at her.

And now he couldn't look her fiancé in the eye.

Crap.

He needed to stop kidding himself that the Bridget issue would simply fizzle away the longer he was with Emma.

He probably needed to find another job, for starters.

For now, he had to start acting remotely normal so that Ben stopped eyeing him suspiciously and he could join in with the conversation.

'Things are all sweet now with you and Orla?' Paolo was asking Sam.

Sam shrugged. 'Not sure you can move past something like that overnight, but we're getting there.'

'And you never said anything to that Jim bloke?'

'Nah. Can't see how that would help. Other than giving Orla another reason to be angry with me, and feel sympathy for him. She's left the gym, cut off all contact. He was a side-effect. We're working on the root of the problem.'

'Man, not sure I could be so forgiving if it was some guy and Bridget.' Paolo shook his head. He glanced at Cooper, flicking his eyebrows in a way that made Cooper nearly choke on his beer.

'Don't get me wrong. If I hear he's tried to get in touch with her, I'll be paying him a visit.' Sam grimaced, shifting his injured leg between the chairs. 'Or I'll send some people who can walk there unaided to do it for me.' He took another sip of his drink. 'But what happened is best left in the past. There's no undoing our mistakes.

We can only learn from them, keep loving each other and keep moving forwards, make sure our family ends up stronger because of it.'

'Wow.' Ben sat back in his chair. 'I mean, I don't know all the facts here, but how do you move forwards from your wife messing about with another man and end up stronger, rather than a total wreck?'

The other men looked at him, as if trying to place who he was and why he was even part of this conversation.

'I'm serious. I genuinely want to know. Because I've seen a lot of mistakes made in a lot of marriages, and I've never seen how anyone comes back from them with anything more than pain and bitterness. If you genuinely know how to work past that, without empty platitudes and twisted acts of revenge and a secret drinking problem, I might reconsider my sworn commitment to avoid all commitment.'

Sam looked at Paolo and Moses, as if they had the answers. He blew out a sigh. 'Probably best to ask me that in another eleven years. I might have an answer by then. All I know is I love her, she's it for me. I didn't marry her on the condition she was perfect. So we'd better figure out a way to be happy, or else it's going to be a long, miserable life.'

'It does help when some of the finest women to walk this earth decided for some unfathomable reason to pick us.' Moses grinned. 'As long as we keep remembering that, and remembering to show them that we haven't forgotten it, it's all good.' He thought for a moment. 'Well, mostly good.'

'Cheers for the advice.' Ben held his bottle up in a toast, and the other men joined him. 'I'll bear it in mind. If I ever find a woman to match the Donovan sisters.'

'Maybe you should try the Compatibility Project?' Paolo smirked. 'Send Bridget your details.'

'Uh oh.' Moses sat up straighter, putting his drink on the table and shoving it over to look as if Sam had been drinking it. 'I think this is one of the exceptions to the mostly good.'

Sofia was striding over, pushing a double buggy, her face a blank mask that seemed somehow more disquieting than if she'd been scowling.

'Darling.' Moses smiled, doing a sterling effort at hiding the tremor in his voice.

'Moses.' Sofia stuck one hand on her hip. 'Jen informs me that we're looking after the twins for the weekend.'

'Uh, yes?'

'Why?'

'Well.' Moses glanced around at the other men, shuffling his chair closer to Sofia. 'I thought it would be good practice. Well. Not a *practice* as such. A good... test? Trial?'

'You have borrowed someone's babies as a trial.'

'I just wanted, you know, to see how it would be, to look after someone else's children. See where we needed to get things ready, how it would work with little ones in the flat.'

'Moses, you have to stop this.'

Moses' face dropped. 'I thought we agreed to fostering? It was your idea.'

'We agreed to investigate the possibility of fostering. Not to start trialling it out with random kids.'

'I thought it would help. Give us something to feel hopeful about again. Help us move on from the grief.'

'Moses, I love you, but honestly I don't know how you can be so wise and so stupid at the same time.'

'Okay. I'm sorry. I'll call Jen.'

Sofia took hold of the pushchair. 'No, you won't. She's already booked a spa day. But we need to talk about this. Properly.' She nodded at Moses' drink, now sitting in front of Sam. 'Finish your beer and then I'll meet you by the car.' She swivelled the pushchair around and started marching away.

'I'll talk to Eli's dad, see if he's ready to allow him home again,' Moses called after her.

Sofia twisted her head over one shoulder, still walking. 'Don't you dare. That boy has a home under my roof for as long as he needs it.'

* * *

Orla arrived not long after that to help Sam back to the car, the younger children proudly displaying their tiger and unicorn faces, Harry eagerly telling his dad about how he'd helped man the inflatable.

'Do you know where the others are?' Paolo asked Cooper, almost managing to sound as if he wasn't bothered about him having spent the day with Bridget.

'Probably clearing up.' Cooper stood to leave. 'I'll see if anyone needs a hand.'

But Cooper found neither Bridget nor Emma in the barn, by the van, in the house. And when Annie emerged, looking flushed and dishevelled, from an upstairs bedroom, she'd not seen them either.

He got out his phone, automatically clicking through to Bridget's number before he checked himself, instead hurriedly calling Emma.

No answer.

Five minutes later, she sent him a message:

I'm at the Cakery. Sorry, when loaded the van couldn't spot you anywhere. Loads to sort, please don't wait up x

He didn't wait up, although he meant to stay awake so he could see her when she got home.

Only by the time the clock read three, she still hadn't arrived.

The next thing he knew after that, it was after seven, and the other side of the bed still lay empty.

* * *

Emma

I spent the night curled up in a Cakery armchair. Well. In the armchair, pacing the floor, opening and shutting the fridge door in a vain search for comfort food.

Once it was six o'clock, I gave up on pretending to sleep, freshening up as best I could using a sink and paper towels, then changing into a clean chef outfit without thinking too hard about wearing the same underwear two days running. After confirming that wire icing-nozzle brushes make a poor toothbrush substitute, I stuck on the coffee machine and collapsed into a chair.

Thank goodness it was Sunday so the shop was closed. If Nita spied me here, I'd tell her I wanted to get some admin done. Either that, or I was hiding from my husband, having just discovered that he was in love with my sister.

Cooper messaged me at seven:

Are you ok???

I thought of a dozen different responses, including turning my phone off and sticking it in one of the ovens, but if I wanted time and space to get my head straight I needed to put him off coming to look for me.

Yes, so sorry – ended up dozing off in the armchair!

He replied a couple of seconds later:

Ah yes. From what I remember it's a perfect chair for napping. Coming home soon?

My fingers trembled as I typed out a reply:

Nita's invited me in for breakfast. See you at church?

A much longer pause, that time:

Might give it a miss this week. Need to get back in gear for work tomorrow.

We signed off with brief pleasantries, and I embraced a wave of relief that I had a few more hours to think.

By think, I of course mean obsessively go over every interaction I'd had with Bridget about Cooper, or Cooper about Bridget, or both of them together, and then go over them all again while comparing them to every interaction between Cooper and me.

I went online and scrolled through the photos Ben had taken at our wedding, and in the weeks since, hunting for clues. But in the limited number of pictures containing both of them, the vast majority of which also included me, along with various other members of the family, I couldn't find any.

Surely if it had been that obvious, one of my sisters – I mean, the loyal, morally upright sisters who loved me and had my best interests at heart – would have said something.

I stared at my phone, tears plopping into my coffee cup, heart feeling as though it were cracking in two.

Another message. To the SisterApp, this time. From Bridget:

Hey. I won't be at church or lunch today. Short version is that me and P split up last night. I'll share the long version when I'm ready. Please don't tell Mamma yet, I've told her it's my stomach again. I love you.

I put down my mug, bending over double as my conversation with Bridget the day before surged back into my head.

Once I'd stopped crying in Dad's bedroom, I'd found her in the kitchen washing up, asking if she'd come into the study so we could avoid interruptions.

'We need to talk about you and Cooper.' I stood, leaning against Dad's desk.

'What?' Bridget's face capsized in on itself. Her hands gripped together so tightly her knuckles cracked.

'Let me rephrase that.' I took a deep breath. '*You* need to talk about it. Now.'

'I can't talk about it! That's one of the worst parts. Well. Not the worst, but still totally horrible. If I say anything to you, I'll lose you. So it's this massive secret slithering inside my head like a python, squeezing my brain so hard I can't think straight, and I can't even look at you any more. Or talk to you about anything else. There's nothing to talk about anyway. Outside of what's in my head.'

I shook my head, disgusted. 'It's too late for that. Your face said enough. So here's my first question: how long have you been in love with my husband?'

Bridget's chin dropped to the floor. She closed her eyes. 'How long have I loved him, or how long have I realised that I do?'

I didn't reply. I wasn't the one needing to expand here. She opened her eyes again, her gaze flitting everywhere but at me. 'I guess I've always loved him. I just didn't realise in what way.'

'Did you know when we got married?'

'No!' She finally looked at me, her face aghast enough for me to believe her. 'No. Of course not! If I'm honest I only really knew when I saw you this morning.'

I flipped my mind back a few hours. 'When you saw us kissing?'

She nodded, the tears flowing freely now. 'I know. I know it's hideous. *I'm* hideous. I hate myself. If I could undo all of it, any of it, I would.'

'Which bits?' My voice cracked, with rage, resentment, desolation. 'Would you undo me signing up to the compatibility project? You choosing to plough on, regardless, even when you match me to the man you've been in love with forever? Promising me he's *perfect* and will make the *best husband*? Marrying me off to him, and somehow deluding yourself that it'll all work out in the end? That I'll never notice? That HE will never notice? How did you think this could end up any way other than a total, ugly, twisted mess? As if it wasn't bad enough having the love of my life leave me for that bitch Helen Richards, now my own sister wants my husband! WHAT THE HELL WERE YOU THINKING? I *TRUSTED* YOU!' Bridget wasn't the only one crying, now. 'I *trusted* you. With the most important decision of my life.'

She reached out one hand, face stricken. I shrugged it off and shook my head, fiercely. This wasn't going to be smoothed over with a sorry and a sisterly hug.

'I'm so, so, sorry. You have to know how sorry I am. I don't *want* to feel like this! I didn't even know that I did!'

'You didn't think to stop and make damn sure before you paired us off?'

She said nothing, pressing her hands up against her face to contain her sobs. I'd never once seen my baby sister upset and not provided comfort. I knew I could be the bigger woman here, offer a thread of hope that I would try to one day understand. Sisters before mister.

Screw that.

'You can undo one part of this. There's still time to do the right thing by one person, at least.' I wiped the tears from my face, the pain solidifying into cold, hard anger. Bridget stilled from behind her hands, listening. 'You need to call off the wedding.'

Her hands fell away, mouth dropping open. 'No, Emma, no. I couldn't do that to him. Not two weeks before... you of all people know what that would do to him...'

'It'll crush him. But I can promise that discovering your fiancé is in love with someone else hurts a hell of a lot less than discovering your husband or wife is. If you care at all about me, or Paolo, then you need to tell him. Tomorrow. Tonight! I don't care how hard it is or how much courage it takes. Time to finally grow up, Young One.'

'Okay! I'll talk to him. I know I have to break it off. But you can't tell Cooper, Emma. He's done nothing wrong. Please don't tell him. It'd only make everything worse.'

'Don't you dare try to tell me what I can say to my husband. And really, you think that there's any way that this could be worse?'

With that, I turned and walked away, leaving my heart a splattered mess on the yard behind me, a gaping, agonising wound where it had used to be.

* * *

I didn't know what felt worse or whose betrayal hurt more. I still hadn't concrete confirmation from Cooper about how he felt, or what he wanted to do. While he could potentially brush off a simple gesture as meaningless, having seen it, I knew what it meant. The thought of how he might react, what he would feel when he found out Bridget had ended things with Paolo, made me want to throw up. Had she told him already?

Was Cooper and Bridget both missing church just a coincidence?

Were they together, now? Packing a bag? Tucking each other's hair behind their ears?

The messages of encouragement and sympathy started pinging through to the app. If I read any more of Annie and Bridget arguing about whether Annie was coming round or Bridget was fine by herself for now, thanks, I would definitely vomit.

I was about to turn my phone off when Sofia messaged me separately:

Hey, are you ok? Or are you with B?

While I was thinking how to reply, she followed it up:

Or is there another reason you haven't replied to her message? If you need to talk I'm free from 4

I blinked back a fresh rush of tears.

Thanks Sis. I'll see you then xx

By some sort of miracle, I made it through church, and on to Sunday lunch. One small consolation being that my parents didn't know, so we couldn't talk about it. Mum's consternation that Cooper was working, the same day that Bridget and Paolo were AWOL and Dad was too fatigued to join us, was thankfully balanced out by Greg and Annie's rays of loved-up happiness and Sam's presence at the table.

Sofia and Moses gave me a lift straight to their flat.

'Here.' Sofia handed me one of the babies. 'You look like you could do with a no-strings cuddle.'

I pressed my cheek against his soft, sweet, baby head and wept.

Once the twins had left, and Moses taken Eli out for a bike ride, Sofia fetched drinks and soy ice cream.

'So, what's going on? I've been trying to guess what could have happened between you and Bridget that was so big you aren't with her the day after she broke up with Paolo.' She pulled a wry face. 'And that sort of led me to an inevitable conclusion.'

'She's in love with Cooper.' I put my bowl of ice cream down. I hadn't been able to squeeze anything past the ache in my throat all day.

'Oh, Emma. I'm so sorry.'

I briefly filled her in on what had happened.

'So you've not spoken to him?'

'I can't face it. I don't know what to say.' I pressed my hands against my face, as if that would lessen the pain. 'We're married. We made vows. And if you and Annie and Orla can work through your problems, then I have to at least try. But it hurts so much, Sofia. I really thought that I'd finally found the answer... that this time I might be enough... and now here I am. Second choice again, only this time facing begging a man to stay with me when he really wants to be with my *sister*. If he leaves me for her, I don't think I can bear the humiliation. I'll have to go back to Ireland for good.' I got up, unable to remain still as my pain twisted back into anger. 'Leave my business behind. I mean, can you imagine it, the three of us at Sunday lunch? Sat on the same row at church? And I'm sorry, but I won't be video calling to join you for Wednesday Wine! And what if they end up getting married? I mean, how could they not? Am I supposed to go to the wedding? Forgive and forget? She's not only ruined my life, she'll have destroyed our whole family!'

Sofia handed me a tissue. 'That's if she ever says anything. No one needs to know how she feels about Cooper. And you don't know yet how he feels about her. Remember, he chose you.'

'This is Bridget we're talking about! It'll be completely obvious.'

I did another lap of the living room.

'I don't know if I want him to go, so I can crawl under a table and cry by myself for the next few years, then pack up and move on to my life as a divorcee, or for him to choose me.' I sucked in a deep breath. 'I know it will break her heart, but I can't help wanting him to choose me. For all the wrong reasons. Not because I love him more than her. I know that I don't. I barely love him at all. I just don't think I can stand it if someone else doesn't choose me. And besides, we're *married*. That means something.' I came to a standstill beside her fireplace. 'If he wants to stay married, do I have to stay with him? I mean, Orla and Sam did, and Bridget and Cooper haven't even done anything. Only felt it. If he admits that he loves her, but wants to keep working on things with me, what then? How can we make that work? We'll probably have to move away. And then I give up my business for a man I hardly know, who has already broken my heart in the first five weeks of marriage, who might one day decide he's changed his mind and wants Bridget instead. Leaving me with nothing. What am I supposed to do? Marriage is *sacred*. I meant what I promised.'

Sofia took a moment to answer. 'You need to talk to him. Find out what he wants at least, as difficult as that might be to hear – it's always better to know than deal with speculation and what ifs.' It was her turn to take a deep breath then, looking up at me from under her fringe as she prepared to speak again. 'But before you do, I need to tell you something.'

'Bloody hell, Sofia. Did you know?'

'No! Not that! You know I'd have told you. Or insisted they did. But if you're making a decision about whether to stay together based on the fact that you're married. Well. That isn't exactly—'

'The registrar!' I didn't know why this was the one clear, rational thought I'd had all day, but there it was, like a revelation bursting through the fog of despair. 'Ginger said that Bridget and Paolo had booked a registrar. But Moses is going to marry them.' I followed that thread to its conclusion. 'Moses isn't a licensed registrar, is he? Which means I'm not legally married! That whole trip to the church to sign the certificate was a big charade. What the hell, Sofia? Were you ever going to tell me or were you going to let me think I was married for as long as we both shall live?'

'I was going to tell you! It was just in case things didn't work out.'

'Well, thanks for the vote of confidence!'

'We thought that if you were still together then we'd own up on your first anniversary, throw a proper big party with all the family and you could renew your vows, only making it legal this time. You were marrying a stranger, Emma. There's a fine line between confidence and having a sensible backup plan.'

'Who else knew?'

'I told Dad and Mamma.'

'And Annie, too?'

'We haven't spoken about it.'

'So I'm not legally married. And everyone knew except me. Oh, my goodness! *Does Cooper know?*'

Sofia shook her head. 'I don't think he'd realise the difference between Moses and a bog-standard vicar.'

'Bridget?'

Sofia shrugged. 'I honestly don't know.'

I didn't know what to make of this. I might be angry with Sofia and Moses when I thought about it properly, but, honestly, when they'd been so blatantly proven right I could hardly be that annoyed. But more importantly, what did it mean for me and Cooper? Would I have stayed with him this long, had I known? If he knew, would that be all the push he needed to end this absurd experiment?

If Cooper told me that he'd fallen for me, that he only saw Bridget as a friend, that he would leave the university and limit all contact with Bridget to minimal family occasions, would I be pleased with that outcome?

Or, as I'd shared with Sofia only weeks before, was there a part of me that knew I'd never love Cooper as a wife should, and that despite the heartbreak and the humiliation, and my utter devastation at the damage it had done to my relationship with Bridget, that not-so-tiny part of me was actually relieved?

I collapsed back onto the sofa, suddenly ready to scarf a bowl of melted ice cream. As I shovelled in a spoonful, a realisation slowly dawned.

'But I made those vows, and I meant them.'

'Can you remember what you said?' Sofia asked.

'No, actually.'

'You remember Moses and I rewrote them, so you didn't have to promise something that wasn't true.'

I did remember.

'Well, we kind of rewrote them so you didn't have to promise anything that would mean your marriage was binding forever, either. There was no "as long as we both shall live". "I promise to support you, to accept you as you are and be honest and open with you. I commit to making the most of what our future may bring, as we move forwards together. I will treat you with the respect, compassion and kindness you deserve for taking this chance with me. Blah, blah, blah." I can't remember the rest, but you get the drift.'

'Wow. I'm not married. I didn't even promise to stay married.' I looked at my sister. 'So, what do I do?'

'I think you know. But first, go home and talk to Cooper.'

'Are you going to talk to Bridget?' I stood up, glancing around for my jacket and bag.

Sofia winced at me. 'I think you know the answer to that, too.'

'I'm sorry you're going to end up caught in the middle of this. I guess everyone is.' My voice cracked at the thought of it.

'It's not your fault, Old One.'

'Well, considering I'm the one stupid enough to marry someone I'd barely met, I think it probably is.'

Cooper couldn't remember the last time he'd felt this stressed. This was worse than when he'd whistle-blown on his research partner and been forced to resign. Worse than deciding to marry Emma. Worse than the day his aunt Louisa left. Because all those things, although nerve-wracking and at times panic-riddled, they'd at least held some hope. The reassurance that came with doing the right thing.

This was... just vile in comparison.

He'd spent the day trawling for jobs. Starting local, then moving outwards as his search became increasingly bleak. Initially focussing on employment that he was qualified for, interested in and that matched his current salary, he soon progressed to scrolling through the kind of work he used to do before he graduated.

Disgusted with himself, he slapped the laptop shut and closed his eyes, flopping against the back of the sofa. How was he to explain to Emma that he was leaving his new and promising role in his chosen field to work on a factory line for minimum wage, or in a bar?

He'd be better off asking her to hire him as a kitchen hand.

But would a job change be enough? Did they need to move away, to restrict contact with Bridget to special occasions and video chats?

He'd cut off all contact with her for four years, and that hadn't sorted it. If he was being honest, and perhaps it was time to be, if anything it had made his feelings for her even stronger.

How could he explain to Emma that they needed to move away from her thriving business, her family and her friends, for him to take on a worse job, doing something he hated?

Even if he could convince her that he'd developed a sudden passion to live in Newcastle and work in a call centre, without the Cakery income how could they afford to live there?

It was a complete and utter mess.

Cooper had spent a lot of years hating himself. Had been told enough times that he was nothing, a waste of space.

After that one day, where nothing had happened and yet everything had changed, he finally accepted it was true, and would always be true.

And the least he could do now was the one last decent option open to him. To face the shame and the hurt he would cause, own up and take the consequences, whatever they might be.

Around five, Emma came home. He purposely hid in the bedroom when she arrived, trying to haul his shambles of a self together.

A few minutes later, Ben knocked on his door. 'Hey, are you decent? It's interview time.'

Just what he needed, a camera in his face.

'Does it have to be now? I'm working,' he croaked back.

'Wife's orders.'

'What?' Dread skittered up Cooper's spine. What possible reason would Emma have for wanting to do an interview? She hated them. Unless... had Bridget said something? Had one of the others guessed? Emma hadn't come home last night.

Cooper swallowed back the bile rising in his throat, tried to assume an appropriate expression and, for the first time in a long time, muttered a heartfelt prayer. Not for himself. He knew he deserved everything he got. But if there was any way that in all of this Emma could get spared some pain...

'Hi.' She was sitting on one side of the sofa, a mug of tea in her hand. If he hadn't already been suspicious, one glance at her brittle expression, the shadows underneath bloodshot eyes and the tense set to her shoulders confirmed this wasn't good.

Cooper sat next to her, offering a weak smile that did nothing to ease the strained atmosphere.

'Right. Ready?' Ben asked, the face behind his camera serious for once.

Emma nodded.

Cooper shrugged.

Emma looked him right in the eye. 'It has come to my attention that you're in love with my sister.'

Cooper's brain froze. He looked at Emma, at the bravery and fear swirling behind her eyes, and his internal organs were suddenly too heavy for his body. He opened his mouth. Sucked in a pointless breath. Tried to find something to say, anything, to make this not as bad as it was right now.

Emma's bottom jaw trembled. She looked down, her fists clenching the loose fabric of her black trousers as she battled to regain control. Cooper's skull burned with the rising pressure of unshed tears.

'Okay. I guess that confirms it.' She glanced at Ben, then back to Cooper. 'I think you owe me an explanation.'

Cooper nodded. He knew he wouldn't be able to find the words to make it a good one, but he would at least try to make it honest.

'I did love her. For a long time. It's one of the reasons I took the job in Cardiff.' He paused to clear his throat. 'I thought, when I came back, that I could... move past it. I shut those feelings down and focussed on starting over. I really, really care about you, Emma. I admire so much about you. You're beautiful, in every way. I don't connect with people. But with you, I felt like things could be different. They *are* different.'

'So, all that's wrong with me, then, is that I'm not my sister.'

'There's nothing wrong with you.'

'But those feelings popped back up.'

'Yes.'

'Like, the times when I kissed you and you froze. You were thinking about Bridget.' A slow tear made its way down her cheek.

'Not consciously, no.'

She swiped at the tear, impatiently. 'So, what happened yesterday?'

He took a deep breath. 'I don't know what happened. Bridget was different. It was as if she saw me differently. Like she saw me the way I'd always longed for her to. I don't know. It threw me. I felt confused and... I was – I *am* a wreck. Emma. I am only beginning to learn how to love, and to be loved. My biggest reservation about marrying you was that I wouldn't stand a chance of being worthy of you. And I was right. I've failed you. And while I know sorry can't be enough, I am truly sorry.

'If you still want to stay married, I will do whatever it takes to try to put this right. I'll resign from my job. Delete her number. Cut off as much contact with your family as you want me to. We'll emigrate if that helps. I will promise you 100 per cent of me from now on.'

Emma wrinkled her nose. 'I'm not sure you want to make me that promise. If you did, you'd already have deleted her number.' She turned to Ben. 'Can you stop filming now, please?'

Ben nodded, before disappearing out of the room.

'Would you still make me that promise if you knew Bridget broke up with Paolo last night?'

What?

Cooper sat back, stunned. He pressed his hands against his head as if somehow that would help stop it spinning.

'And how about if we weren't, in actual fact, legally married?'

'What do you mean? We signed the certificate.'

'It was a fake certificate. Moses isn't a licensed registrar.'

'What? How? Did you know?' Cooper was aghast. He couldn't think. Couldn't breathe.

'Not until this afternoon.' She threw him a bitter smile. '"I promise to be open and honest with you." We didn't even make proper vows to each other. I think we can end this now and still treat each other with the kindness and compassion we deserve, as promised.'

There was a long silence.

Cooper cleared his throat again. As he started to speak, the tears finally sprang out, burning his eyes.

'Do you want to end this?'

When Emma replied, it was close to a whisper. 'Are you in love with my sister?'

'I...' He shook his head. 'Yes.'

'Then the next obvious question doesn't even matter, does it?'

'What's the next question?'

'Are you in love with me?'

He reached out to take her hand. To his surprise, she let him. 'I know I could be.'

'She's my sister, Cooper. We could move to Australia and her shadow would still haunt us. Would you have me give up my family for you? Are you that sure this will be worth it? Because as long as we're in contact with them, she'll always be there.

'You've loved her for seven years. With no hope of anything in return but her friendship. She's single now. She loves you. We aren't married. If you think I could continue this, if I could let myself fall in love with you, knowing that, then you have seriously overestimated my strength and my self-worth.'

He blew out a shuddering sigh. 'So we're over.'

'Yes. And let's be grateful we don't have to go through the agony of a divorce. I'm going to stay with Nita for a bit. I don't want anyone in the family to feel they're choosing sides.'

'Emma.' Cooper tugged on her hand. 'Please don't hate her. She didn't do anything. You know she'd never do anything to hurt you.'

'Only she did.' Emma stood up, smoothing her hair back and wiping her face. 'And for what it's worth, if things had been different, I think I could have fallen for you, too.'

* * *

Emma

Bridget's break-up meant that I found myself with a lot of unexpected free time over the next fortnight. This was a mixed blessing. On the one hand, it allowed me plenty of time to lie in Nita's spare bed, stare at the ceiling and contemplate my own failings. On the other, well, I wasn't a woman who thrived on having nothing to do and no energy to do it.

On the first Friday, prompted by a text from my mother announcing her imminent arrival, I finally dragged myself up and into the shower. Not knowing quite what to do with myself next, I resorted to what I did best, shuffled across to the Cakery and began to bake.

An hour or so later, Mum joined me. Doffing an apron and scrubbing her hands, she took a bag of flour out of the walk-in pantry.

'Here. We're going to make sfogliatelle. My nonna's recipe. And her nonna's before her. For generations of Barone women, through each and every trouble and sorrow that came our way. Idiot husbands who gambled the house, rebellious children who ran off to Roma and got themselves pregnant. The babies we lost too soon. The men who went to fight and never came home. The years the purses were empty. The days we said goodbye to our mothers, and our sisters, who were also our best friends. The times we gave our hearts to men who turned out to be unworthy of our love. We dealt with this with a rolled-up sleeve and a clenched fist and we kneaded and rolled that dough, and then we gently painted each delicate layer with butter, salting it with our tears and sweetening it with our undaunted spirit and unbowed love for our family. I cannot believe I never showed you how to make it. So, anyway, in case it's useful for you one of these days, you might need a pencil and paper to write it down. First of all...'

And that, by some miracle, was all she had to say on the matter of my own doubly broken heart.

Half an hour later, Sofia swung by. 'I heard historical family recipes were being handed down.'

An hour later, Annie and Orla joined us. 'Budge up, then. You're not the only one in need of disaster-rectifying recipes.'

Perhaps inevitably, as we prepared to roll out the second batch, the empty space at the worktop was filled when my youngest sister tentatively pushed open the kitchen door. 'Room for one more?'

My mamma and sisters didn't even break their stride, seamlessly adjusting their positions to allow Bridget to squeeze in next to Annie. No one even looked at me, let alone gave me the chance to say, 'No! There actually isn't any room in my kitchen for traitorous sisters, who stabbed me so hard in the back the blade sank all the way into my heart.'

Our family was founded on love and forgiveness, and, while I couldn't bring myself to speak to or even glance at her, I did pass her a pastry brush, so I suppose that was a start.

We baked four batches of sfogliatelle riccia, layers of pastry stuffed with custardy, cinnamony deliciousness, until Mamma decreed we'd got it right. Divvying the leftovers between the families, and lonely singletons, three of my sisters hugged me, blotting our tears on their aprons, and headed home. The fourth sister lingered in the shop until everyone else had left.

'I got a new job.'

I managed a brief nod of acknowledgement.

'It's with Professor Ernestine Lavinski. Prof Love. In Bristol.'

'Do you want my congratulations?' I sighed, exhausted more than angry at this point.

'No! I only wanted to tell you I'm moving out next Saturday. So you can move back in. I mean, unless you want me to go earlier. In which case I'll stay at the farmhouse or something, that's not a problem. Not that it matters if it *is* a problem, given that this is all my fault, and it's your home and you should move in whenever you want, just say the word and I'll make myself scarce. It's all yours. I just wanted to let you know.' Her voice, finally, collapsed into a squeaky sob. 'Right. Bye, then.' She took a shuddering breath, plastered a weak and watery smile over her tears and turned to go.

'You can tell the letting agent we're handing in our notice.'

'What?'

I shrugged. 'Probably time we both had a change. You know I've always dreamed of buying a cottage somewhere. It seems ridiculous now that I thought I needed to get married first.' I did my best to offer something akin to a smile in return. I was still very, very hurt and upset. But after days under Nita's goosedown duvet, thinking, I wasn't sure that one terrible mistake, one that had resulted in everyone suffering, came anywhere close to erasing the lifetime of love and joy leading up to it.

* * *

I skipped Sunday lunch – without a word of complaint from my mother – but Orla called to say that a friend of hers had a cottage on the edge of Hatherstone whose long-term tenants had suddenly left. If I liked it, she might even consider an offer to buy. I had packed, driven over and unpacked by Monday lunchtime. It was too far to run to work any more, but running through the woods where I'd roamed as a child, first thing in the morning or with the summer sunset lighting my path, soothed my soul in a way that pounding the streets of Nottingham never did.

My second week off, I spent some evenings with Sofia, talking a lot and crying not quite so much. A couple of afternoons I walked into the village to pick up Harry, Lottie and Oscar from school and take them to the park for an ice cream. Annie brought over Indian takeaway and her scissors, cutting my hair and painting my nails while we watched old episodes of *The Great British Bake Off*. I sat in the farmhouse garden with my father nearly every day, drinking tea and watching the bees humming in the flower beds while Mamma gardened. Sometimes she'd hand me a trowel or some pruning shears and I'd join her until the ache in my bones drew me back to the wicker sofa.

I didn't see or speak to Bridget. The SisterApp was silent. I concluded we were communicating independently these days.

The weekend before I was due back at work – the weekend of Bridget's not-wedding – the family gathered for Bridget's farewell barbeque at the farmhouse. We also combined it with saying goodbye to Greg and Annie, who were heading back to New York, for now at least.

I managed a couple of hours, most of which I spent playing with my niece and nephews or hiding in the kitchen. I'd acquired this magical power to thicken the atmosphere in any room as soon as I

entered. And if Bridget was there, the power magnified exponentially.

No one mentioned the fact that I hadn't made a cake.

We did have trays and trays of sfogliatelle.

I held my tears back until Nita drove me home. I never would
have imagined that I'd fail to cry at Bridget's leaving party, but any
tears shed would have been about far more than her move. Anyway,
in all the ways that mattered I'd lost my sister two weeks earlier,
when she smiled at my fake-husband in a way I never could have.

'Stop!' Nita nearly swerved into the hedgerow when I yelled.

'Calm down, I'm already on it.' Without waiting for me to
explain, she whipped her BMW around in a three-point turn and
screeched back the way we'd come. I leapt out of the car before
she'd had a chance to put the handbrake on, crashing through the
front door, my mother and sisters appearing at the kitchen door to
see what was going on.

Saying nothing, shaking my head for reasons I was in no state to
figure out, I clattered down the corridor.

Bridget met me halfway, her chin pressing into my bare
shoulder as her arms held on tight, our tears blending together
where her cheek pressed against mine.

'I love you so much. How the hell am I supposed to manage
without you?'

'Your genius brain will work it out.'

'Will you come and visit me?'

I inhaled deeply, the scent of her almond and coconut shampoo
as familiar to me as my own skin. 'Probably not. But I'll see you
when you come home.'

'Okay.'

It really wasn't. But one day it would be.

27

The Monday evening after the woman Cooper had thought was his wife moved out, someone buzzed the flat intercom. He'd called in sick that day at work. Sick of himself, more than anything.

Ben looked up from his laptop. 'Expecting someone?'

Cooper shook his head, grimly. He was pretty sure it wouldn't be Emma. But the other possibilities didn't bear thinking about.

When he looked through the spyhole, his heart plummeted to somewhere around the basement car park, before rebounding back up again and jamming in his windpipe. He opened the door before he had a chance to think about whether that was a good idea or not.

Bridget stepped inside. 'Hi.'

'Hi.'

She looked about as wretched as he felt. The main difference being that she was still beautiful.

He led her into the kitchen. The grim look from Ben as he peered through the living-room door to see who it was said it all.

'Do you want a drink?' His voice was shaking. A dozen conflicting thoughts and feelings roared through his head.

'No. Thank you.' She peeped at him through her hair. Her

cheeks were a soft pink, and Cooper suddenly realised that she was feeling shy. His head wanted to bundle her out of the building to where she was safe from him. His heart wanted to wrap her up in his arms and never let go.

'I came here to say... well. I'm really, really sorry. For everything. For being an idiot and a despicable human being. Let alone a friend. I know that not intending to hurt anyone means nothing when you end up destroying everything anyway. But when it's the two people I love the most in the whole world. Well, I'm so ashamed. I'm beyond devastated. I've made multiple, monumental mistakes. And all I can say is I'm sorry. And. Um. I don't know what Emma or anyone else has said, or if you've even heard. But...'

Cooper thought his chest would explode waiting to hear whatever she said next. If it was the words he'd always hoped to hear, then it could ruin any chance of Bridget and Emma mending things. And after everything he'd done, he would sacrifice hearing those words in a heartbeat, for the sisters' sake.

'You might have heard that I'm not marrying Paolo. I thought it was only fair and right, given that I'm the one who caused all this mess, that I told you I ended it with him because I didn't want to marry him. I didn't end it because, well, I wanted to be with you.'

He didn't ask if she did want to be with him.

It didn't matter now.

She took in a long, shaky breath, before steeling her shoulders and fixing her gaze about a foot above his head. 'Whether I want to be with you is irrelevant. Because I can't. Ever.'

As usual, Cooper agreed with Bridget's conclusion 100 per cent.

It didn't stop her taking his heart with him as she left, all the same.

* * *

Wednesday, he forced himself to go to work. As much as he deserved to end up homeless and broke again, ditching his job would be one more dishonourable item on his self-hate list, and it was already full to the max.

Bridget's workbench was empty. Her desk cleared, locker swinging open.

It took until Friday before he could trust himself to ask someone where she'd gone.

He swallowed hard, rolled up his lab-coat sleeves and did what he'd always done without her: ploughed on, one stumbling step at a time through the darkness, and tried to be the kind of man she'd always believed him to be.

* * *

Two weeks after that, as the July heat rose steaming from the city pavements, and every available green space filled up with sunbathers and picnics, Emma messaged him asking if she could pick up the rest of her stuff. He offered to bring it to her instead, so they arranged to meet at her old apartment. It would be the first time he'd been there.

It was exactly the kind of place he'd imagined Emma living – huge sash windows, airy ceilings and original features.

Only she clearly wasn't living there. She'd welcomed him into an empty living space – boxes lined up where furniture should have been, pictures propped against one pale wall beside a roll of bubble wrap instead of hanging on the walls.

'You're moving.' He put the holdall containing her books, photographs and the kitchen implements she'd left behind on the bare wooden floor.

'I never moved back in. I'm renting a little cottage near the farmhouse.'

He nodded. No further explanation needed as to why she didn't want to move back into the home she'd shared with Bridget.

'I had to pick up the rest of my things, and thought it would save you coming out all that way. My sisters offered to come and fetch everything, but I've got a reputation to maintain as the organised and efficient one. Plus, I didn't really trust them to uphold my strict packing procedures. They weren't even interested in looking at my spreadsheet.'

He shook his head, wincing. 'Come on now, surely every responsible packer knows you have to stick to the spreadsheet. Otherwise, before you know it they'll be folding not rolling your jumpers. Putting items from the bedroom and the kitchen in the same boxes. It'd be utter carnage.'

She raised her eyebrows, quirking her mouth in response. 'Hmmm. I maybe would have trusted you to do it. Eventually. If you approach packing as seriously as you do baking.'

'I've never moved more than a couple of bags, but if I did, then I'd certainly follow your instructions to the letter.'

'That's why we were 94 per cent compatible.' She gave him what appeared to be a definite smile then, and a weight the size of a giant suitcase tumbled off his back and he found himself blinking back tears. Now probably wasn't the time to mention that he'd fiddled their compatibility score.

'Do you want a drink while you're here? Or something to eat? I thought a meal would be a bit too full-on, but I'm experimenting with a vegan version of Mamma's sfogliatelle. I seem to be making it a lot these days, so you'd be doing me a favour if you ate some.'

She flicked on the kettle. 'I've only got tea. The coffee machine moved at the same time as me. And no milk.'

'Black's fine.' He'd have happily drunk own-brand instant coffee if it meant accepting a peace offering.

They settled back against the dark blue kitchen cabinets, each holding a mug in one hand and a pastry in the other.

'Would it ruin the atmosphere if I dragged up again how sorry I am?'

'Yes!' Emma exclaimed, rolling her eyes. 'I thought it was an unspoken agreement that we never spoke of such things ever again. Part of our fake-divorce settlement.'

'Okay. But I think there was a minor subsection permitting me this one, brief, statement. Despite me not being in any way deserving of it.'

'Go on, then. If you absolutely must.'

'I must.' He finished the last chunk of sfogliatella, dusting off his hands before speaking. 'I wanted to say that, as gutted as I am, if gutted is in any way an appropriate word to convey something so massively huge and life-altering, as gutted as I am about us not working out—'

'You not working out, because you were in love with my sister all along.'

'Yes. I wanted to say that the thing I'm sorriest about, and ashamed and furious at myself about, is what I've done to you and Bridget.'

'That kind of implies that me – us – what we could have been, didn't mean that much to you, then.'

'No. It's not that. But I knew I didn't really deserve you. I'm conditioned to expect my life will turn back to crap. But this is the first time I completely ruined someone else's.'

She downed the last of her tea and dumped the mug on the worktop. 'It's not your fault. Well. Not entirely. Or even mostly. Personally, I think the walrus's share of the blame falls squarely on the smug shoulders of Professor Cole.'

Cooper thought about that. About whether to accept this token of grace graciously, or continue to argue for his prosecution. Being part of the Donovans had clearly had some impact. It wasn't that difficult to choose grace.

'He won't be quite so smug when he has to face Prof Love at the awards dinner and explain the outcome of his bet.'

Then, Cooper did something he hadn't thought he'd do for a long time. Something he hadn't thought he'd ever do with Emma again: He laughed.

She laughed too. Another chunk of bitter regret crumbled away, and then the front door crashed open.

Emma sprang away from the worktop, eyes wide with alarm. Scanning around, she grabbed one of the biggest books. Footsteps thudded closer.

Cooper went to stand in front of her, but he needn't have bothered. The intruder wasn't there for her.

Paolo stormed through the kitchen door, reaching Cooper in three strides and taking four more to have him up against the floor-to-ceiling cabinet by his T-shirt. 'I heard a rumour you'd slimed your way back to the surface.'

'Paolo! Stop it!' Emma cried, clutching at his forearm. 'Cooper never did anything with Bridget! He's not responsible for her breaking up with you.'

Paolo pulled his face a few inches closer. He reeked of sweat and fury. Cooper remembered the scent of violence in a man well. He probably could have fought him off in seconds. He'd lived the kind of life where he'd learnt to defend himself. Only he found he didn't have the energy. This punch, or whatever it would turn out to be, had been a long time coming. He'd accept his due punishment. Besides, he knew what it felt like to be mad with grief for losing Bridget even though she'd never been his in the first place.

'Paolo! What will Dad say if I have to call the police on you? That's the last thing he needs, to have to fire his manager.'

There was a long, lingering moment. Paolo's bloodshot eyes glittered as they bored into Cooper's. Eventually, he stepped back, collapsing against the wall and sliding to the floor, where he shook the perspiration from his forehead and buried his head in his hands.

'Sorry. I know you did nothing wrong. Never tried to steal her off me, and I always knew how you felt. If I'm honest, I knew she might've loved you back. I'm not a total idiot. But then you left, so it didn't matter any more. And now nobody wins. Everyone's on their own, you included.' He paused, looking up. 'Seriously though, marrying her sister? That was not cool.'

Cooper had to agree.

* * *

Emma

Before I knew it, July had rolled through to August. Buried in work, I managed to resist breaking out into bitter cackles and shrieking, 'Good luck with that!' as I handed over wedding cakes, tucking my cynicism behind warm wishes and my widest fake-smile until the spike of grief and anger began to soften into mere sadness.

I nodded along to bridal plans and dreams in my design appointments, and as the weeks went by I began to allow myself to believe in them again.

When Annie announced her pregnancy over a Sunday lunch call in early September, Greg's hand gently resting on her perfectly flat stomach, the joy was enough to fill up another fissure in my cracked heart.

The twin faces of my twin sisters sharing the split screen as they shared snapshots of a life I could only imagine took some getting used to.

Bridget was doing okay. Working for a non-narcissistic, misogynistic or megalomaniacal professor was proving to be a nice change. Rebuilding her self-confidence, rekindling her spark and learning to love herself again would prove more of a challenge.

Sofia and Moses had signed up for fostering training, zipping through the process in record speed. For some reason, no one but them had wanted to take part in the house auction for a wreck of an ex-drug-dealing den where three people had been murdered, which also happened to be in one the most notorious, crime-riddled streets of Nottingham. The first and final bid was cheap as chips. It took no time at all for the members of the New Life Church to rip out the manky, reeking carpets and replaster the crumbling walls. One of Moses' uncles sorted the rewiring while another showed him how to plumb in a bathroom. Paolo worked every one of his days off sanding wood and installing kitchen units, all the materials at a family discount, because, well, being part of the Donovan family had nothing to do with whether you'd ended up marrying one of them or not.

In the end, quite probably helped along by a cheque offered and accepted in the privacy of my father's study, they had a five-bedroom home with clean white walls waiting to be covered with memories, and a playroom longing to be filled with the laughter and tantrums of the children who would need it the most.

By September, Sam was down to one crutch and one therapy session a week. Ready to return to work, Orla decided that it was about time they had another woman working in Donovan's DIY, and somehow muscled her way in as Assistant Manager before Paolo had a chance to check her CV.

* * *

As for me, well, I ran each morning and I baked most days. I spent my occasional days off digging up an abandoned vegetable patch in the cottage garden, readying the soil for seed planting in the spring.

I strung a hammock between two birch trees, and started reading again, revelling in having an outside in which to dream and doze.

As for my evenings? I found myself needing Wednesdays more than ever. I dipped in and out of the SisterApp, like a mole poking her nose out of her hole. Over the weeks I found seeing Bridget's bright, beaming picture beside a comment was less inclined to cause my insides to seize up. My shoulders grew slightly less hunched in automatic response to her name being mentioned.

I loved my sister. I still liked her. I missed her with an ache that burned through my bones. So, meeting up with Sofia and Orla, despite the hole on the sofa where Bridget used to be, was like a tincture to my bruised emotions.

We laughed, and ranted about my mother and worried about my father, still so frail, still so stoically stubborn.

We gossiped and remembered who we were before our family had been splintered in two. We took the pain and sorrow of disaster fake-marriages and almost-affairs and the babies who would never be born and the sisters who weren't there to share it with us, and we dug through the wreckage and we salvaged the scraps until each of us grew stronger than before. We learned to laugh at our mistakes, because, honestly, we'd had enough of crying about them.

How did people get through life without fabulous sisters to love them and laugh with them and boot them up the backside when they needed it?

* * *

With all this loving and laughing, before we knew it, Christmas was here and Bridget was coming home. I had the seedling of an idea while rolling out marzipan for another batch of cranberry

Christmas cakes. It took root inside my brain as I pounded through the frosty footpaths around my new home.

I sent a Christmas card to my youngest sister. Inside I wrote an invitation to which she said yes.

Bridget came to stay on Christmas Eve and left on New Year's Day, and I have honestly not talked as much about so many things as I did that week. It took three days before we could speak about Cooper, and Paolo, and everything that had happened and why. Only once we had, we found we couldn't stop. I was done with trying to keep up appearances, be the big, wise Old One who knew what she was doing.

Bridget was most definitely done with being nice and lovely and cheerful 100 per cent of the time, she assured me.

Mamma cried so hard about her girls being reconciled that Sofia and Moses' foster placement, a four-year-old girl, started crying along with her. And that only made the rest of us cry along with them. 'If you do not put in the papers to adopt this beautiful child and have her become one of the family forever, then I will do it!' Mamma whispered, as soon as the children had gone into the other room to watch a film.

'That's not how fostering works!' I tutted at her, because I was clearly now an expert, being one of Sofia and Moses' chosen support carers. 'They can't adopt every placement they get.'

'No, but we're pretty sure we're asking if we can adopt this one,' Sofia admitted, Dad popping open another bottle of fizz before she'd had time to finish speaking.

'Oh, this is so wonderful!' Mum yelled, toasting us all. 'All we need now is for Emma and Bridget to find themselves separate, different, not the same men, who they actually want to stay married to, and then our family will be almost completed!'

28

Valentine's Day, Bridget came to stay with me again. Neither of us had, or wanted, any prospects of romance on the anniversary of Bridget's engagement, and, more importantly, Bridget had a fancy dinner to attend the next day for which she needed a whole two days of sisterly empowerment to give her the courage to get through it.

On the day itself, Nita and I delivered a wedding cake to a hotel in the city centre. It being one of the most popular wedding dates of the year, and a Friday, this was the last of a long day of deliveries, and the wedding guests were already milling about with drinks in their hands when we arrived.

'Ugh!' Nita grimaced as she pushed through an archway made of hearts and flowers. Actual replica biological human hearts. The couple were cardiologists, and had thought it a 'cute' personal touch. Nita had not considered creating an anatomically correct heart for a cake in any way cute.

'No one wants to eat fake blood and gore at a wedding! This is a mass murderer's cake. The kind of cake I would expect to deliver to Sofia's estate on Halloween, not the swankiest hotel in Nottingham.'

'Most of them are doctors,' I replied, scanning around for the cake table. 'They'll appreciate the joke.'

'And what about those children?' Nita retorted. 'This is not a PG cake!'

'The children will probably love it the most.'

Then my words dried up in my mouth.

Nita followed my dumbstruck gaze to where Ben was charming the hat off an older woman. Literally, as we watched she tugged off her hat, tossed her hair like an advert for grey hair-dye, and batted her eyelashes, tittering.

Ben grinned back at her, camera clicking.

'Wow,' Nita said. 'I think maybe you need to rescue him.' We watched as the woman leant forwards, displaying a cleavage that appeared to go all the way down to her waist. 'I never thought I'd say this, but I think Ben has unleashed a beast even he can't tame. I think he needs rescuing.'

'Not my problem.' I started hurrying over towards the cake table as quickly as possible when carrying a giant-sized replica human heart in a box, valiantly attempting not to dwell on Ben's beautiful arms, his broad shoulders, his perfectly lovely face that made my heart bounce about somewhere below my stomach. Had he been this gorgeous back when we were housemates?

'You could make it your problem,' Nita replied once she'd caught up with me.

'I don't think so,' I said as, at the same time, Nita started waving her arms in Ben's direction, hooting and hollering his name. He looked over, smiled and waved, then looked back at his camera.

Phew. That was a close escape. From what, I wasn't sure – a quick conversation with a nice, kind, easy-going man I knew and hadn't seen for a while?

Then he paused, for a millisecond (yes, I was still looking at him, thinking how pleased I was that he hadn't come over) before snapping his head back over in our direction.

Those eyes. That gaze. It was like an ultra-sexy laser-beam, locking me in. We both stared at each other for long enough that I started to hope he couldn't move either, so we'd just be stuck there on opposite sides of the room.

Then, dashing my hopes, he started walking towards us.

That walk. So cool and assured and focussed and chilled all at the same time. I carefully placed the cake box on the table, using up the rest of my faculties on breathing and remaining upright.

My feelings about Ben were vastly complicated. My memories of him were mixed up with a whole load of issues and guilt and self-doubt. I couldn't see Ben and not remember Cooper. But without Cooper to consider, I was suddenly seeing Ben in a whole new light.

And then he was there in front of me, and grinning with what my heart was sure was a genuine, happy-to-see-me grin, not a charming, get-the-customers-to-relax one.

And, like always with Ben, in an instant my nerves and angst and uncertainty mostly dissolved and I simply felt happy to see him.

'Hey!'

'Hi.' I gave in to the urge to smile back.

That smile!

'How are you? How've you been?'

'Good.' Which, right then, was perfectly true. 'How about you?'

His grin turned rueful. 'Well, my documentary took an unexpected twist, leaving me morally obligated to wipe all footage. So, I'm still filming weddings. But actually, I'm learning to embrace it.'

'What? The super-sceptic Ben is learning to embrace happy-ever-after?'

'He is. I am.' He looked me right in the eye and my stomach dissolved into a puddle of goo.

'Time for a drink?'

'Here?' I looked around at the room, bursting with wedding guests and medical paraphernalia disguised as decorations.

'There's a much quieter bar in the back.'

'Aren't you meant to be working?'

He shrugged. How could a shrug be sexy? 'I'm due a break.'

Nita poked me in the back with the leg of a cake stand. 'OW!'

'Off you go, I'll set up here. When I'm done I'll take the van back and pick you up on the way to Hatherstone Hall tomorrow.'

'But how will I get home?'

'You'll figure it out.' Then she winked at me, and Ben grinned innocently. I was so embarrassed I went with him for a drink just to stop having to talk about it any more.

We settled on a sofa by the open fire with a G and T and a cider. It took a while to get through the requisite catch-up – my new home, my family, his plans to set up his own studio.

'So, how's Cooper?' I mean, I had to ask, didn't I?

'He's okay. Took him a while, but he's getting there. A little less RoboCoop as the months go by. He's even joined a pub quiz team. And I think he smiled a couple of weeks ago.'

I guess that answered the unaskable question about whether or not he was still single.

'He's got that dinner tomorrow night, the one where I was supposed to be showing the film, so he is extra grumpy today. Not that he's the one having to humiliate himself in front of his arch-nemesis, but having been a vital component of the project's success means he's been bearing the brunt of the prof's simmering rage ever since. No telling at what point in the proceedings it'll boil over.'

I carefully put my glass down on the table. 'Bridget's going to the dinner.'

Ben looked at me. 'Is she, now?'

'He still loves her, doesn't he? I mean, of course he does!'

'It's not exactly prime topic for conversation, but I'm guessing that, yes, he will love Bridget for a long time yet.'

'She still loves him.'

Ben widened his eyes. 'You sure?'

'She told me. At Christmas. It all felt too complicated and painful for it to ever be able to mean anything. But now? Maybe it's Valentine's Day and a second gin and tonic, but now I'm wondering why on earth two people who've been in love with each other forever, are both single, both good people, shouldn't be together.'

I took another sip of my drink, hardly able to believe I'd just come out with that statement. Head whizzing as I tried to probe the furthest corners of my brain to double-check if I'd really meant it.

'Is that completely absurd?'

'Of course it's absurd. Which doesn't mean it shouldn't happen anyway.' He glanced down at his bottle of cider, picking at the label. 'Except for the one, insurmountable thing stopping that from ever happening, of course.'

'Which is?'

'You.'

* * *

We gave it another half an hour before Ben went back to the wedding to take a few more photos, capturing the bride's dissection of the heart cake and the first dance. I lingered in the bar. Thinking. Stressing out. And then I made a decision, and in an instant my insides stopped quaking, so I knew it was the right one.

Ben arrived back a few minutes later. 'Right. I'm signed off for the night. Do you want another drink?'

'Actually, I think I need to go home. This is my fifth wedding of the day.'

'Home alone on Valentine's Day?'

'Bridget's spending the evening at my parents' house. I'll get an Uber and join her.'

'Okay.' Ben had stopped smiling. He shuffled on the seat next to me, scratching at his head. It was so unlike him it took me a few moments to realise that he was nervous. So now I felt nervous. I started gathering my coat and bag together.

'How about another time?' Ben blurted.

'Um.' It took a couple of seconds for my brain to catch up. 'You mean a drink?'

He attempted to grin. It came off sheepish. 'Yeah. Or... dinner. A film. A walk along the river.'

'You mean a date.'

He nodded, biting his bottom lip. Who was this Ben, such a contrast to the casual guy who'd asked me out the first time I met him?

I thought about his question, the silence stretching out between Ben's lip-chewing and my coat-button fumbling.

But I knew what the right answer would be:

'Thank you. But no. Thank you.'

He sat back, starting to run his hand through his hair and it ending up stuck there on the top of his head. 'Because of Cooper.'

'No. Not because of Cooper.'

'So, it's because of me.' His hand found its way out, then, dropping into his lap.

'I don't want to say it's not you, it's me. But it genuinely is. I really like you, Ben. If I was interested in a date, you'd be top of the list. But if this year has taught me anything – and I pray it has, because not having learnt anything from a failed fake-marriage is too depressing to think about – well, it's taught me that maybe you were right. If I need to find someone else in order to feel whole, then that means there's something wrong with me. Long-term commitment, sharing your life with someone, clearly isn't the right path for everyone. I've been raised to think that finding a man, getting married, having children, is the end goal. Like it's the only destiny mapped out for me.

'I think that's why it seemed the only option, like nothing else was worth considering, because I never took the time to imagine any alternative.

'But these past few months, I've been building my own picture of a future that doesn't seem terrible. It feels like mine. I want to do up my house, get a dog. Grow my business. Travel more. Properly get to know my niece and nephews. Spend more time helping my mum with fundraising. Meet my neighbours and become part of the community and make some proper friends I'm not related to. Be spontaneous without having to tell anyone.

'Making a conscious choice to build a life for myself that is satisfying and full to the brim even without a romantic relationship in it doesn't feel like a loss. I feel *free*. I feel giddy with excitement at the thought of not having to worry what anyone thinks about how I spend my time or what I look like or whether they'll love me enough.

'And while, yes, I know you weren't proposing marriage – you'd never do that, anyway – I'm not sure casual dating wouldn't bring with it some of those hopes and expectations. They've been so deeply engrained in me for so long, I know they'll be loitering around for a while, yet.

'I think you're gorgeous, and maybe one day I'll be ready to meet up for dinner with you. I know I'd enjoy it. But until I know I can do it and know it's just dinner, then my answer'll have to be a no.

'Sorry – are you asleep yet? I guess by this point the offer of a date is retracted anyway, after that insight into my highly boring and overly intense inner workings.'

Ben sighed, managing a slight smile at the same time. 'The offer of a date is unretracted. It's actually open-ended. Because while I totally agree with everything you're saying, that the presumption that getting hooked up with someone has to be the end goal, and no one can be fully happy without it, is a load of rubbish... while you *know* how fully I subscribe to that theory, what I didn't factor into my hypothesis on long-term relationships was how it has the potential to be utterly derailed by another person. You're fine by yourself, all complete and happy and sorted, and then suddenly you meet someone, and you start thinking about them. And then you meet them again. And you're thinking about them when you wake up, and then it's when you go to bed. And the more you get to know them, the more you want to be the man standing up with a glass of some rip-off, fairly nasty champagne, telling your family and friends, and their family and friends, that you will love and care for, and give your very all to her, because she's quite simply the most wonderful woman you've ever met. Your heart has found a new owner and you didn't even notice it. Let alone plan or want it. So, while this isn't a marriage proposal, in the interests of full disclosure, for the first time in my life I'm open to the possibility that it might lead to one. And, to be honest, while on the one hand I fully endorse this new, freeing, fabulous theory of yours, I'm also gutted.'

'When did this happen?' I managed to croak out.

'I asked you out the first time I saw you, if you remember. And you'd recently crawled out of a skip at the time. It's not too implausible to say you only got better from there.' He shook his head. 'But when I saw you on your wedding day, leading your dad across the courtyard, it felt like everything I'd ever known to be true flipped over in an instant.'

I sat back, my coat poking awkwardly at my chin because I'd buttoned it up wrong. 'Now you tell me?'

'You were sort of married to my housemate before.'

I let out a long sigh, blowing out some of my bewilderment and shock. Then I kissed Ben on the cheek, told him that was the loveliest thing anyone outside my family had ever said to me, wished him well for the future, said that maybe one day I'd be in touch, and I set off on a whole new, solo adventure.

There was no pre-dinner pep talk for Cooper at this year's Henry Munch Conference Dinner. Wearing the same suit as last year. New shirt. No tie. He tried and failed not to think about the difference between this year and last.

At least he had a job, this time. And despite being irrevocably in his boss's bad books due to his role in Professor Cole's imminent humiliation in front of numerous peers, and most importantly his arch-nemesis and spurner of his romantic advances, Cooper's other project was turning out surprisingly promising so far.

He had a decent place to live, with a housemate who was also a genuine friend. His football team were second in the league, although his quiz team had lost three weeks in a row. He was a year older, eons wiser, and he'd readjusted to living life solo.

On the whole, not bad.

Except that this year he would be playing the role of Cole's minder. He would be smack bang in the middle of the farcical feud that everyone was talking about. And there'd be no Bridget.

His proposed methodology for the evening?

Head down, mouth shut, brain off, all helped along by a very expensive bottle of whisky.

Professor Cole decided to handle things with his usual bulldozing belligerence, charmless repartee and by chugging back two thirds of Cooper's whisky.

After about four thousand hours of small talk and awkward jokes and Professor Cole's increasingly embittered snipes at anyone and everyone who wasn't him, the food was over and the awards began. This moment had been much discussed in the corridors and laboratories of the Nottingham University Neuroscience Department. Hushed whispers about what might happen. The general conclusion: as much as some members of the department might furtively and fervently hope that it would all kick off, what everyone expected to happen was a big-fat-no-mention-at-all of last year's disruption.

But those people hadn't factored in the 20 per cent increase in tickets sold.

The scientific people wanted a show.

And, boy, were they going to get one.

Prof Love was only hosting the whole awards.

With a huge grin on her face, a split in her skirt all the way to her sixty-something-year-old hip, she handed out the first six awards with a bewitching combination of mischief, sophistication and TV personality pizzazz.

'And finally, professors, doctors and science aficionados, we now come to the final award of the evening. This year's Henry Munch Lifetime Achievement Award for an outstanding contribution to neuroscience and behavioural science goes to... oh – hang on a moment. Before we get around to announcing that, I think we have some unfinished business from last year.'

The collective gasp of half-sozzled scientists reverberated through the hall. Everybody froze. Professor Cole slowly swivelled to glare at Cooper, as though Cooper had known about this in advance.

'Professor Cole. How lovely of you to join us. I believe we have a bet to settle?' Prof Love smiled her stunning, wicked smile. 'Come on up and tell us all about it.'

'Cooper,' Cole ground out between purple lips.

'What?' he whispered back, his voice drowned out by the escalating chant of 'Coley! Coley! Coley!' started from somewhere in the direction of Prof Love's table.

'Up you go.'

Cooper's mouth dropped open. 'Nobody wants me up there, Professor. If you don't go, some of your numerous enemies from the psychology department are going to drag you up there themselves. You might as well get it over with.'

Cole's sigh twisted into a frustrated snarl halfway through. 'Well, you're coming up there with me.' He stood up. 'Unless you want me to announce the real reason the Compatibility Project was a total fail.'

Cooper came up with him.

Once the catcalls, whistles and abusive heckles had died down, Prof Love poked the microphone into Cole's face.

'Let's hear it.'

Cole cleared his throat. Ran one finger inside the rim of his shirt collar. Blotted his brow with a chequered handkerchief.

The audience rustled in anticipation.

Cooper cracked, grabbing the microphone before his more rational side could stop him. 'Due to the exceptional progress made on our most significant project, investigating potential treatments for Myalgic Encephalomyelitis, which clearly must take precedence over a... over smaller projects with less... without so much... promise... Professor Cole along with the rest of the department agreed that the ME study must take priority, for now, and therefore—'

'It was my fault!'

Cooper nearly choked on his own half-baked excuse.

Bridget stood up, waving her arm in the air to ensure she caught everyone's attention. As all eyes swung around to her, he took the opportunity to remind his diaphragm that it was supposed to keep moving.

She wore a bright yellow dress, her hair curled up on top of her head like an old-time Hollywood starlet. Eyes shining with emotions that he couldn't begin to try to fathom with three shots of whisky clogging up his neurons.

'Totally, all my fault,' she called again. 'I was in charge of the project, and I messed it up. Subconscious sabotage. After weeks of failing to find any suitable candidates, in a moment of unprofessional desperation, I chose my oldest friend as one of the research subjects.'

The neuroscientific and behavioural scientists murmured their disapproval at this revelation.

'Oh, wait. It gets worse!' Bridget flapped her hands in a shushing motion. Cooper's heart had become wedged in his throat, severely impacting its ability to beat.

'I paired subject one, my oldest friend, with subject two – *my own sister*.'

The murmur became a rumble.

'So...' Bridget had to shout now to be heard '... it was me who rendered the project invalid, wilfully deceiving Professor Cole in the process. As soon as the revelations came to light, being the kind and generous man that he is, he allowed me a dignified relocation to another university. Who, I must add, are fully aware of my previous misdemeanour and are supervising me accordingly. Anyone with an ounce of scientific professionalism and a working brain must concede that the only fail Professor Cole made here was in trusting me with his project.'

'Very well,' Professor Love replied, eyeing up Cole's expression and the mood of the room in one swift glance. 'Given that I'm a fair and honourable woman, I'm prepared to give you another go, Angus. Another year to try again. What do you lot think?' she asked the crowd, perfectly arched eyebrows raised.

It was impossible to decipher any of the words being thrown at the stage, but Cooper got the general gist. Professor Cole looked on the brink of apoplexy.

'Unless you wish to concede defeat now?' Love batted her eyelashes at her rival. 'Admit that the psychology of compatibility is a true science, equal in validity, depth and complexity to any branch of neuroscience. And that I was, and am, fully deserving of the lifetime achievement award, due to my ingenious research into making our world a more romantic place. Not to mention passionate!' she added, sparking a wave of whistles and whoops.

Cole nodded his head, his eyes shrivelled into slits. 'Yes, whatever.' He took a step towards the edge of the stage, but Prof Love halted his retreat with a bark into the microphone. 'Uh-uh! I haven't finished. *Finally* I would like you to explain to our good colleagues that this whole debacle was purely due to me having spurned your fumbled advances thirty-four years ago.'

'I will not!' Cole looked ready to explode in a purple smoke-bomb of rage. 'You only rejected me because I didn't pass your stupid questionnaire!'

'Oh, Angus, Angus, Angus.' She tittered. The audience tittered too, not knowing why but knowing it would be good. 'I rejected you because you are an unpleasant, egotistical narcissist who bullies women. I didn't need a test to tell me that. In fact, my new head of research, Dr Donovan, has compiled a very thorough and quite frankly fascinating report detailing how you're still an arrogant, self-obsessed bully to this day. We'll see what your vice chancellor has to say about it.

'And on that note, I think it's high time we moved on. This year's Henry Munch Lifetime Achievement Award goes to...'

Cooper never did find out who it went to.

The energy that had been building inside him since Bridget had stood up reached critical levels, propelling him off the stage and towards her. As the smatter of applause surrounded them she grabbed his hand, and, exchanging a look that contained a thousand words, they began weaving in and out of the tables until they reached the exit.

'Hi!' She gasped, once they were safely tucked away in a store-room full of cleaning supplies.

'Hello, Widget.' He knew he should probably stop staring at her, at least blink or something, but, standing a mere foot away, her soft, warm hand still enclosed in his, he was mesmerised. There was nothing but her.

'A bit embarrassing.' She rolled her eyes, but her smile was like the sun bursting through months of thunderclouds.

'You didn't have to do that.' He sounded breathless. He *was* breathless.

'Yeah, I did. And it's fine. Ernestine knows what really happened.'

They stood there, gazing at each other, and for the first time all pretence tumbled away. Bridget's eyes said all he needed to know.

Here she was, his heart. And she loved him.

'I wanted to call you.'

'I'm so sorry.'

They spoke at the same time, both breaking off into a second of silence while they waited for the other to continue.

But a second was enough. The quiet of the cupboard was broken by twin beeps.

Bridget sighed and pulled her phone out of the hidden side-pocket in her dress. 'It's Emma.'

She looked up at him, a question in her voice.

Cooper checked his own phone, nodding in confirmation.

They read the message at the same time.

It didn't take long.

Don't you dare leave that dinner without having kissed

Another message:

This is purely for selfish reasons

Message three:

I can't move on and be happy knowing you aren't together because of me

And one final ping:

No excuses! You've wasted enough time (mine included!) FIND EACH OTHER AND SAY WHAT YOU REALLY THINK! Oh, and have a wonderful evening. I love you both xx

Bridget looked at him, still gripping her phone. Tears began to spill over and tumble down her cheeks. Somehow she managed to keep smiling. 'So. Big sister's orders. What do you think?'

Cooper took a step forwards, gently placing one hand on the exquisite spot where her jawline met her neck. He took a slow breath. His heart pounded against his ribcage, but, for the first time in forever, Cooper felt an overwhelming sense of calm.

'I think that I was born to love you.'

She tipped her head, resting her cheek against his palm. 'I think that I've been waiting for this moment for seven years,' she whispered. 'My whole life.'

Then, for the second time whilst Bridget Donovan cried in a cleaning cupboard, Cooper leant across and gently kissed her.

This time, she didn't pull away, leaving him to be the one to eventually break off the kiss. After what felt like a lifetime later, Cooper stepped back.

'I think I might ask Prof Lavinski for a job and move down to Bristol.'

Bridget grasped both his lapels, tugging him close again. 'I think that would be a really good idea.'

He was the one to break off the kiss for the second time, causing Bridget to let out a squeak of annoyance.

He rested his forehead against hers. 'Will you marry me?' A ridiculous question, but Cooper couldn't help himself.

'I thought you'd never ask.' She pulled back, laughing. 'Genuinely, up until those messages, I really thought you'd never be able to ask me.'

'You haven't answered yet.'

'Hmmm...' She pressed one finger to her lips, pretending to think. 'We probably ought to check how compatible we are, first. Maybe we should try the Cole Compatibility Function.'

'I already did.' Cooper's eyes danced. 'We scored 23 per cent.'

'Well, it beats the woman who wanted to marry a hobbit. I guess I'd better say yes.'

Not for the first and most definitely not for the last time, Patrick Charles Cooper agreed with Dr Bridget Donovan 100 per cent.

ACKNOWLEDGMENTS

Thanks again to the consistently fantastic team Boldwood – especially Sarah Ritherdon, who is simply everything I could have asked for in an editor. Thanks also to my wonderful agent, Kiran Kataria for her input and encouragement.

I'm very grateful to Dr Gareth Hathway, Associate Professor of Neuroscience at Nottingham University, who allowed me to look around a lab for the first time in twenty years and also spent time patiently answering all my random questions.

Emily Sturgess generously gave her precious time and energy in reading through some early extracts. Her thoughts on the topic of living with ME/CFS were extremely helpful. As always, to everyone who has read my books, taken the time to write a review or get in touch – I'm so very grateful. Knowing you are out there reading and loving my books means more than I can say.

This book has family at its heart, as do I. I am so incredibly thankful to belong to a family full of love and laughter. For Ciara, Joseph and Dominic – may you love wisely and well.

And for George, who I fell head over heels for at first sight – twenty-five years later I'm still falling.

AUTHOR'S NOTE

ME (myalgic encephalopathy or encephalomyelitis) is a complex neurological disease that affects up to a quarter of a million people in the UK, and 20 million worldwide, with 25% housebound or bedbound. Historically, ME has been widely misunderstood and research has been severely lacking in funding, so to date there is no known cure or effective treatment. The ME Association has invested over £1million in biomedical research in recent years. For more information or to make a donation, please visit meassociation.org.uk. Similarly, the Open Medicine Foundation (OMF) is spearheading research via collaboration with leading scientists and clinicians around the globe. You can find out more about this vital work at www.omf.ngo.

MORE FROM BETH MORAN

We hope you enjoyed reading *Take a Chance on Me*. If you did, please leave a review.

If you'd like to gift a copy, this book is also available as an ebook, digital audio download and audiobook CD.

Sign up to Beth Moran's mailing list for news, competitions and updates on future books.

http://bit.ly/BethMoranNewsletter

Explore more uplifting novels from Beth Moran.

ABOUT THE AUTHOR

Beth Moran is the author of eight novels, including the bestselling *Christmas Every Day*. She regularly features on BBC Radio Nottingham and is a trustee of the national women's network Free Range Chicks. She lives on the outskirts of Sherwood Forest.

Visit Beth's website: https://bethmoranauthor.com/

Follow Beth on social media:

f facebook.com/bethmoranauthor

twitter.com/bethcmoran

BB bookbub.com/authors/beth-moran

ABOUT BOLDWOOD BOOKS

Boldwood Books is a fiction publishing company seeking out the best stories from around the world.

Find out more at www.boldwoodbooks.com

Sign up to the Book and Tonic newsletter for news, offers and competitions from Boldwood Books!

http://www.bit.ly/bookandtonic

We'd love to hear from you, follow us on social media:

facebook.com/BookandTonic

twitter.com/BoldwoodBooks

instagram.com/BookandTonic